UNDER TWO FLAGS

Also by WILLIAM M. FOWLER, JR.

WILLIAM ELLERY: A RHODE ISLAND POLITICO AND
LORD OF ADMIRALTY

REBELS UNDER SAIL: THE AMERICAN NAVY DURING THE REVOLUTION

THE AMERICAN REVOLUTION: CHANGING PERSPECTIVES
(edited with Wallace Coyle)

THE BARON OF BEACON HILL: A BIOGRAPHY OF JOHN HANCOCK

JACK TARS AND COMMODORES: THE AMERICAN NAVY, 1783–1815

UNDER TWO FLAGS

The American Navy in the Civil War

William M. Fowler, Jr.

W · W · NORTON & COMPANY

New York   London

Printed in the United States of America.

The text of this book is composed in Baskerville,
with display type set in Cochin Old Style.
Composition and manufacturing by
The Maple-Vail Book Manufacturing Group.
Book design by Jacques Chazaud.

First Edition

Library of Congress Cataloging-in-Publication Data

Fowler, William M., 1944–
Under two flags : the American Navy in the Civil War /
William M. Fowler, Jr.
p. cm.
Includes bibliographical references.
1. United States—History—Civil War, 1861–1865—Naval operations.
2. United States. Navy—History—Civil War, 1861–1865.
3. Confederate States of America. Navy—History.   I. Title.
E591.F77   1990
973.7′5—dc20   89–29462

ISBN 0-393-02859-3

W. W. Norton & Company, Inc., 500 Fifth Avenue, New York, N.Y. 10110
W. W. Norton & Company, Ltd., 37 Great Russell Street, London WC1B 3NU

1 2 3 4 5 6 7 8 9 0

To
SHIRLEY AND BOB

To
SHIRLEY AND BOB

Contents

—————◆—————

Photographs appear following page 155

Preface

———————

Lincoln's tall, gaunt figure towered over everyone in the White House reception room. It was shortly after his inauguration, and the new president was there to greet the senior members of his administration. Among those present were the secretary of the navy, Gideon Welles, and senior navy officer Captain Joseph Smith. As the three men stood together, each grimly aware of the crisis facing the nation, Smith, with a boldness born of age and seniority, told the president, "[W]e will perform our duty, and expect you to do yours." Lincoln did stand true to his duty, unto death, and so did the navy.

Along the Atlantic and Gulf coasts the Union navy blockaded the South and assaulted its shores. On the inland waterways Federal gunboats steamed up and down rivers, helping the army strike at the heart of the Confederacy. And on distant stations off Australia, off the Cape of Good Hope, in the Atlantic, Mediterranean, and Indian oceans Union steamers pursued the wily Confederate raiders. Without a powerful navy the North could not have won the war.

The South's seacoast was far longer than that of the North, and its interior was crisscrossed by navigable streams. Confederate strategists knew that they must control the waterways. But the South had too few sailors to put theory into practice, and it lacked the resources—of iron in particular—to make up for its scanty manpower. Still, the Confederate navy deserves to be remembered for its flamboyant—if ultimately unsuccessful—exploits.

Although writing can be a lonely business, no author really writes alone. It has been my continuing good fortune to have the support and encouragement of numerous people and institutions. Whenever I have signaled for assistance, they have always responded. Nancy Borromey skillfully manages the History Department's office at Northeastern University so that my work always gets done, while Jane Heine has patiently typed the manuscript (many times). Linda Smith Rhoads, my associate on the *New England Quarterly*, has uncomplainingly taken up the slack whenever I have been called to other duties. To James Ewin and Jack Post I owe a special debt. Both these friends had ancestors who played key roles in the navies of the Civil War, Jim's for the South and Jack's for the North. They shared their ancestors' experiences with me. To Bill Dudley at the Naval Historical Center I say thanks for taking time from his demanding schedule to read my manuscript and provide comments. Gerry Hayes and Dianne Thomas managed my schedule in the Office of the Provost so that I had time for writing, and I thank the provost, Robert Lowndes, for allowing me the time to continue to be a "scholar." Kenneth G. Ryder and John A. Curry, the former Northeastern's recently retired president and the latter the new president, both deserve a strong note of thanks. Both men have made this university a haven for teachers and scholars.

Northeastern University has, as always, been generous in its support. The librarians at Dodge Library have scoured the country to find the titles I need. What they have not found I have invariably discovered at two institutions that have been serving scholars for nearly two centuries: the Massachusetts Historical Society and the Boston Athenaeum. Access to the collections at the latter has been made possible by the generosity of my good friend Jason Aisner.

I have also had access to the fine collections and assistance of the librarians at Mystic Seaport, Connecticut. One final institution needs mention: the United States Navy. The Naval Historical Center is a place all naval scholars have come to hold in high regard both for its collections and for its most valuable resource: skilled historians and archivists.

It has been my great good fortune in this effort, as in others, to have once more the support of the American Philosophical Society. Its generosity has made it possible for me to gather and consult vital materials.

At W. W. Norton I have been fortunate to work with two superb editors, Hilary Hinzmann and Rose Kernochan, whose skill at editing is matched only by their diplomacy.

Every author, like every sailor, needs a snug harbor. Mine is provided by a wife and family who provide a home where I can always find love and humor. Thanks.

Chronology

1860

6 November   Abraham Lincoln elected president.

20 December   South Carolina becomes first state to
                  secede.

1861

4 March   Lincoln takes oath as president; Gideon
                  Welles becomes secretary of the navy.

12 April   Fort Sumter attacked.

17 April   Confederate President Jefferson Davis
                  invites applications for letters of marque
                  and reprisal.

19 April   Lincoln issues blockade proclamation.

---

20 April	Norfolk Navy Yard put to torch by retreating Union forces.
7 May	Flag Officer William Mervine ordered to establish blockade at Gulf of Mexico.
13 May	Queen Victoria proclaims British neutrality.
16 May	Commander John Rodgers ordered west to establish naval armament on western rivers.
28 June	Confederate privateer *Jefferson Davis* sails from Charleston.
30 June	CSS *Sumter,* under Commander Raphael Semmes, runs past blockade at mouth of Mississippi River.
5 July	Blockade Board makes its first report.
21 July	First Battle of Bull Run.
1 August	Lincoln appoints Gustavus Fox as assistant secretary of the navy.
29 August	Forts Hatteras and Clark surrender to Flag Officer Silas Stringham and General Benjamin Butler.
5 September	Captain Andrew Hull Foote arrives to relieve Commander Rodgers of naval command on western rivers.
17 September	Confederate forces evacuate Ship Island, Mississippi.
18 September	Flag Officer Samuel F. du Pont appointed to command South Atlantic Blockading Squadron.

18 September	Flag Officer Louis M. Goldsborough appointed to command North Atlantic Blockading Squadron.
26 October	CSS *Nashville* runs past blockade at Charleston.
1 November	General George B. McClellan appointed to succeed General Winfield Scott as general in chief.
7 November	Union navy captures Port Royal, South Carolina.
7 November	Battle of Belmont, Missouri.

1862

9 January	Flag Officer David Glasgow Farragut appointed to command Western Gulf Blockading Squadron.
16 January	Seven armored river gunboats commissioned for Union navy.
30 January	USS *Monitor* launched.
6 February	Union forces under Flag Officer Foote and General Ulysses S. Grant capture Fort Henry on the Tennessee River.
8 February	Union forces under the command of Flag Officer Goldsborough and General Butler capture Roanoke Island.
16 February	Grant and Foote capture Fort Donelson on the Cumberland River.
4 March	Union forces under Foote occupy Columbus, Kentucky.

8 March	CSS *Virginia* attacks at Hampton Roads and destroys USS *Cumberland* and USS *Congress*.
9 March	*Monitor* versus *Virginia*.
13 March	Confederate forces evacuate New Madrid, Missouri.
17 March	CSS *Nashville* runs past blockaders at Beaufort, North Carolina.
4 April	McClellan begins Peninsula campaign.
4 April	USS *Carondelet* runs past Confederate batteries at Island Number Ten.
6–7 April	Battle of Shiloh.
7 April	Island Number Ten surrenders to Union forces under Foote.
11 April	Fort Pulaski at mouth of Savannah River surrenders to Union forces.
24 April	Farragut's fleet passes Forts Jackson and St. Philip.
25 April	Farragut captures New Orleans.
3 May	Thomas ("Stonewall") Jackson begins Shenandoah Valley campaign.
10 May	Confederate forces first destroy and then withdraw from navy yards at Norfolk, Virginia, and Pensacola, Florida.
11 May	CSS *Virginia* blown up by her crew to prevent capture.
5 June	Confederate forces evacuate Fort Pillow, Tennessee.

6 June	Union gunboats under Charles Davis and rams under Charles Ellet, Jr., defeat Confederate gunboats and capture Memphis, Tennessee.
17 June	Union gunboats attack Confederate fort at St. Charles on White River, Arkansas.
25 June	Seven Days Battles begin.
28 June	Farragut's fleet passes upstream under the guns of Vicksburg.
1 July	Farragut's and Davis's forces meet above Vicksburg.
15 July	CSS *Arkansas* runs past Union force at mouth of Yazoo River, Mississippi.
16 July	Farragut promoted to rear admiral.
24 August	Raphael Semmes takes command of CSS *Alabama*.
26 August	Franklin Buchanan promoted to rear admiral, Confederate States navy, and posted to command naval forces at Mobile, Alabama.
17 September	Battle of Antietam.
5 October	Galveston captured by Union naval force under command of Commander William Renshaw.
10 October	Western gunboats transferred to Navy Department.
12 December	USS *Cairo* sunk in Yazoo River by underwater mine.
13 December	First Battle of Fredericksburg.

29 December	Union forces under William Tecumseh Sherman withdraw after being repulsed at Chickasaw Bluffs, thus ending Grant's first attack on Vicksburg.
31 December	USS *Monitor* lost in storm off Cape Hatteras, North Carolina.

1863

1 January	Confederate forces retake Galveston, Texas.
11 January	Fort Hindman at Arkansas Post, Arkansas, surrenders to Union forces under command of Rear Admiral David Dixon Porter and Major General John McClernand.
11 January	CSS *Alabama* sinks USS *Hatteras* off Galveston, Texas.
31 January	CSS *Chicora* and CSS *Palmetto State* attack Union blockaders at Charleston, South Carolina.
7 February	Yazoo Pass expedition gets under way.
17 February	Union gunboats retreat from Fort Pemberton. Yazoo Pass expedition is a failure.
14 March	Farragut passes under guns at Port Hudson, Mississippi.
7 April	Du Pont's ironclads attack forts at Charleston, South Carolina, but are forced to withdraw.
16–17 April	Porter's gunboats pass below Vicksburg.

2–4 May	Battle of Chancellorsville.
22 May	Grant begins siege of Vicksburg.
17 June	CSS *Atlanta* surrenders to Union naval force at Warsaw Sound, Georgia.
24 June	Rear Admiral John Dahlgren appointed to command South Atlantic Blockading Squadron.
1–4 July	Battle of Gettysburg. Lee withdraws.
4 July	Vicksburg surrenders to Grant.
9 July	Port Hudson, Mississippi, surrenders to Union forces.
10 July	Dahlgren's ironclads bombard Battery Wagner on Morris Island, South Carolina.
1 August	Rear Admiral Porter relieves Farragut.
6 September	Confederates evacuate Morris Island.
19–20 September	Confederates under General Braxton Bragg defeat Union forces at Chickamauga, Tennessee.
25 November	Battle of Missionary Ridge. Confederates forced to withdraw from Chattanooga.

1864

17 February	Confederate submarine *H. L. Hunley* sinks USS *Housatonic* off Charleston, South Carolina.
9 March	U. S. Grant given commission as lieutenant general, moves east, and sets strategy for final defeat of Confederacy.

12 March	Porter's gunboats begin to move up Red River, Louisiana.
19 April	CSS *Albemarle* sinks USS *Southfield* off Plymouth, North Carolina.
5–7 May	Battle of the Wilderness.
7–20 May	Spotsylvania campaign.
13 May	Porter's gunboats escape down Red River.
3 June	Battle of Cold Harbor. Lee and Grant both suffer heavy losses.
15 June	Siege of Petersburg begins.
19 June	USS *Kearsarge* sinks CSS *Alabama* off Cherbourg, France.
5 August	Battle of Mobile Bay.
2 September	Atlanta falls to Sherman.
7 October	USS *Wachusetts* captures CSS *Florida* at Bahia, Brazil.
19 October	CSS *Shenandoah* commissioned at Madeira Islands.
27 October	Lieutenant William Barker Cushing destroys CSS *Albemarle* off Plymouth, North Carolina.
15 November	Sherman begins march to the sea.
13 December	Farragut promoted to vice admiral.
21 December	Sherman takes Savannah.
24–25 December	Unsuccessful Union attempt against Fort Fisher.

1865

13–15 January   Naval forces under Porter and the army under General Alfred Terry capture Fort Fisher.

17 February   Confederates evacuate Charleston.

22 February   Confederates evacuate Wilmington, North Carolina.

3 April   Union forces enter Richmond.

9 April   Lee surrenders to Grant at Appomattox Courthouse.

14 April   Lincoln shot at Ford's Theater.

3 May   Stephen Mallory submits resignation to Davis.

28 June   CSS *Shenandoah* captures eleven whalers.

6 November   CSS *Shenandoah* reaches Liverpool and lowers her flag.

UNDER TWO FLAGS

1

The Union Dissolves

12 APRIL 1861, 3:30 A.M.

"**B**y authority of Brigadier General Beauregard, commanding the Provisional Forces of the Confederate States, we have the honor to notify you that he will open the fire of his batteries on Fort Sumter in one hour from this time."[1] For Major Robert Anderson, commanding officer of Sumter, and his besieged garrison of barely one hundred men, this demand came as no surprise. Since just after Christmas the Union soldiers in Sumter had watched as Confederate soldiers in Charleston mounted heavy guns and trained them toward the Union forces. Fort Sumter was so vulnerable: small and precariously perched on an island in the middle of the Charleston harbor. Anderson understood his plight, and so did his superiors in Washington. At best, provisions might last for a week. But if he were brought under fire, he and his men could not hold out more than a few hours. The only possible hope—a forlorn one—was that the navy might be able to speed past the

Confederate guns and relieve the garrison. That hope rested with ill-informed politicians and officers in Washington, who had never seen Pierre G. T. Beauregard's sturdy fortifications.

At 4:30 A.M. the Confederate batteries opened fire. Meanwhile, offshore the long-awaited Union "relief" arrived. It was a fleet of three vessels: the unarmed merchantman *Baltic*, the small revenue cutter *Harriet Lane*, and the steam frigate *Pawnee*. When they realized it was hopeless to try to run the Confederate gauntlet, these ships tacked and steamed back and forth out of range. Their crews crowded the bulwarks, trying to catch a glimpse of the drama in the harbor.

All through the day and night the Confederate batteries kept up their fire. The masonry walls of the fort slowly crumbled while Anderson and his men did what they could to return fire. In the darkness arching mortar rounds flew over the harbor and exploded within the walls of the fort. The bombardment continued through the morning of the thirteenth. Anderson had done all that he could; it was pointless to resist. At three in the afternoon Fort Sumter raised the white flag. After the usual ceremonies the three Union vessels standing away were permitted to approach and embark the major and his garrison. The Civil War had begun.

The Union debacle at Sumter was even more of a defeat for the Union navy than it was for the army. While the army had struggled and resisted, the navy had not even fired a shot. The three navy vessels had only helped the army to retreat.

Some Americans could still remember the heady days of the War of 1812. Where, they asked, were the Stephen Decaturs, the William Bainbridges, and Isaac Hulls? Where was the courageous navy of Washington Irving's and James Fenimore Cooper's novels? In the 1840s and 1850s the navy had been the darling of the public. The navy had successfully defended the Republic against pirates in the West and East Indies, and helped spread trade and commerce; it had successfully shown the flag around the world. In an age when readers devoured travel books, officers such as Alexander Slidell Mackenzie drew considerable audiences by spinning tales of their travels to exotic climes. It was a time, observed a writer in a contemporary magazine, the *American Quarterly*, when "Sailors wash the tar from their hands and write verses in their log-books; midshipmen indite their own adventures; and naval commanders not content with discovering countries and winning battles, steer boldly into the ocean of literature."[2]

High among the American navy's claims to prominence in the antebellum years was its role in scientific exploration. Spurred on by the urge to compete with other nations, the United States used its navy to explore, chart, and carry scientists to the far regions of the globe.

In 1848 Lieutenant William Lynch led a small party that surveyed the Sea of Galilee. From there, via the Jordan River, they entered the Dead Sea. Commander John Rodgers was dispatched to survey and chart the North Pacific, while Lieutenant William L. Herndon was sent off to explore the Amazon. At home Lieutenant Matthew Fontaine Maury was appointed superintendent of the Depot of Charts and Instruments, a post from which he exerted great influence as he gathered data from merchant and naval officers. Thanks to his vast store of information, Maury could carefully chart winds and currents. He was able to direct American captains to the fastest passages to their destinations. Maury's efforts made his office an important scientific resource. And science, of course, was not the only reason for these expeditions. The presence of American warships and officers served to encourage commerce. The American navy was keen to support and encourage overseas trade, for it benefited both the nation and the navy.[3]

The navy was also making advances and gaining public approval in its system of education. By tradition, officers in the American navy were trained on an apprentice system. A young man, usually with good family connections, was taken into the service and placed aboard ship as a midshipman. The name itself defined his position, for in the hierarchy of shipboard life this young man stood somewhere between the enlisted men in the forecastle and the officers who lived aft. His job was to learn navigation, ship handling, and the other skills necessary to command at sea. After an appropriate but indefinite period of time he would receive his commission and move into the world of the naval officer.

Not everyone, however, was pleased with this system. Some, such as Secretary of the Navy Samuel Southard, thought that naval officers were poorly educated. Shipboard training, in his view, was inadequate and uneven. In 1823 the inadequacy of the system was proved when the service had to report that of eighty-nine midshipmen, only thirty-nine had sufficient knowledge to pass an exam which led to promotion. Perhaps it was this embarrassment to the service that prompted Southard to observe in a report to Congress: "Instruction is not less necessary to the navy than to the army." The army already had West Point. What Southard wanted was an academy for the navy.

Conservatism, however, held sway, and Southard's dream of a naval academy was not realized for more than twenty years. Those opposed to an academy argued that "book learning" was not needed by seagoing officers. Senior officers saw this business of reform as an insidious attempt by civilian politicians to change their beloved navy. They, and they alone, should determine who joined the ranks of their fellow officers.

The naval academy remained only a dream cherished by reformers. Then, in December 1842, the nation was startled by the tragic events aboard the brig *Somers*. In September 1842 this vessel, under the command of Alexander Slidell Mackenzie, had sailed from New York bound toward Africa with dispatches for the African Squadron. Though she was a small vessel, *Somers* was packed with a heavy crew of 120, largely a cargo of apprentice sailors. Only 9 of these men were experienced seamen.

One of the young men on board was Philip Spencer, the son of the secretary of war. Spencer's reputation was tarnished at best. As a midshipman he had been in and out of a good deal of trouble, usually involving drinking, but he had managed to stay in the service thanks to his father's influence. On the homeward voyage toward the Virgin Islands, this troublesome midshipman sowed discontent among the young and inexperienced apprentices on board the brig. Spencer's activities did not go unnoticed, and on 26 November Mackenzie ordered the midshipman seized and placed in irons. An investigation and court-martial followed; Spencer was convicted of mutiny, along with two fellow plotters. All three were hanged.

The *Somers* mutiny rocked the navy and spilled over into politics. Spencer had his champions, as did MacKenzie. In the midst of the raging debate over the *Somers*'s mutiny, a general consensus emerged: Educating midshipmen entirely on board ship left a good deal to be desired. Neither education nor discipline was well served by sending inexperienced boys to sea, particularly when they were crammed into a craft like *Somers*. The service was finally ready for reform, and its secretary, George Bancroft, was ready to carry it out.

Bancroft was a graduate of Harvard College and the founder of the famous Round Hill School in Northampton, Massachusetts. He was probably best known, however, as the author of the multivolume *History of the United States*. As an experienced educator Bancroft understood the need for more professional, rigorous, and regular education for naval officers. He was also an astute politician, able to chart a fine course that would avoid opposition to reform within the service and allay Congress's parsimonious reluctance to fund reform. Through some fiscal legerdemain, Bancroft secured funds from existing appropriations to support faculty salaries. At the same time, with the cooperation of the War Department, he found a location for his new school at a little-used military facility on the Severn River in Annapolis, Maryland. Bancroft appointed Franklin Buchanan, a well-regarded and senior officer, the first superintendent. The curriculum, Bancroft specified, should consist of mathematics, nautical astronomy, theory of morals, international law, gunnery, use of steam, Spanish, French, "and other branches essential in the present day to the accomplishment of a naval officer."

On 10 October 1845 the school officially opened. By the following year, fifty-six midshipmen had enrolled. With the academy now a fait accompli, Bancroft asked Congress directly for regular appropriations to support the school. Congress agreed. Bancroft's small school on the Severn was on its way to becoming an important influence on the United States Navy.

Of all the navy's activities during the antebellum years, the best known and most popular were the expeditions of Charles Wilkes and Matthew Calbraith Perry.[4]

In the summer of 1838 Lieutenant Charles Wilkes set forth from Norfolk on an epic voyage. With six vessels at his command, he was under orders to explore various parts of the Pacific and to push into the South Polar seas. Known officially as the United States Exploring Expedition, Wilkes's venture was the most important scientific undertaking conducted by the American navy in the nineteenth century. The voyage lasted nearly four years, covered more than eighty-five thousand miles, charted 280 islands, collected thousands of scientific specimens, and sighted—at last—the Antarctic continent. Wilkes's reports were published and widely read.

Equally well known was Perry's expedition to Japan, an event that changed the destiny of two nations. Leaving from Norfolk in November 1852 with a squadron consisting of the side-wheel steamers *Mississippi* and *Susquehanna* and the sailing sloops *Plymouth* and *Saratoga,* Perry entered Tokyo Bay in July 1853 to begin efforts at opening relations with the Japanese. Impressed by Perry's firm and dignified manner and alert to their own interests, Japanese officials accepted a letter from President Millard Fillmore to the emperor. Perry then informed them that he would return in the spring to receive a response to the president's letter.

In mid-February Perry returned with a force even more powerful than the original. Dropping anchor, this time off

Yokohama, Perry entered into three weeks of elaborate negotiations designed to impress the Japanese. It worked, and on 31
March he signed the Treaty of Kanagawa, which opened the
ports of Shimoda and Hakodate to American trade and promised fair treatment for shipwrecked American sailors. Having
completed his mission, Perry returned home in triumph. Not
to be outdone by Wilkes, he spent the remaining three years of
his life preparing his three-volume *Narrative of the Expedition of
an American Squadron to the China Seas and Japan . . . 1852–1853,
and 1854. . . .*

While collecting scientific data, charting oceans, and nego-
tiating treaties were laudatory and useful ventures, they were
not the navy's principal mission. As always, its first assignment
was to defend the nation at sea. But it had rarely been called
upon to perform its first duty. Although some officers who were
to play key roles in the Civil War, such as Raphael Semmes and
David Dixon Porter, did get a taste of combat in the Mexican
War (1846–1848), it was tantalizingly brief. For the most part
it was the army that fought Mexico, leaving the navy to play a
very supporting role. Putting down random attacks of piracy—
another peacetime occupation—required no great force either.
Lulled by the comfort of peace, the navy ignored many of the
technological advances which were being made overseas in
gunnery, armor, and propulsion, advances that were changing
the face of war at sea.

Contemporary European commentators were apt to write
off the American navy because of both its small size and its lack
of modern ships and weapons. In the 1850s, for example, paddle wheels were still popular in the American navy, though it
had become clear how vulnerable they were to enemy fire. One
British observer remarked that the American navy was the last
one still planning to sail into battle in side-wheelers. Even the
more modern screw-propelled steamers in the fleet—*Merrimack, Roanoke,* and *Minnesota*—were criticized by sophisticated
foreign observers. One British reviewer noted that the screw
frigate *Niagara* had "no beauty to recommend her." Beauty or

not, though, the steam frigates at least were a far step ahead of side-wheelers and sailing frigates. Their one big handicap, which revealed itself after 1861, was their deep draft. Designed as blue water craft, ready to assail the seaborne trade of any would-be enemy, these frigates drew too much water to allow them to come in close to shore, where they might help blockade ports.[5]

In the matter of armament, the navy had made some strides, thanks primarily to John Dahlgren. Dahlgren, an expert on ordnance, entered the navy in 1824. It was he who designed the large-bore guns, nine inches and eleven inches, capable of hurling both solid and shell shot, which armed the navy's vessels at mid-century. While Dahlgren's guns were placed aboard, senior officers still insisted, against his advice, on putting a variety of guns in each broadside. This resulted in supply problems since various shot were required for each size gun. It also raised the possibility in drill or battle "of mismatching powder charges and projectiles."[6] Dahlgren also recommended the use of rifled guns, but more senior officers resisted the innovation.

In retrospect, however, the most glaring mistake of the U.S. Navy in the years before the Civil War was its reluctance to recognize the overwhelming superiority of armored—that is, ironclad—vessels. The Crimean War (1854–1856) had provided bloody proof that exploding shot could annihilate wooden hulls. Anyone needing further evidence had only to look at the experience of the Russians. In 1853 the Russians, with modern shell guns, destroyed a Turkish fleet of wooden vessels at Sinope in the Black Sea. Two years later the victors found themselves the vanquished at the Battle of Fort Kinburn near the mouth of the Dnieper River. The French attacked the Russians in the fort with three crude ironclad floating batteries, *Devastation, Lave,* and *Tonnant.* The three rafts stood only eight hundred yards off the fort. Within a few hours they had totally demolished Fort Kinburn, with almost no damage to themselves, despite more than two hundred direct hits from Russian guns. The lesson was unmistakable. Assessing the situation, one naval writer noted that "it would be impossible to find men stupid enough to go into action against this new form of gunnery in unprotected ships, and that he who compelled men to do so would be guilty of a crime."[7] In subsequent years all European navies equipped themselves with armored vessels and shell guns.

The navy needed modern ships and armaments; chiefly, however, it needed leadership. The civilian secretaries changed with each administration; during the 1840s and 1850s the average secretary served less than two years. He could hardly be expected to provide the kind of long-term guidance which the neglected navy required. Even when a secretary offered sensible leadership, his program often ended with his tenure. Real control of the service rested in the bureaucratic system. Since 1842 five bureaus, all reporting to the secretary, held administrative responsibility for the navy: Construction, Equipment, and Repair; Medicine and Surgery; Ordinance and Hydrography; Supplies and Accounts; and Yards and Docks. Each bureau, under the direction of a senior officer, became something of an independent satrapy, and short-term civilian secretaries were ill prepared to deal with such firmly entrenched and wily bureaucrats.

The American navy on the eve of the Civil War was light of head and weak in the body. In battle it was by no means a match for its European counterparts, but that was not its mission. It had defended American rights in distant places, kept order when necessary, and conveyed scientists and diplomats on important journeys. Unfortunately what was acceptable in peace proved wholly inadequate in war.

President James Buchanan was as weak as his navy. He merely stood by, wringing his hands, while the Union disintegrated. On 20 December 1860 South Carolina voted to leave the Union. In January Mississippi, Florida, Alabama, Georgia, and Louisiana joined the Palmetto State. In February Texas left. With the Deep South gone and the Upper South (Virginia, Arkansas, Tennessee, and North Carolina) wavering, the Union was effectively dissolved, yet Buchanan did virtually nothing. In early February delegates from the seceding states met in Montgomery, Alabama, and formed a new government, the Confederate States of America. They elected Jefferson Davis of Mississippi its president.

While the authorities in Montgomery moved vigorously to create a new government, a sluggish feebleness infected Washington. President-elect Lincoln, who was not to take the oath until 4 March, could do little to stop its course. Two departments in particular, critical to the preservation of the Union, felt Buchanan's flaccid hand: the War Department and the Navy Department.

Some contemporaries suggested that more than simple bewilderment and ineptness had paralyzed the War Department. Accusations of treachery were directed at the secretary, John B. Floyd. This former governor of Arkansas and ardent states' rights Democrat was alleged to have made sure that Federal arsenals in the South were well stocked with munitions before he casually surrendered them to Confederate authorities.

The situation in the Navy Department was somewhat different. Clearly, Secretary Isaac Toucey, a Connecticut Democrat with southern sympathies, was not a knave; he was simply a fool. With a crisis so apparent and so long in coming, any prudent secretary would have called his vessels home. Toucey, however, left his navy scattered across the globe. Twenty-seven vessels—more than half the American navy—were on foreign station: in the East Indies, in the Mediterranean, off Brazil, on the African coast, and in the Pacific. Had Toucey acted more wisely, a sizable fleet might have been concentrated at key southern locations before the Confederates had time to erect powerful fortifications. The secretary's failure to act in time provided the Confederates ample opportunity to prepare a warm welcome for any would-be naval intruder.

Congress noted Toucey's misconduct. Only two days before Lincoln took office it voted "censure" against the secretary.[8] It was a small penalty for such gross negligence.

Meanwhile, at home in Illinois Lincoln was trying to assemble a more effective government. The new secretary of the navy would be a critical ally. Lincoln needed to find someone who was both competent and politically acceptable. The latter would be the most difficult quality to find. The Republican party was still quite new, and it was riven by factions. The party was a fragile coalition united only by the fear of an expanding southern slave power. Free-Soilers, Democrats, and Whigs ranked among its members, and Lincoln needed to be mindful of all factions if he wished to govern effectively. To alienate any one element of the party was to risk collapsing the entire structure. For this reason Lincoln insisted that his cabinet must reflect the composition of the party. As he looked about for a secretary of the navy, he took notice of an old Democratic wheelhorse, Gideon Welles of Connecticut.[9]

Welles was born in 1802 in Glastonbury, Connecticut, into a reasonably prosperous family. After his graduation from the local Cheshire Academy, he went to visit relatives in Pennsylvania. While traveling, he took to writing descriptions of the places he visited and people he met. Several of these sketches were picked up and published by the *New York Mirror*. But writing was hardly a respectable or rewarding career, and once he was back in Connecticut, his family insisted that he find a profession with more status. Welles floated amid business ventures and small-town politics, served a stint as a sergeant in the militia, and was once the Fourth of July orator. Then, in 1824, he made a bold decision. Though he was surrounded by Federalists, he threw in his political lot with the Democrat Andrew Jackson. He was now, and remained at heart for the rest of his life, a Jacksonian Democrat.

The new Democrat allied himself with another Connecticut politician, John Niles, publisher of the *Hartford Times and Weekly Advertiser*. Niles, who recognized Welles's skill as a writer, put him to work churning out biting editorials. Those who felt the sting of his pen called him an "illiberal pedagogue," but Welles also earned respect as a partisan editor. Together Welles and Niles assembled a powerful Democratic party organization in Connecticut. In 1829, thanks to his support of Jackson, Niles became postmaster of Hartford. In 1835 Niles was elected U.S. senator, and Welles moved into the postmastership. Welles lost his job with the Whig victory of William Henry Harrison in 1840 but then recouped in 1844, when his support of the victorious Democrat, James K. Polk, was rewarded with an appointment to the Navy Department. Four years later, when the Whigs and Zachary Taylor came to power, Welles returned to Connecticut politics in the pages of the *Hartford Times.*

Like many northern Democrats, Welles supported the doctrine of states' rights, but he disapproved of the apparent southern desire to nationalize the institution of slavery. Saddened at the direction his party was taking, he broke publicly with the Democrats in 1855 and joined the newly formed Republican party. The following year he accepted the party's nomination for governor. It was a race he was sure to lose, but he won national attention in the process. His efforts earned him a seat on the Republican National Committee, which ensured him a critical place at the party convention in 1860. There he opposed Lincoln in favor of Salmon P. Chase, a candidate even more clearly opposed to slavery.

In forming his cabinet, Lincoln sought the advice of his vice president, Hannibal Hamlin, from Maine. Hamlin put forth three names for the Navy Department—all New Englanders: Charles Francis Adams, Nathaniel Banks, and Gideon Welles. Adams and Banks were both ex-Whigs and close allies of William Henry Seward, Lincoln's choice for the secretary of state.

Welles had his doubts about Seward, a former Whig. Welles's Jeffersonian idealism ran counter to Seward's Hamiltonian view of the Republic. Welles believed in states' rights while Seward saw the states as frequent obstacles to progress. To Welles Seward appeared to be without any fixed points, always shifting, devious, and opportunistic. In a letter to his friend Francis Blair, Welles referred to Seward as that "obnoxious centralist."[10]

Lincoln, however, knew Seward to be able and clever, if

haughty and arrogant. Seward would bring talent to the administration, as well as Whig respectability. Lincoln, who saw similar qualities in Seward and Welles, appointed both to the cabinet. Gideon Welles was to be the new secretary of the navy.

From the outset Welles was distrustful of Seward. Faced with the crisis at Fort Sumter, Welles advocated firmness; Seward seemed conciliatory. At first Lincoln seemed to favor Welles and even agreed to a plan put forth by the secretary and Gustavus Fox, a recently arrived former naval officer and well-connected Massachusetts businessman. Fox offered Welles and Lincoln a scheme for relieving Sumter. With so little else to clutch at, the president and secretary listened to Fox, agreed with his plan, and then ordered him to New York, where he was to prepare a naval force for Sumter.

Seward, taking advantage of the indecision of the new administration, behaved more and more like Lincoln's prime minister. With the help of naval Lieutenant David Dixon Porter, he set out to direct not only the war but the Navy Department as well.

Welles got wind of Seward's meddling one evening while he was dining at Willard's Hotel. His meal was interrupted by the president's secretary, who carried a sheaf of papers. These contained orders which were being sent out to naval officers over the president's signature. It was the first time that Welles had seen these documents. Immediately he recognized Seward's hand. Furious at being outflanked, Welles went to the president and learned from him that the secretary of state and Porter had been interfering in his department's business. Chagrined at his own ineptitude in the matter, Lincoln assured Welles of his confidence in him and withdrew all the orders pending approval of the secretary. But Seward, never one to be stayed from his course, continued his intrigues against Welles. The secretary of state, always confident of his own judgment in any realm, viewed Welles as a ponderous bumpkin and believed that his interference was justified.

Welles had faith in Fox's plan to relieve Sumter. Fox proposed sending four ships—*Powhatan, Pawnee, Baltic,* and *Harriet Lane*—to make a quick dash to the fort with supplies. Critical to the mission was the powerful steamer *Powhatan*. Welles and Fox thought she was assigned to them. But Seward cleverly managed to persuade Lincoln to issue orders to turn the ship over to Lieutenant Porter. The lieutenant, he decided, would not join Fox at Sumter but instead would sail to Fort Pickens at Pensacola, Florida. A bit of comedy ensued. Welles found out about Seward's plan and got the orders rescinded, but not in time. Porter had sailed. Welles sent dispatch boats. When they reached Porter, he refused to believe the new orders. He held his course for Florida.

Fox, as a result, was left with three rather than four ships, although it made little difference. *Powhatan*'s absence was immaterial. She would only have carried more Union spectators to the fiery show over Charleston Harbor.

Gideon Welles's new navy had begun the war in disorder and defeat. Welles's task now was to organize and rally his fleet. His troubles, though, paled before those of his Confederate counterpart. Stephen Mallory, secretary of the Confederate States navy, had to create a navy where none existed.

2

Strategic Views

I

While Gideon Welles was floundering in Washington, Stephen R. Mallory, secretary of the Confederate navy, was struggling to stay afloat in his own sea of difficulties.[1]

Mallory was a convivial, high-living raconteur from Key West, Florida. He was born on the island of Jamaica; his father was a civil engineer from Connecticut, and his mother was an Irish immigrant. When he was about one year old, Stephen and his family moved to Key West. At the time Florida was still a sparsely inhabited territory of the United States. Key West in 1826 was little more than a small collection of buildings perched on a coral outcropping far from the mainland.[2] Aside from wrecking, not much happened there. Wrecking was a profitable and busy enterprise; passing vessels often ran aground on nearby coral reefs. If the crew or captain stayed with the stricken vessel, they might ask the locals to help salvage the cargo, perhaps even the ship. But if the crew abandoned the vessel, she was fair game for the wreckers of Key West. Mallory's hometown was exotic, piratical, and remote. It would be hard to imagine a place more different from Welles's Connecticut.

Local politics attracted young Stephen Mallory, and through his town connections he secured for himself the post of customs inspector. It was hardly a demanding job, and while collecting his government salary, Mallory began to study law with William Marvin, the United States district court judge at Key West. Mallory also found the time to go soldiering in the Second Seminole War (1835–1839). On board a small whaleboat, Mallory patrolled the Everglades, up winding shallow streams near Tampa Bay, and along the endless sandy coast.

On his return from the war, Mallory passed the bar and began to practice maritime law. Soon he became one of the state's leading Democratic politicians. Even as Welles grew suspicious of southern motives, Mallory grew impatient with northern hostility. In 1850 Mallory became a candidate for U.S. senator, and after a fierce battle the state legislature elected him senator.

In the Senate Mallory took a post on the Naval Affairs Committee; not long after that, he became chairman. His own background suited him well for the post, and Mallory became knowledgeable in naval matters. Indeed, Mallory probably knew more about developments in naval technology and weapons than any other civilian in Washington, including the various secretaries of the navy.

When Florida seceded on 10 January 1861, Mallory's course was clear. With considerable sadness, but confident in the rightness of his cause, the senator went south. On 20 February 1861, almost immediately after the creation of the Navy Department of the Confederacy, President Davis named Mallory its secretary.

When the government moved to Richmond in May 1861, Mallory took his offices in the Mechanics Institute, located on Ninth Street between Main and Franklin.[3] His two chief aides were Edward M. Tidball of Winchester, Virginia, and Commodore French Forrest, a former Union naval officer.

As Union secretary Welles could work within an established organizational framework; it was solid, although a bit shaky in places. Mallory as Confederate secretary had to create a whole new structure on what soon proved to be a pitiful foundation.

Mallory's first task was to set in place an administrative structure. What better model to follow than the one he had known in Washington? The Confederate States navy, like so much of the Confederate government, seems remarkably like its northern counterpart. Four bureaus were created to administer it. The Office of Orders and Detail was primarily responsible for matters related to personnel. A second bureau, the Office of Ordnance and Hydrography, was charged with providing munitions as well as nautical instruments and charts. The Office of Provisions and Clothing dealt with issues of food, clothing, and pay. Finally, Mallory relied on the Office of Medicine and Surgery to provide medical care for men in the service.

Mallory's organization had much to recommend it. But it suffered from the two chronic weaknesses of the Confederacy itself: poverty and states' rights. Without an adequate budget, Mallory was chronically hobbled. Poverty was complicated by the independent attitudes of the southern states. Having left the Union because they believed their rights as sovereign states were endangered, the members of the Confederacy were not likely to grant another central government power over them. The government in Richmond had neither the money nor the legal and political power enjoyed by the government in Washington.[4]

Even if Mallory had been blessed with a bountiful treasury, he would still have had trouble finding resources from which to build his navy. In the antebellum years the South hadn't needed to know how to build ships. There were a few yards devoted to small-boat construction along the Atlantic and Gulf coasts. But the South had little else by way of a shipbuilding industry. Inland, southern yards had built shallow-water rivercraft, but their flimsy construction and weak power plants hardly suited them for combat. The Confederate army had fortunately fallen heir to the mighty store of weapons left behind by the retreating Union forces. Only one Union naval vessel, however, fell into southern hands. *Fulton,* an aged steamer, had been laid up at Pensacola. In addition to *Fulton,* the Confederates seized four small revenue cutters, three slavers, and two privately owned steamers. On the day Stephen Mallory took his oath of office, he became the commander of a ragtag collection of ten vessels mounting fifteen guns. The Union navy may have been ill prepared for war, but it was mighty compared with Mallory's fleet.

As Mallory pondered these problems, he had also to deal with internal difficulties. Since the South had so little maritime tradition (compared, for example, with New England), Mallory had to persuade those around him that the South needed a navy. In the minds of most southern leaders, Jefferson Davis among them, the South's survival depended upon land warfare. Too often Davis, a West Point graduate, saw the navy as a mere auxiliary for the army.

Through the spring months of 1861 Mallory argued his case for a navy in the councils of the Confederate cabinet, in the halls of the Confederate Congress, and with his own staff. His effort met with success, and within a short time work began on Confederate vessels at Norfolk, New Orleans, and Memphis.

But resources would always be scarce. Because Mallory understood this, he paid special attention to strategy, hoping that whatever he had might be used wisely. In those spring months plans that were to guide the southern navy for the duration of the war took shape.

Central to Mallory's plan was maintaining contact with the outside world in the face of the northern blockade. Somehow, for the South to survive, the Union blockade would have to be broken.

One tactic the Confederates could try, obviously, was to draw the enemy's ships away from the coast. The American navy had fought this way in both the Revolution and the War of 1812; it had sent warships, singly or in small squadrons, to attack the enemy's commerce. The theory was that as soon as merchants saw their trade jeopardized, they would demand protection; the government, under heavy political pressure, would then have no choice but to withdraw ships from blockade duty to protect the sea-lanes. American experience in both wars had shown, however, that this tactic was not particularly successful in the long run since it meant chasing down one rascal while several others were escaping to sea. The Union's best defense against high-sea raiders was to bottle up the home ports, thus preventing enemy ships from either getting to sea or returning home. Nevertheless, whatever the realities, Americans, who had been brought up on swashbuckling stories of romantic privateers and John Paul Jones, found it hard to resist the lure of raiding at sea. Stephen Mallory, too, dreamed of Confederate warships pillaging Union trade on the high seas.

Secondly, the Confederate sailors might attack the blockaders themselves. Although the Union navy was a superior force, the South might, with the help of energy, imagination, and surprise, achieve local superiority. If Union ships could be destroyed or driven away for a period of time, the South might expect to reap some considerable propaganda value and be able to move its own vessels in and out of port. Mallory placed considerable emphasis on this tactic.

Whether he depended on harassment or on outright attack, one thing was clear: Mallory would need ships.

Despite its overwhelming financial problems, the South did, to a greater degree than anyone might have anticipated, build a considerable number of warships. Some such as *Virginia* were built in government-operated yards, some in private facilities under naval supervision, and some were built under contract in private yards.[5]

Mallory also sought to purchase warships. Before the surrender of Fort Sumter and the beginning of the war Confederate naval agents were dispatched to southern and even to northern ports, looking for candidates to purchase. The difficulty was that vessels constructed for commerce were almost uniformly ill suited for war; they were too small, lightly constructed, and slow. Agents were also sent abroad to purchase vessels and to find yards willing to build warships for the Confederacy. Several yards, particularly in England, were interested in undertaking building contracts, provided that they could find the means to circumvent international law, (which generally prohibited neutral countries from building warships for belligerents) and that the Confederacy could find the cash to pay for its purchases.

Unfortunately for Mallory's peace of mind, his shortage of cash and ships was not matched by a shortage of officers. The southern navy lacked everything except officers. More than 125 captains, commanders, and lieutenants had resigned their commissions in the Union navy and come home to the South to offer their services. Finding naval billets for such a plethora of officers was, of course, impossible. Many naval officers found themselves assigned to duties inland. Often, because of their expertise in ordnance, naval officers were sent to command coastal and river fortifications. In April 1862 the Confederate Congress increased the tiny navy's officer corps by authorizing the appointment of 9 admirals, 6 commodores, 20 captains, 20 commanders, 20 first lieutenants, 65 second lieutenants, and 60 masters. These officers, exiled from shipboard, grew restive; their thirst for rank, even without the command to match it, was unquenchable.[6]

Amid the swarm of officers there were men with talent, and it was the Confederacy's good fortune that several of these men, including such soon-to-be-famous commanders as Raphael Semmes and Franklin Buchanan, did receive commands.

Through all his labors Mallory took it as a fundamental principle that the South could never win a naval race with the North. It was pointless to try to best the giant at its own game. On 10 May 1861 Mallory wrote a prescient letter to Charles M. Conrad, the chairman of the House Committee on Naval Affairs.

After providing a brief history of the development of naval technology in the 1850s, Mallory wrote:

> I regard the possession of an iron-armored ship as a matter of the first necessity. Such a vessel at this time could traverse the entire coast of the United States, prevent all blockades, and encounter, with fair prospect of success, their entire Navy. If to cope with them upon the sea we follow their example and build wooden ships, we shall have to construct several at one time; for one or two ships would fall an easy prey to her comparatively numerous steam frigates. But inequality of numbers may be compensated by invulnerability; and thus not only does economy but naval success dictate the wisdom and expediency of fighting with iron against wood, without regard to first cost.
>
> Naval engagements between wooden frigates, as they are now built and armed, will prove to be the forlorn hopes of the sea, simply contests in which the question, not of victory, but of who shall go to the bottom first, is to be solved.
>
> Should the committee deem it expedient to begin at once the construction of such a ship, not a moment should be lost.[7]

Despite Mallory's exhortations, more than moments were lost. Within a few days of his letter the whole Confederate government was on the road from Montgomery to Richmond, the new capital, a place chosen because it was the state capital of Virginia, the oldest and most powerful member of the Confederacy. Equally important, the new capital stood a bare hundred miles from Washington. The choice of Richmond was an act of deference to Virginia and defiance to the North. Mallory arrived on 3 June, and that night, having not yet even completed unpacking, he was visited by Lieutenant John Mercer Brooke, formerly of the Union navy.

Brooke, like Mallory, was a believer in ironclads, and he laid before the secretary his plan for an ironclad ship. Intrigued, Mallory asked the lieutenant to prepare additional plans and calculations. It was a task that Brooke relished. Mallory, too, was excited. Not only did he now have a plan for an ironclad, but he also had facilities for construction. Thanks to Union bungling, the Confederates had been able to take the Norfolk Navy Yard.

Fronting along the Elizabeth River, the Norfolk yard was strategically located about midway on the Atlantic coast. Stocked with enormous quantities of supplies, it was a prize which the Confederates eyed greedily. Washington knew this but did nothing. As long as Virginia remained in the Union, the Union authorities were reluctant to remove the stores or to send reinforcements to secure the yard. Such actions they feared might only provoke the Virginians and precipitate secession.

After the fall of Sumter, Virginia followed its sister states into secession. By then it was too late to evacuate the yard completely. The Union forces, under the command of the aged and incompetent Captain Charles S. McCauley, made some feeble attempts to destroy the riches of Norfolk. On 20 April, with Virginia's forces at the gates, the yard was put to the torch. The results were not, however, what were expected. To his delight Mallory received the following report on the yard's condition from Lieutenant G. T. Sinclair:

The *Pennsylvania, Merrimack, Germantown, Raritan, Columbia,* and *Dolphin* are burned to the water's edge and sunk. The *Delaware, Columbus,* and *Plymouth* are sunk. All can be raised; the *Plymouth* easily; not much injured. The *Germantown* crushed and sunk by the falling of shears. Her battery, new and complete, uninjured by fire; can be recovered. . . . Destruction less than might be expected. . . . About 4000 shells thrown overboard; can be recovered. The *Germantown's* battery will be up and ready for service tomorrow. In ordnance building all small arms broken and thrown overboard will be fished up. The brass howitzers thrown overboard are up. The *Merrimack* has 2,200 10 pound cartridges in her magazine in water-tight tanks. Only eight guns, 32 pounders, destroyed; about 1000 or more from 11 inch to 32 pounders taken, and ready for our cause.[8]

II

For Mallory this was glorious. But Welles was in agony. Horace Greeley, editor of the *New York Tribune,* echoed the views of many when he wrote: "No man fit to command a sloop of war could have thought of skulking away from a possession so precious and important. . . . This was the most shameful, cowardly, disastrous performance that stains the annals of the American Navy."[9]

While the debacle at Norfolk weighed heavily on Welles, he could scarcely afford to spend time in reflection. On 19 April Lincoln had proclaimed a blockade of the Atlantic and Gulf coasts from South Carolina to Texas. A week later (27 April) he extended the blockade to include the coasts of North Carolina and Virginia. With the blockade proclaimed, it was Welles's duty to make the president's words ring true. In this regard he had some help from an unexpected quarter, the army.

General Winfield Scott was a year older than the federal Constitution. Having made his reputation in the War of 1812, he was promoted to general in chief in 1841 and held that rank at the outbreak of the Civil War. It was Scott who early conceived a grand strategy for the Union, while Welles still had no strategy whatsoever.

Scott took an opportunity to air his thoughts about how the

war should be fought shortly after the fall of Sumter, when he entertained three cabinet officers: Secretary of War Simon Cameron, Secretary of the Treasury Salmon P. Chase, and Secretary of State William Seward. Scott laid out before his distinguished guests a plan which might isolate and strangle the Confederacy. Eighty thousand men would march down the banks of the Mississippi, supported by gunboats, while the southern seacoast was covered by a strict naval blockade. Scott predicted a three-year war and recommended that the Union marshal its resources for a prolonged fight.

But Scott's audience was not receptive to the old man's vision. They were politicians, not strategists, and they wanted quick results. The press was screaming, "On to Richmond"; neither Lincoln nor the electorate could accept such a defensive plan.

When the newspapers got wind of Scott's strategy, they derisively dubbed it the "Anaconda Plan," a reference to the South American snake that kills its prey by slowly crushing it.[10] Welles also had his doubts. Many months later he confided in his diary: "I had, in the early stages of the War, disapproved of the policy of General Scott, which was purely defensive non-intercourse with the insurgents, shut them from the world by blockade and military frontier lines, but not to invade their territory. The anaconda policy was, I then thought and still think, unwise for the country."[11] Welles understood that the fault in Scott's plan lay in its lack of aggressiveness. Though he was a superb battlefield commander, with a string of victories from Lundy's Lane to Mexico City, Scott was a master of maneuver, more inclined to husband resources than to throw them into decisive battle. However, time and events proved Scott right on a good many points. His notion of isolating the Confederacy was sound, and when combined with invasion by land and water, it was the strategy that carried the North to victory.

Welles might have been more at ease during this trying time if he had people upon whom he could rely. Unfortunately he simply did not trust many of those around him. Years of brawling in local politics had made Welles a suspicious man.

And in the current climate there was good reason for his fear. Though 25 percent of the naval officer corps had "gone south," many of those left behind were southerners by birth. Could these men be trusted? In the miasma of suspicion hanging over Washington, Welles could not be certain.

And so far the bureaucratic system had not provided him with professional aides who could be trusted. Thanks to the inefficient organization of the Navy Department, there was really no one to recommend policy to the secretary, no subordinate who could sift and evaluate the schemes at hand. Some unofficial candidates had come forward, however, and among them was the man who had launched the Sumter expedition, Gustavus Vasa Fox. Fox was a Massachusetts businessman with naval experience. He also had impeccable political and social connections: His wife's sister was married to Montgomery Blair, Lincoln's postmaster general. Armed with talent, shipboard experience and political leverage, Gustavus Fox was a man to be reckoned with.[12]

When Hobart Berrien, the chief clerk of the Navy Department, resigned to move to the Treasury, Fox wanted his job. Though his title at first glance seems unimpressive, the chief clerk was, in fact, the second highest-ranking civilian in the department and functioned effectively as assistant secretary. But Welles had his own man in mind. William Faxon, a member of Welles's Hartford circle, was a close personal confidant. He had already been appointed clerk of the second class and was looking forward to a promotion. Knowing that he must pacify Fox, Welles proposed to Lincoln that Fox be reinstated at his old naval rank and given a command of his choice. The president nodded his assent.

In this instance Welles's usually astute political instincts failed him. Montgomery Blair was not a man to be trifled with, and it was his earnest desire that his brother-in-law have the chief clerk's post. Blair had easy access to the president, and he told Lincoln unequivocally that posting Fox to a command at sea would be a waste of his wonderful talent for organization. His skills were

needed to fight the bureaucratic battles of the Potomac, not to
patrol some distant shore. Here Lincoln agreed.

Not wishing to offend his secretary of the navy, the president was cautious. He seems not to have ordered the appointment of Fox but merely to have asked Welles to consider it.
Welles appreciated his situation and looked for a solution to
please both his old friend and his president. His problem was
solved on 24 July, when, as part of a general bill expanding the
navy, Congress authorized the appointment of an assistant secretary of the navy. To no one's surprise, and everyone's relief,
Fox was nominated. It was a superb choice. Fox's knowledge of
naval affairs, his wide contacts in Washington, and his own strong
personality made him an invaluable aide to Welles. Together
they formed a harmonious team that brought energy, integrity,
and skill to the administration of the navy.

Their first task was to establish the blockade. On 17 April
Confederate President Jefferson Davis had called for volunteers to take out letters of marque, commissions allowing private southern vessels to attack Union shipping.

Lincoln hoped to bottle up the troublesome vessels before
they got to sea. It was Welles's unenviable task to fashion a
blockading force from the scant resources at hand. As a symbol
of determination on 10 May the steam frigate *Niagara* arrived
off Charleston to begin the blockade of that port. Her arrival
gave substance to Lincoln's proclamations. Three days later the
Union was buoyed by an announcement from Great Britain:
Queen Victoria had recognized the Union blockade and for-
bade her subjects from any attempt at reaching the closed ports.

At least for the moment, British recognition of the blockade guaranteed its status in international law, but Welles knew
all too well how fickle the world of international diplomacy could
be. The queen's ministry had acceded to the Union blockade
only because it feared angering the North, upon which it
depended economically more than the South. Should that situation change, or should the Union blockade prove ineffectual,
there was every likelihood that Great Britain would choose

another policy. There was no time to lose. Welles had to strengthen the blockade with strategy and ships.

In some ways, finding ships proved easier than deciding how to use them. At the outbreak of the war the American merchant marine was second only to Great Britain's in tonnage and number of vessels. The sudden disappearance of the southern trade (particularly cotton, the largest single commodity carried in American bottoms), as well as the threat of hostile action at sea, kept merchant vessels at the dock. Chartering or buying these idle vessels was the quickest and easiest way to create a fleet.

Initially Welles depended upon naval officers to charter and purchase privately owned vessels. However, his naval officers had very little experience judging vessels outside the narrow band of warships. For reasons of economy, construction, tactics, and supply, navies build only a few types of vessels, while the variations in merchant vessels seemed almost limitless. Shipowners anxious to rid themselves of idle ships delighted in dealing with novice customers from the navy.

Friends in New York and elsewhere soon told Welles tales of how his officers and the department were being cheated. After looking at the evidence, Welles was forced to conclude his officers were falling victim to "a palpable and gross" fraud.[13] The best way to deal with those "clever" tricksters was to send people just as clever to deal with them. Welles turned to some old New York friends in whom he had great trust. The first was his own brother-in-law George D. Morgan, a merchant of the city, who, long with William Aspinwall, another well-known merchant and shipowner, was asked to handle business at the port. The other port at which a considerable number of vessels were being chartered was Boston. There the secretary turned to a hard-nosed Yankee from one of the city's's best-known families, John Murray Forbes. So complete was his trust in these men that Welles gave them no explicit instructions. They were merely to strike the best possible deal for the navy.[14]

Morgan's appointment brought an avalanche of complaints from critics who cried "Nepotism!" It is true that Morgan made a handy profit for himself. He received a 2.5 percent commission, which, over the course of the nearly six months in which he acted, netted him about seventy thousand dollars. This figure drew even more attention when it was revealed that Forbes took no commission at all. Nevertheless, Welles persisted in his plan, even in the face of criticism from the press and Congress. Altogether Morgan arranged for eighty-nine vessels to enter the service, everything from double-ended ferryboats to large merchantmen.

The Navy also needed to build new vessels, and here Welles wisely decided to depend upon experts in his department. Two men are worthy of special note. John Lenthall, chief of the Bureau of Construction, Equipment, and Repair, although not particularly imaginative or innovative, was steady and dependable. He was first appointed to his post in 1853 and enjoyed an international reputation as a naval architect. Welles's other mainstay in these matters was Benjamin Franklin Isherwood, whom he had appointed engineer in chief. Isherwood was a well-known and respected civil engineer when he entered the navy in 1844 as a first assistant engineer. His outspoken nature did not endear him to everyone in the service, but his talents were unmistakable.[15]

It was clear to Welles, Isherwood, and Lenthall that the makeshift fleet improvised by Morgan and Forbes could never perform as well as real warships might. One type of vessel seemed especially essential: a small, fast shallow-draft well-armed steamer, which could scout and blockade the southern coast. Curiously, Isherwood had recently been involved in building just this sort of vessel, not for the American navy but for the czar of Russia.

The Russian navy had dispatched Captain Davidoff to the United States to contract for two gunboats to be used on the Amur River. Davidoff's design called for screw steamers of 691 tons, capable of making roughly ten knots. The Amur design was ideally suited for American coastal work, and Isherwood persuaded Welles that it would be wise for the navy to buy a few. Within ninety days the first of this class was delivered, thus earning the nickname ninety-day gunboat. By the end of the war twenty-three of these fast, heavily armed shallow-draft vessels had been commissioned.

The double enders conceived by Isherwood were larger than the ninety-day gunboats, but still designed for work near the coastline. These were side-wheelers, with rudders at both ends, well suited for narrow waterways where turning might be impossible. At eleven hundred tons they were fairly large and well armed and could make eleven knots.

In the fall of 1861 Isherwood put his hand to vessels designed for the high seas. In February 1861 Congress had authorized construction of seven sloops of war; only four of them were actually built. These were fast vessels of 1,560 tons, one of which—*Kearsarge*, built at the Portsmouth Navy Yard—went on to fame as the destroyer of *Alabama*. Ten sloops of war of similar design, but considerably larger, 1,934 tons, were also built under Isherwood's direction. Later in the war Isherwood turned his attention to still larger and more capable vessels, culminating in the *Wampanoag* and her sisters. These were superb ships far ahead of their time. Their launching unfortunately coincided with the end of the war and the beginning of an American naval ice age.[16]

While agents scurried around looking for vessels to bring into service and Isherwood labored to build new warships, Welles still had to plan a basic strategy. How could he best employ his rapidly expanding fleet? The blockade was his first concern.

Detailed knowledge about the coastline would be the key to the blockade, and no one knew more about this than the superintendent of the Coast Survey, Alexander Dallas Bache. Bache, the great-grandson of Benjamin Franklin, was first appointed to the Coast Survey in 1843. He was a skilled administrator and an able politician who managed to maintain his agency as an independent civilian operation reporting directly to Congress. As superintendent Bache was responsible for the ongoing charting of the American coasts. To this end he employed a large number of surveyors, including dozens of naval officers assigned to survey work. Bache was well known and much admired among the American naval officer corps.

Bache's credentials made him the obvious person for Welles and Fox to turn to for advice. Bache recommended forming an advisory committee.

Welles agreed. Bache, Captain Samuel F. du Pont (a naval officer), Major J. G. Barnard (of the Topographical Service), Commander Charles H. Davis (another naval officer), and Gustavus Fox were appointed to the new board.

Under tremendous pressure the board displayed a remarkable capacity for work. It met several times a week, usually at the Smithsonian, where Bache was a regent. While blockades were as old as naval warfare itself, the board had to contend with new developments. The most important of these was the wide use of steampower, which had freed vessels from their bondage to the winds and tides and gave both blockaders and the blockaded the ability to move their vessels at will. At the same time it limited the blockaders, who found problems of refueling. Sail power might take the blockaders to their stations, but once there, they could remain effective only by keeping a head of steam up, ready to pursue. Unless there were coal depots nearby, resupply would require long voyages and tons of coal. Many ships would be needed, so that the navy could keep a reasonable number on station. Clearly the board would have to solve this important problem.

Hours were spent poring over charts, examining surveyors' reports and notes, discussing tides, currents, weather, distances, and the myriad other items affecting the movements of vessels. Then the industrious board produced five reports, which were presented to Welles on 5, 13, 16, 26 July and 9 August.[17]

Fernandina, on the Atlantic coast of Florida at the mouth of St. Marys River, was the principal subject of the 5 July report. Long recognized as a haven for freebooters and pirates, the town stood at the northern end of Amelia Island. The board suggested that its location on an island made it an ideal place for a secure supply depot which could service the southern end of the Atlantic blockading force. Typically the board's view was exclusively naval and somewhat myopic; it neglected the real possibility of moving inland from this enclave to wage war on the enemy. Although brief reference was made to an operation of "a purely military character" which might be conducted simultaneously, this suggestion never found its way into policy.

Eight days later the board submitted its second report. It concentrated on approximately a hundred miles of coastline fronting South Carolina, with particular emphasis on three locations: Bulls Bay (north of Charleston), St. Helena Sound (between Charleston and Savannah), and Port Royal (slightly north of Savannah). All these were suitable for a base, but the board recommended either Bulls Bay or St. Helena; Port Royal was too strong to venture an operation against.

Only three days after the second report the board presented a third paper. In the opening sentence it put forth a key recommendation: "that the Southern Atlantic coast be divided into two sections, one of which will extend from Cape Henry to Cape Romain [also known as Cape Roman] about 370 miles, the other from Cape Romain to St. Augustine, about 220 miles."

These two stretches of coastline had quite different geographical features. The northern sector was characterized by "narrow belts of sand which separate large inland waters from the ocean, and are divided at irregular intervals by openings or inlets through which the ocean tides ebb and flow and access is obtained to the enclosed sounds." The southern portion was, according to the board, "distinguished by the ordinary ports and bays."

For the northern tier of the coast the board proposed what it called the most expedient and least costly method of closing it: sinking hulks in those passages which ran through sandbars. Relatively small tides, slow currents, and shallow channels made the idea attractive. Admittedly, currents and tides would eventually carve new channels, but they, too, when required, could be blocked. The report cited thirteen specific locations and in each case made mention of the appropriate means for block-ading. In one instance (Loggerhead Inlet), the board admitted that it was "Not well known by us" and declined to make any comment. The other twelve were marked for obstructions.

Ten days later the board members devised a fourth plan for the southern end, the region "distinguished by ordinary ports and bays." Here they divided the coast into three subsections. "The first of these sections will extend from Cape Romain to Tybee Island and embraces the greater part of the coast of South Carolina; the second, from Tybee Island to Cumberland Sound, St. Mary's entrance, Fernandina, covering the whole coast of Georgia, and the third, from Fernandina to Cape Florida, including all the east coast of Florida."

Having already dealt on the thirteenth with the first of these, the board concentrated on the remainder of the coast. The coast of Georgia seemed especially important. The board took special note of the inland passage available from Savannah to St. Marys River, along which relatively shallow-draft steamboats could move. It compared this region with the coasts of Holland and Belgium, pointing out the similarity of its protected coast-line with frequent openings to the sea. After a long description the board concluded this section of the report by warning Welles: "A superior naval power must command the whole of this division of the coast. It will be occupied by the party or nation, whichever it may be, that chooses to place armed steamers of suitable draft in its interior waters, and fortifications of suffi-cient strength at the mouth of its inlets. And the naval power that commands the coast of Georgia will command the State of Georgia."

The third part of the coast, although by far the largest of the three, was also the simplest, for while the stretch from Fer-nandina to the tip of the Florida peninsula was long, it was also barren. The only places worthy of consideration were St. Johns and St. Augustine, to be blockaded "in the usual manner"—that is, with ships standing offshore on a regular basis. The rest of

Florida's east coast might easily be watched by two steamers on patrol.

Report number five, on the Gulf coast, longest of all the groups, was presented on 9 August. Here the board envisioned six major subdivisions:

1. The Florida keys and reefs.
2. The west coast of Florida, from Cape Sable to Cedar Keys.
3. Northern division of Florida, from Cedar Keys to the River Perdido.
4. Coast of part of northwestern Florida, and the coasts of Alabama and Mississippi, from the river Perdido to Ship Island. This section includes Mobile Bay and Mississippi Sound, with its numerous and very important subsidiary bays and dependencies.
5. The coast part of Mississippi and the coast of Louisiana, from Ship and Cat islands to Atchafalaya, Cote Blanche, and Vermilion bays inclusive.
6. And, lastly, a part of the coast of Louisiana and the whole coast of Texas, from Grand Pass, Vermilion Bay, to the Rio Grande del Norte.

It seemed, on the face of it, by far the most ambitious report. However, this last document did not dwell on a possible policy for the entire coast. Instead, it concentrated on New Orleans, made some brief remarks concerning Mobile, and virtually ignored the remaining area which they board viewed as too remote and inaccessible to be of any importance. Thanks to Bache, the board was able to present an impressive amount of hydrographical and topographical information concerning the complicated geography of New Orleans, much more in fact than the charts revealed, which suggests that the board may well have had access to people with "local knowledge," most likely Yankee captains or officers who had run in and out of the port on cotton packets during the prewar years.

As was its wont, the board construed its task as a purely naval one:

> The question is, whether the present plan of proceeding should embrace the conquest of this city [New Orleans] or the sealing up its trade and navigation. We regard its conquest as incompatible with the other nearer and more urgent naval and military operations in which the Government is now and will be for some time hereafter engaged. It is an enterprise of great moment, requiring the cooperation of a large number of vessels of war of smaller class, but of formidable armament, a great many troops, and the conduct of sieges, and it will be accomplished with slow advances. . . . We recommend, therefore, that the subject of the capture of New Orleans be deferred for the present; be deferred at least until we are prepared to ascend the river with vessels of war sufficiently protected to contend with the forts now standing and the temporary fortifications which, in the event of invasion, would be established at every defensible point.

A bit carelessly the board noted that New Orleans had lost much of its importance as an entrepôt for the farmers of the West and Northwest since "[t]hey are bound to the East and to the Atlantic Ocean by railroads and by water connections, through canals and the Great lakes, which render them in a measure independent of the Mississippi for the means of access to the sea." One can only wonder what a westerner such as Lincoln might have made of this easy dismissal of an artery so vital to his region. The board targeted Ship Island in the Mississippi Sound as the proper base for the blockaders and suggested that it be taken and fortified as quickly as possible.

Mobile was dealt with summarily in five paragraphs (compared with eleven printed pages for New Orleans) and with no recommendation for action.

For the most part the board's recommendations were sound, and most were carried out. However, two flaws are worth noting.

First, as previously mentioned, the plans were limited in scope. The Union navy should close southern ports and seize sufficient coastal enclaves to support its fleet. The plans made no mention of exploiting its opportunities and moving farther inland, operations that would have required army cooperation. What the navy, and the Union administration, failed to realize, and later learned at great cost, was that the most effective way to close a port was to capture it.

A second flaw was more tactical than strategic. In its deliberations the board was clearly concerned about the nature of the age-old ship-to-shore duel. Most senior naval officers subscribed to the notion that to reduce a shore emplacement successfully, guns afloat to guns ashore needed to be in the ratio of five to one. That assumption grew out of the board members' own experiences, which were limited primarily to sailing vessels and solid shot. But the wide use of steam-powered armored vessels and the introduction of more powerful guns and exploding shot had changed the old ratio forever. In fact, some advantages had shifted toward the seaward side. Although the navy had yet to realize it, the time had come when a naval squadron could actually deliver a nearly overwhelming volume of firepower.

Welles, who had been watching the board's work carefully, was pleased. So were Fox, the cabinet, and the president. By mid-July the Navy Department was already preparing to act on some of the board's recommendations. It was the coast of North Carolina that drew its attention first.

3

First Victories

I

On 28 June 1861 the people of Charleston bade farewell to the Confederate States privateer *Jefferson Davis*. Captain Louis Coxetter set his course for the North. Over the next seven weeks Coxetter, using a small sailing brig armed with five ancient cannons, took nine Union vessels, including one almost within sight of the New Jersey coast.

Not since the days of the War of 1812 had American merchants felt the sting of privateers in home waters. Northern shipowners were nearly hysterical, and they demanded that Welles launch a counterattack. On 25 July the privateer *Mariner* took a small Yankee schooner off Ocracoke Inlet, North Carolina, and the same day another Confederate rascal captured a brig off Cape Hatteras. Where, many asked, was the Union blockade?

News of these captures also inflamed the fears generated by recent reports. According to these, the Confederates were preparing other vessels behind the shelter of the North Carolina sand barriers and building fortifications to protect these privateering bases.[1] An attack on the North Carolina coast was obviously in order.

Among those urging action was Major General Benjamin F. Butler, a scheming politician from Massachusetts, who saw an opportunity to recoup in North Carolina a reputation that had been damaged by his recent mishandling of troops in Virginia.[2] The decision was made. Hatteras Inlet would be the target, and in mid-July Welles approached Captain du Pont, who was growing heartily tired of Blockade Board meetings, and asked if he would command the naval force accompanying Butler's attack. Du Pont declined, perhaps viewing the proposed expedition as something of a sideshow and preferring to await the better command, which he hoped was forthcoming.[3]

Welles then turned to Commodore Silas H. Stringham, commanding officer of the Atlantic Squadron, at the time flying his flag aboard USS *Minnesota* at Hampton Roads. Stringham was a naval relic who had first seen combat in 1811 aboard the American frigate *President* when her captain, John Rodgers, had attacked and subdued the British sloop of war *Little Belt*. For more than half a century he had served ably. Welles respected him and had sought his counsel during the Fort Sumter crisis. Stringham was reflective and cautious; his only great handicap was a noticeable lack of energy.

On 25 July Stringham received orders to report immediately to Washington. At the Navy Department Welles and Fox laid before him the outline of a plan to seize the Hatteras Inlet and then sink hulks in the channel to block passage. Stringham returned to Hampton Roads to begin his preparations.[4]

Like everyone else, he assumed that this operation would be a typical army-navy attack. Naval gunfire would be used to suppress the fort's guns and do as much damage as possible, but the actual capture would be accomplished by land attack. This scenario had prevailed since guns first went to sea.

To his delight, Butler was given command of the land force:

860 infantry and a company from the Second Artillery at Fort Monroe. His mission was to land and to seize Forts Clark and Hatteras, the two strongholds which guarded the inlet.[5]

Butler's troops traveled light: only ten days' rations and water; only 114 rounds per man. Supplies were kept to a minimum because the intent was to hold the forts only long enough to bring in stone-laden hulks and sink them in the channel. Stringham and Butler planned to execute a raid, not an occupation.

After a brief delay caused by a strong east wind, the fleet finally sailed from Hampton Roads at noon on Monday, 26 August. Stringham and Butler were aboard the flagship *Minnesota* in company with the U.S. steamers *Wabash*, *Monticello*, *Pawnee*, and *Harriet Lane* and the sailing frigate *Cumberland*. The chartered transports *Adelaide* and *George Peabody*, towing schooners with surfboats aboard, carried most of the troops, while behind them steamed *Monticello* and *Pawnee*, towing more surfboats to be used in landing on the beach. Borne by light airs from the south and east, the fleet sailed south toward Cape Hatteras. Through a heavy ground swell, they rounded the cape about noon on the twenty-seventh and came to anchor just south of the cape at 5:00 in the afternoon. Surfboats were hoisted out and brought alongside the transports in preparation for ferrying troops ashore. Soldiers and sailors were roused at 4:00 A.M., given a hearty breakfast, and told to go to their stations. At 6:45 Stringham gave the signal to disembark troops.

Butler planned to land his main body on a beach about three miles north of Forts Clark and Hatteras, while Stringham intended to use most of his squadron to bombard the forts. With *Monticello*, *Pawnee*, and *Harriet Lane* laying down covering fire, the troops were to climb into the boats. But heavy swells and green troops did not mix well, and it took more than four hours for the soldiers to disembark. On their way to shore, their troubles really began. A heavy breaking surf rolled in; the clumsy surfboats were tossed high by the breakers and smashed onto the beach. Fortunately the water was shallow. With dripping wool uniforms, soaked packs, and waterlogged weapons, the soldiers dragged themselves ashore. Another method of approach was tried. Two hulks were brought alongside, loaded with men, and sent drifting toward the shore. Some distance from the beach they dropped anchor, and then, with the aid of a windlass mounted on deck, they payed out a cable and backed toward the shore. This approach proved even worse. By early afternoon Butler had managed to put ashore only 318 men, all wet, tired, and scared.[6]

At Stringham's end of the beach things were going better. *Wabash* with *Cumberland* in tow steamed toward the forts at eight forty-five. By ten they were within range and opened fire. At eleven they were joined by the newly arrived *Susquehanna.* In a move reminiscent of the allied bombardment of Odessa during the Crimean War, Stringham ordered his squadron to steam in an elliptical pattern, firing on the fort as each came around within range. However, their deep draft (eighteen to twenty feet) kept the ships a considerable distance offshore, and in fact, only Fort Clark, the smaller of the two emplacements, fell within range. This simplified target selection, and Clark soon had the undivided attention of Stringham's gunners. At twelve twenty-five Confederates could be seen running from the fort toward Fort Hatteras. Five minutes later Stringham ordered a cease-fire, and not long afterward Butler's advance guard entered the abandoned fort.

With Fort Clark in his possession, Stringham ordered *Monticello* into the channel near Fort Hatteras, hoping to flank her. But as soon as the vessel got within range, the Confederates' withering fire forced a retreat. The Federals opened fire at about four and kept up a steady but ineffectual bombardment until a strong easterly breeze came up, making it hazardous to keep station close to shore. While the main force moved offshore, the lighter-draft vessels—*Pawnee, Monticello,* and *Harriet Lane*— remained close in during the night to cover the troops ashore in case of Confederate attack. It was a long, cold, and hungry night for the Federal troops holed up in Fort Clark. Had the

Confederates attempted to retake the fort, they might well have succeeded, but at dawn, as the vessels raised anchor and moved in, Federal officers were relieved to see the Stars and Stripes still flying.

Monticello and *Pawnee* remained off the landing site, standing by either to remove the troops or to provision them. The remainder of the force responded to Stringham's signal "Attack batteries, but be careful not to fire near the battery in our possession." After a few minutes of firing, it was clear that once more the rounds were falling short. Stringham ordered a cease-fire and then signaled his captains to "use 15 second fuse only, with ten inch guns." This decision turned the day. By firing their large ten-inch guns at maximum elevation, the Federals could rain exploding shot on the fort, wreaking heavy damage and causing numerous casualties. In fewer than two hours the garrison hoisted a white flag.

Forts Hatteras and Clark were bought cheaply—there was not a single Union casualty—but this did not diminish their value to their captors. In fact, though Stringham and Butler had at first agreed to abandon the posts and block the channel, they began in unison to press for a different course. Stringham urged his superiors to keep the forts, going so far as to assert that the inlet was "second in importance [only] to Fortress Monroe and Hampton Roads."

Welles was persuaded and managed, after some considerable discussion, to bring along Lincoln and the remainder of the cabinet. It was a half hearted decision that did, in fact, close Pamlico Sound, but Stringham and Butler also missed a great opportunity. They could easily have sent in a few small steamers to take control of Pamlico and Albermarle sounds, as well as the surrounding area. However, this move would have required additional troops, which General Scott was not willing to send. Furthermore, Lincoln and others would have opposed any diversion of vessels from the blockade. Under diplomatic pressure from European powers that sought to weaken the blockade, Lincoln and Seward were in no mood to agree to any plan that might take so much as a rowboat away from the essential duty of isolating the Confederacy.

Compared with the other great battles of the war, the capture of the Hatteras forts was, as du Pont perhaps guessed, a mere sideshow. For the Navy Department, however, the expedition was crucial. This victory, which came soon after the army's defeat at Bull Run, focused favorable attention on the navy, the more so when it became known that the forts had fallen to naval gunfire alone. Politically astute as always, Welles and Fox moved quickly to exploit their first success in an effort to secure backing for an even more ambitious venture farther down the coast.

I I

For centuries sailors had clung to an adage: "A ship's a fool to fight a fort." It seemed that the superior firepower of land fortifications would always be able to withstand fire from afloat. Landlocked cannon could devastate weak wooden hulls, whose mobility was subject to the whims of winds and currents. At Hatteras, Welles and Fox believed, they had witnessed a balancing, perhaps even a reversal, of the odds between ships and forts. The secretary and his assistant were intoxicated by the possibilities of steam power. Given sufficient mobility and firepower, the Union navy alone might reduce and occupy almost any Confederate fortification within reach of its guns.[7]

Mobility was critical. Had Stringham's force been composed of sailing vessels (only *Cumberland* was an all-sail vessel), the outcome would have been significantly different. Upon coming within range, Stringham would probably have decided to reduce sail and simply slug it out with the forts. In such a situation the forts would have had a clear advantage since the wooden hulls of the fleet were far more vulnerable than the earthworks of the shore. Stringham could have kept his sailing vessels moving, but that could prove risky and painfully slow.

Trying to bring broadsides to bear while coping with perverse currents, tides, and wind made it impossible to deliver heavy, accurate fire.

But steam power made all this labor unnecessary. When Stringham ordered his vessels to engage the enemy, they had only to pass repeatedly by the forts at distances of well over a mile. Confederate gunners had a devil of a time trying to fix the range of the Federals and found it virtually impossible to score any hits on moving targets more than a mile offshore. Steam gave attackers the power to choose their range and position, thereby allowing a much heavier—and more accurate—concentration of firepower.

Weapons, too, were central to deciding the issue at Hatteras. In the decades before the war, three crucial developments took place in naval gunnery: the introduction of larger guns, development of rifled cannon, and adoption of exploding shells.[8] These advances had a profound effect on the war afloat.

John Dahlgren was the person most responsible for the American emphasis on heavier guns.[9] Dahlgren realized the need for heavier guns aboard ships, and it was he who partially solved the problem of increased weight that came with such guns. He devised a casting system that produced a cast-metal homogeneous gun that was considerably thicker at the breech, where the pressure was greatest, and then tapered toward the muzzle. This unusual shape gave the gun its nickname: soda-water bottle. Guns of nine inches, eleven inches, and eventually fifteen inches were manufactured using this method. Dahlgren also invented a small-boat howitzer weighing only 220 pounds that proved useful and popular in the Mexican War. At the outbreak of the war in April 1861 he was second-in-command to Franklin Buchanan at the Washington Navy Yard. When Buchanan "went south," Dahlgren became commander of the yard. Ruggedly handsome and charming, Dahlgren was one of the city's social lions and a personal favorite of Lincoln's.

Although Dahlgren guns had considerable advantages and

were good seagoing weapons, most were still muzzle-loading smoothbores. Parrott guns, on the other hand, were rifled cannon. Rifling gave the projectile a spin that increased the range but, even more important, enhanced accuracy. Invented by R. P. Parrott, a Union army officer from New Hampshire, these guns, like the Dahlgrens, were muzzle-loaders with a very distinctive appearance. In order to sustain the increased pressure caused by the tight fit of the rifled projectile, the Parrott had a heavy wrought-iron band near the breech, where the pressure was greatest.

The expanding size and range of the cannon were crucial, but so was the destructive power of the projectiles themselves. Unreliable fuses and crude black powder had kept shells far less effective than they might have been; nevertheless, they were, in the words of Confederate General Thomas Drayton, well able to "disorder the stoutest men." Confederates, huddled behind earthworks in their bunkerlike bombproofs, could testify to the terrible sounds and effects of exploding shells. Ordinary solid shot fired against soft earth were swallowed up like rocks in molasses; it took the tearing effect of an explosion to blow earthworks apart, driving walls of dirt into the men and disabling their weapons.

I I I

Hatteras was a victory for the Union offense. But as is so often the case in war, losers can learn more from defeat than victors from triumph. Confederate engineers learned how to build earthen defenses which were capable of absorbing a Union pummeling. Now that they were protected from Union bombardments, Confederate soldiers could repel a land attack whenever it came.

In their exaltation the Federals failed to appreciate the true potential of their victory at Hatteras. Neither Washington nor the fleet gave much thought to exploiting the position at Hatteras and moving inland along the waterways to subdue the countryside. For the time being, it seemed that mere possession of coastal enclaves was enough.

Some in the press and the administration might continue to dismiss Scott's Anaconda, but their actions belied their rhetoric. What Stringham and Butler were about was strangulation à la Anaconda; it did not require invasion, only isolation and patience. As a result, at Hatteras and elsewhere along the coast, Union forces failed to collect the dividends due them.[10]

Commodore Stringham became an unrecorded casualty of the campaign as journalistic encomiums turned to criticism. His failure to move beyond the sand barriers into the sounds brought stern reproofs in the Union press. So did his hasty departure from the scene of battle. As soon as the articles of surrender were signed, Stringham loaded prisoners and wounded on board *Minnesota* and sailed north. Welles and Fox were publicly embarrassed; the commodore in command of the southern blockade should not ride at anchor in New York Harbor. When Stringham telegraphed from the city that he most urgently desired to come to Washington for a conference, they suggested to him that his presence would be better appreciated at Hampton Roads.

Their irritation with the aged commodore was doubtless fueled by rising press criticism of the weak blockade. Daily news stories told of merchant vessels passing blithely in and out of southern ports, sometimes even within sight of Union blockaders. Such reports finally prompted Fox (Welles was absent in Hartford) to write a peremptory letter to Stringham. He upbraided him for taking his flagship so far from the area of command, for not maintaining the blockade, and for misconstruing his orders. The letter had the desired effect. Two days later Stringham bitterly asked to be relieved of his command. Although he remained on active duty for the remainder of the war, he never again commanded at sea.[11]

Stringham's departure paved the way for an important

reorganization that had been planned for some time. At his appointment Stringham had been charged with overseeing Union naval forces along the entire Atlantic coast. This command was altogether too large for any one officer. Through July and into August, as the Blockade Board made its presentations, the shape of a better plan began to unfold.

The board had recommended that the East Coast be divided into two commands, one extending from Cape Henry to Cape Romain (370 miles) and the second from Cape Romain to St. Augustine (220 miles). It was a sensible suggestion. But though it made good strategic sense, it might be politically costly. What could the navy do with Commodore Stringham, snug at his anchor in Hampton Roads? He was, after all, the senior officer on the coast, and any division of his command could only be interpreted as a demotion. In a service famous for its factional conflict, removing an officer as well connected as Stringham was bound to have untoward political consequences. His voluntary departure could not have been better timed.

Instead of using Cape Romain as the dividing line, Welles opted for a more balanced command and drew the line at the border of North and South Carolina. The northern sector was placed under the command of Louis M. Goldsborough.

For more than forty years Goldsborough had been in naval service. Like so many in the officer corps, he had impeccable social credentials, not only through his own family but by marriage. He was the son-in-law of William Wirt, an attorney general of the United States (under both James Monroe and John Quincy Adams) and later president of the University of Virginia. Although Goldsborough's roots were in the South, his loyalties were unquestionably with the Union. On 23 September he relieved Stringham at Hampton Roads and hoisted his flag on *Minnesota*.

On the same day (18 September) that the secretary dispatched orders to Goldsborough also sent instructions to the flag officer selected to command the South Atlantic Blockading Squadron: Samuel Francis du Pont.

"J'espère un jour de faire honneur à ma patrie," the young du Pont had written to his mother at the beginning of his naval career. Over his forty-five years of service du Pont had fulfilled his promise; he was undoubtedly one of the service's most distinguished officers.[12] Tall, good-looking, and almost regal in his bearing, he was truly an American aristocrat.

Welles and Fox were well aware of du Pont's talents. Early in August, even before Stringham's departure, they had approached him about an important mission: the seizure of a port along the coast of South Carolina. There were at least four possible targets, as outlined in the board's reports of 5 and 13 July: Bulls Bay, St. Helena Sound, Port Royal (all in South Carolina), and Fernandina in Florida. As noted, the board's report discouraged any attempt against Port Royal; the port seemed too heavily defended to risk an attack. But Welles felt differently. Port Royal was the best deepwater port in the area; since it was most vulnerable on the sea side, naval forces would undoubtedly play the leading role in its capture, and it was so big that its capture would have far more political significance than that of the others. Ever conscious of the need for good press, former journalist Welles saw front-page headlines for the capture of Port Royal. The capture of any other port mentioned would be lucky to make page two. As du Pont listened to these arguments, it was clear that Port Royal should be his target.

On 17 September du Pont wrote to his wife: "I have South Carolina, Georgia, and Florida. . . . The *Wabash* is to be relieved off Charleston and sent to New York, to be my flagship. [Charles H.] Davis goes as fleet captain and [C. R. P.] Rodgers to command the ship, and [Percival] Drayton as ordnance officer."[13]

In giving du Pont such capable officers as Davis, Rodgers, and Drayton, the department had done very well by the new commodore. So, too, had the War Department. It appointed Brigadier General Thomas W. Sherman to command the land forces. He was a West Pointer and a veteran of both the Seminole and Mexican wars.

By the first of October du Pont was meeting with Lincoln,

Welles, Fox, and others to discuss his plans. At these meetings, particularly one with the president, du Pont was taken aback by what he sensed as confusion in the government.

He was not overly impressed with Lincoln. After one meeting with him du Pont described the president as a person always in a "hurry." He did like Fox, with whom he struck up a very cordial relationship. Du Pont viewed Welles as a person not well versed in naval matters. Fox, he decided, was the real power in the department; the secretary merely followed the lead of his assistant. Du Pont was mistaken here, and his underestimation of Welles damaged his cause in days to come. For now, though, he got what he wanted: a strong commitment from the president to provide full support for the expedition. By the eighth he was at New York on board *Wabash*.[14]

On Wednesday, 16 October, at one in the afternoon du Pont signaled the squadron to get under way. From the deck of a nearby steamer Sophie Madeleine du Pont, wife of the commodore, had a wonderful view of this impressive sight. With both pride and sadness she wrote: "When we got on board the steamboat, we saw the *Wabash* had her steam on, and was beginning to move. It was a perfectly beautiful sight to see her and the gunboats and other ships, and I was so glad we had come; it cheered me so to think I was looking at your ship. You can't think how beautiful she looked, or how fine the effect of the salute was where we stood."[15] Thousands of people lined the shore as the fleet passed the narrows and headed for the open sea.

Du Pont's first call was Hampton Roads, where he rendezvoused with additional vessels, including colliers, troop transports embarking Sherman's twelve thousand troops, and supply vessels laden with tons of equipment and hundreds of horses. It was the largest naval force ever assembled in America, a hodgepodge of first-class warships, hastily assembled gunboats, and converted civilian craft. In all, a fleet of nearly eighty vessels was under du Pont's command when, on 29 October, they steamed out of Hampton Roads.[16]

The day before the main fleet departed, du Pont's colliers,

twenty-five schooners, set out under escort of the sailing sloop of war *Vandalia* for Tybee Bar off Savannah. It was a poor deception and fooled no one, particularly the Confederates, who, thanks to northern newspapers, were well informed of du Pont's real intentions. B. S. Osbon, a correspondent for the *New York Herald,* had been sent by his editor to Washington to find out what was going on. While waiting at the secretary's office for an interview with Welles, Osbon noticed a pile of Coast Survey charts laid out on a nearby table. On top of the pile was a chart for Port Royal. Quickly Osbon concluded: "What is uppermost on the pile is uppermost in their minds."[17] When presented to the secretary, he asked Welles for a letter of introduction to the commander of the Port Royal expedition. Welles was taken aback—by both the breach of security and the reporter's temerity.[18] How did he know du Pont was sailing for Port Royal?

"Nobody but the president, Captain du Pont, General Sherman, and myself know that."

"And me," Osborn replied.

"Who told you?

"You, did, Mr. Secretary, just now."

It was a grand bluff, and it worked. Osbon got his letter. To his credit, however, he kept the information confidential. Other reporters, however, were not so circumspect. *The New York Times* published a story describing the force under du Pont while it was still at anchor in Hampton Roads. Du Pont was outraged. He would have been angrier still had he known that before his fleet sighted Port Royal, the Charleston newspapers were reporting his movements and accurately predicting his target.

To the reporters who sailed with the fleet, the expedition seemed like a grand adventure. Osbon wrote lyrically about his first night at sea:

> The sky was as clear as a bell, and myriads of bright, twinkling stars bedecked the deep blue canopy which hung high over our heads. A gentle swell rolled over

the surface of old ocean, rocking our staunch craft. . . . On every hand was heard the rumbling paddles of the host of steamers, and a thousand lights loomed up against the darkened background of the horizon. To our left the green lights on the steamers' paddle boxes looked like bright emeralds set in jet, while to our right the red lights of the steamer bore the resemblance of rubies in a darkened setting. The large passenger steamers, with their cabins brilliantly lighted, looked like a city in the distance, and one could almost imagine himself passing up New York bay. . . .[19]

Meanwhile, on the quarterdeck of *Wabash,* matters were anything but romantic. Du Pont was having a hellish time getting his ships to keep their station. His plan was to proceed in convoy fashion with the transports in three parallel columns. *Wabash* would sail in the van, accompanied by other escort vessels in front, on the flanks, and in the rear. No one in the fleet, including the commodore, had ever organized such a large naval movement. Even in the good weather of the first day, vessels began to straggle and fall out of formation.

In accordance with Rodgers's careful navigation, the fleet set a course that would carry it inside the Gulf Stream but still far enough offshore to avoid the hazards of the waters near Cape Hatteras. By day two, however, Hatteras's dirty weather was upon the fleet, which was making less than five knots, barely enough to maintain headway. Some vessels were out of sight and could not be accounted for. Day three saw gales from the southeast. On day four, 2 November, du Pont recorded in a journal letter to his wife: "L'homme propose, Dieu dispose. The fine ordered fleet, the result of so much thought, labor and expense, has been scattered by the winds of heaven. . . ."[20] The following day *Wabash* was within twenty-five miles of Port Royal, but from her masthead the lookouts could see only seven vessels. During that night and the following day, to the commodore's great relief, more vessels straggled into view. At the final count four members of the fleet were missing. The transport *Governor*, freighted with a battalion of marines, had gone down in a storm. Thanks to the superb seamanship of Cadwalader Ringgold, commander of the frigate *Sabine*, all but 7 of the 650 men aboard were rescued. *Union* and *Osceola* were driven ashore and wrecked while *Belvidere* was forced to turn back. Fortunately for du Pont and Sherman none of the last three was carrying troops. Nevertheless, many tons of supplies and numerous horses were lost.

Sunday, 3 November, was a peaceful day taken up mostly with church services and watching for other vessels to come into sight. *Wabash* was anchored about ten miles off the entrance to Port Royal. A long, low sandbar lay between her and the shore.

Port Royal had a tricky entrance. There were few landmarks on which to take bearings, and the Confederates had removed the navigational aids ordinarily present, including the lightship *Relief*. Du Pont had foreseen this problem, and among the vessels in his fleet was the former Coast Survey steamer *Vixen*, with the survey assistant Charles O. Boutelle on board. On Monday morning *Vixen* moved forward with her men heaving the lead. Within a short time Boutelle had found the channel, set out buoys, and notified du Pont that vessels drawing less than eighteen feet could pass the bar. Light gunboats and transports were signaled to move forward following the buoys, and before dark a good portion of the fleet was riding at anchor in the roadstead, within easy sight of the Confederate positions.

To the port side were Hilton Head Island and Fort Walker with its twenty-three guns, while off to starboard was Phillips Island, where the Confederates had mounted twenty guns at Fort Beauregard and five more at a seaward outwork. Ironically, Brigadier General Thomas Drayton, the brother of du Pont's own ordnance officer, was commanding the defenses. Facing an enemy superior in numbers, firepower, and mobility, General Drayton was in an unenviable position.[21]

Assisting Drayton in his defense of Port Royal was Commodore Josiah Tattnall, formerly of the United States Navy. On Monday evening, with a weak force of converted gunboats, Tattnall made a sortie against four of du Pont's warships. He was easily driven away, and although he and his small force remained in the area and fired occasionally at the Federals, they were no more than a nuisance.

On the fifth du Pont eased *Wabash* over the bar and into a position to lead the attack. Unfortunately it was too late in the day to commence the fight, which was postponed until the following day. On Wednesday, the sixth, the weather turned boisterous, and again du Pont had to wait. Finally, the morning of the seventh dawned clear and calm, and du Pont signaled the fleet to move forward.

Remembering the triumph of Stringham's evolutions at the Hatteras forts du Pont elected to attack using a similar formation. The main battle squadron (*Wabash, Susquehanna, Mohican, Seminole, Pawnee, Unadilla, Ottawa, Pembina,* and *Vandalia,* towed by *Isaac Smith*) was to form a moving ellipse along a northwest to southeast axis. Guarding their northern flank, to prevent any interference from Tattnall as well as to provide enfilading fire, du Pont positioned *Bienville, Seneca, Curlew, Penguin,* and *Augusta.* The main formation would move in a roughly counterclockwise direction and come up midway between the two Confederate positions, firing at both. Once past Fort Walker and Beauregard, the fleet was to come about, head southeast, and close on Fort Walker. As they passed the fort, they were to turn again so that they could bring their broadsides to bear on the Confederate batteries.[22]

Three times *Wabash* poured her broadside into the forts, each time with devastating effect. As General Drayton wrote later, there was "[n]ot a ripple upon the broad expanse of water to disturb the accuracy of fire from the broad decks of that magnificent armada."[23]

For four and a half hours Confederate artillerymen fought a desperate but losing battle against the fleet. Overwhelmed by the volume and accuracy of the naval guns, their own weapons dismounted and destroyed, the defenders of Fort Walker finally retreated from their posts, "which to have defended longer would have exhibited the energy of despair rather than the manly pluck of a true soldier."[24] Captain Rodgers went ashore and hoisted the Union flag over the fort.

Fort Beauregard was even quicker to surrender. Du Pont sent a small detachment across to bombard the fort, but this proved unnecessary. The garrison elected to flee, and the next morning Lieutenant Commanding Daniel Ammen went ashore to raise the Union colors.

Coming so soon after the Hatteras victory, the fall of Port Royal was a wonderful balm to Union pride, sore from recent losses on the battlefield. The ease of victory (du Pont's casualties numbered eight killed and twenty-three wounded) surprised even the commodore himself, who wrote to Fox, "I never thought I could carry it out so fast."[25]

In the days following the Port Royal victory, Sherman's troops began to build strong fortifications in the neighborhood of Fort Walker. With the aid of du Pont's gunboats, the army was able to seize Beaufort and take control of the surrounding countryside. What neither du Pont nor Sherman could know was that the whole interior lay open to them, unresisting. Unfortunately they had neither the inclination nor the manpower to move decisively inland.

Jefferson Davis was quick to realize the threat proposed by the Union navy. While du Pont was still at sea, he sent Robert E. Lee to organize coastal defenses in the Florida, South Carolina, and Georgia area. A keen strategist and trained engineer, Lee knew it would be hopeless to defend a long coast against an enemy who could always choose his own time and place of attack. At Lee's suggestion, the southern strategy was to concentrate on defending a few key places, while holding in reserve forces that could be quickly dispatched to threatened locations. From Lee's perspective, it was a classic case for a mobile defense:

> Wherever his [Union] fleet can be brought to bear no opposition to his landing can be made except within

range of our fixed batteries. We have nothing to oppose
to its heavy guns, which sweep over the low banks of
this country with irresistible force. The farther he can
be withdrawn from his floating batteries the weaker he
will become, and lines of defense, covering objects of
attack, have been selected with this in view.[26]

Such concentration and mobility served the Confederacy well,
and enabled it to hold key ports for nearly the entire war.

Having completed his main mission, du Pont still had two
collateral ventures to which he needed to attend. First he had
to close Charleston Harbor. Twenty-five superannuated New
England whalers were purchased and loaded with stone. Du
Pont ordered his "Stone Fleet" sunk at Charleston. Du Pont
himself seemed somewhat skeptical about the usefulness of the
venture; he called the fleet his elephant. Nevertheless, he knew
that it might serve to close Charleston through the winter. For
that alone, he felt, it was worth a gamble. As it turned out,
du Pont's skepticism was more than justified. The hulks of the
"Stone Fleet" proved tasty to the marine life in the harbor's
warm waters; within a month marine borers and other sea crea-
tures had destroyed many of the hulls intended to block passage. The stone cargo, of course, could not be devoured, but
here again, nature worked in the Rebel's favor. The currents of
the channels in the harbor swirled around the rocks, cutting
new and deeper passages. The whole project turned out to be
a colossal flop and did little, if anything, to foil Confederate
vessels passing in and out of Charleston.

Du Pont's second mission was Fernandina. Although he was
expected to move on Fernandina immediately after taking Port
Royal, neither he nor Sherman was anxious to make the attack.
Both the general and the commodore thought that their forces
needed reinforcement and resupply before attacking again. By
the time they were ready, in March 1862, the Confederates had
virtually abandoned Fernandina, and its capture on the third
was anticlimactic.

By taking the Hatteras forts, Port Royal, and Roanoke

Island, the Union navy had shown its mobility and muscle. From its new vantage points the fleet could sweep the coast and blockade the ports, thus strangling (or so the navy thought) the Confederacy. Whether the North admitted it or not, Scott's Anaconda Plan was indeed a part of northern strategy.

4

Ironclads

Stephen Mallory could ill afford to waste time. Political and popular pressure against him was mounting daily. On 22 November, barely two weeks after the fall of Port Royal, the *Charleston Mercury* was crying out on its front page, "Where is Mallory?" He and his navy were taking heavy blame for the Confederate losses at Hatteras and Port Royal. In contrast with the southern army, still bathed in glory from its decisive victory at Bull Run, the navy seemed woefully inadequate. Despite the editorials, however, Mallory had not been inactive, and he well understood the implications of what had happened at Hatteras and Port Royal. As poor Tattnall's futile sortie had shown, his pitiful navy could never challenge the might of the Union fleet. Nor could the army be expected to hold coastal forts in the face of devastating naval fire. Nevertheless, Mallory was not without hope and certainly not without a plan. If the Federals could not be repulsed, nor the blockade smashed, he would at least make it difficult for the enemy to keep a close station. Mallory was giving serious thought to the use of ironclads.[1]

Welles did not share the southern secretary's prescience as regards ironclads. Only a day or two before the Confederate secretary's letter of 10 May, he wrote Abram S. Hewitt, a New Jersey iron manufacturer, that his department had no plans to construct iron vessels.[2] Welles would learn, but in the meantime, Mallory had the advantage of greater foresight.

On 20 May Mallory ordered Captain Duncan N. Ingraham "to ascertain the practicability of obtaining wrought-iron plates of from 2 to 3 inches in thickness."[3] Even if the plates could be obtained, however, there remained the problem of building or finding a vessel suitable for armoring. For the South, which lacked real industrial capacity, this was not an insignificant problem, and indeed, in the years to come some pointed to Mallory's devotion to large ironclads as a serious strategic error. For the moment, though, thanks to McCauley's mistakes, the secretary had the wherewithal to build a powerful ironclad. Among the vessels scuttled at Norfolk was the steam frigate *Merrimack*. With little difficulty, the Confederates raised the frigate and discovered, to their joy, that her hull was intact and that the engines, though damaged, were capable of repair.

Commander John Mercer Brooke was responsible for *Merrimack*'s conversion to an ironclad. Brooke had approached Mallory with plans for an ironclad early in June. With the assistance of the naval constructor at Norfolk, J. L. Porter, and William P. Williamson, the chief engineer for the Confederate States navy, Brooke presented a design for a casemated ironclad. His original plan called for "a shield and hull, the extremities of the hull terminating with a shield, forming a sort of box or scow upon which the shield was supported." It would be, he noted, "a good boat for harbor defense."[4]

Since Brooke envisioned his "boat" as a harbor defense, he designed it for a shallow draft of about eight feet. Unfortunately the Confederacy could not build such a vessel from scratch; it would have to rely on *Merrimack*, whose draft at twenty-two feet was anything but shallow. Nonetheless, Brooke, Porter, and Williamson created a new vessel from the wreckage of *Merrimack*. In honor of the Old Dominion, they named her *Virginia*.

News of what was happening at Norfolk made its way to Washington. As they heard more and more about the Confederates' plans, Welles and Fox began to think seriously about ironclads. Senior officers in the service, however, were not so easily persuaded. John Lenthall, chief of the Bureau of Construction, Equipment, and Repair, was openly hostile and considered the idea a "humbug."[5] Rather than challenge his staff directly, Welles relied on his bureaucratic instincts and opted to sidestep the issue by throwing it into the lap of Congress. "At the instance of the Department," a bill introduced into the Senate on 19 July called for the secretary to "appoint a board of three skillful naval officers to investigate the plans and specifications that may be submitted for the construction or completing of iron or steel-clad steamships or steam batteries."[6] Welles selected three senior officers for the board: Commodore Joseph Smith, Captain Hiram Paulding, and Commander Charles H. Davis.

During its deliberations the board became interested in two plans. Both were relatively conventional in their approach and called simply for armor-plating standard vessels. One design, later to be built and named *New Ironsides*, bore a striking resemblance to the type of armored vessel then being laid down in Europe. She was a screw streamer with a bark rig. For 170 of her 232-foot length she had 4-inch iron plates, but her bow and stern remained unarmored. She carried fourteen 11-inch smoothbores and two 150-pound Parrott rifles in broadside.[7]

A second conventional design, later to be named *Galena*, sprang in part from the imagination of a Mystic, Connecticut, entrepreneur, Welles's friend Cornelius Scranton Bushnell. Born in Connecticut of an old and distinguished family, Bushnell had wisely invested in railroading. Through that enterprise he had acquired technical knowledge concerning steam engineering and iron construction.

Galena was far smaller than *New Ironsides,* 738 tons versus 3,486; her topsail schooner rig and exaggerated tumble made her home immediately recognizable. Like those of *New Iron-sides,* her engines were designed for a maximum speed of eight knots, and she carried, in broadside, four 10-inch Dahlgren guns and two 100-pound Parrott rifles.[8]

Galena's novel design seemed to disturb the board. She carried a considerable topside weight of armor and heavy guns. Would she be stable? Unable to answer their question himself, Bushnell consulted the Swedish-born engineer John Ericsson. Ericsson was a distinguished inventor with an international reputation and nearly a hundred patents to his name.

Ericsson examined the plans for the new ironclad. To Bushnell's great relief, the inventor told him that *Galena* was not only seaworthy but could "stand a 6-inch shot—if fired from a respectable distance." Ericsson also asked his visitor if he had time to examine a plan for "a floating battery absolutely impregnable to the heaviest shot or shell."[9] His curiosity pricked, Bushnell agreed, and Ericsson laid before him drawings for a vessel the like of which Bushnell had never seen before. It resembled a raft more than a ship. Ericsson's design called for a shallow-draft flat-bottomed wooden hull propelled by a steam screw and covered with iron plates. But the deck arrangement was the most unusual part of the design. It was flush, with very little freeboard and only two structures: up forward a small armored cupolalike position for piloting and, farther aft, a revolving turret housing two large guns. Although he was only a layman in the field of naval architecture, Bushnell knew enough to appreciate the ingenuity of the design. He was also impressed by Ericsson's forceful and articulate presentation. Bushnell asked Ericsson if he could speak to the navy secretary about what he had just seen.

Bushnell came straight to the point with Welles. "The country was safe," he said, for he "had found a battery which would make us master of the situation so far as the ocean was concerned."[10] Welles urged Bushnell to present this exciting new plan to the board, and after a great deal of hemming and hawing, the board agreed to risk the venture. The Union would invest in the new ironclad.

Even before the final contract was signed, plates for the new ironclad were being rolled. With Ericsson's drawings and specifications as the guide, subcontracts were let to various specialty manufacturers. Thomas Rowland at the Continental Iron Works in Green Point, New York, was awarded construction of the hull. Engines went to the New York firm of Delamater and Company, while the turret with its eight layers of one-inch-thick iron plate was assembled by the Novelty Iron Works, also of New York City.

As the ship began to come together, Ericsson gave thought to an appropriate name. He offered his suggestion to Fox in a letter on 20 January 1862:

> In accordance with your request, I now submit for your approbation a name for the floating battery at Green Point. The impregnable and aggressive character of this structure will admonish the leaders of the Southern Rebellion that the batteries on the banks of their rivers will no longer present barriers to the entrance of the Union forces.
>
> The iron-clad intruder will thus prove a severe monitor to those leaders. ... I propose to name the new battery *Monitor*.[11]

Monitor's keel was laid on 25 October, and ninety-seven days later, on 30 January 1862, she was launched.

In command was Lieutenant John L. Worden, a veteran of the navy. Although Worden had twenty-six years of service, he was still far down on the promotion list, and why such a junior officer was given this command is a question open to speculation. The fact that no senior officer raised any objections suggests that *Monitor* was not viewed as a desirable command. And

Worden himself entertained doubts; his orders had made it clear that the business was an experiment.

Worden's first trip out with *Monitor* did little to build confidence. Moving down the East River, the vessel "steered so very badly" that he had to return to the dock. On Sunday, 2 March, Ericsson came aboard to adjust the steering mechanism. Unfortunately there was no time for another trial run. On Thursday, 6 March, *Monitor* was ready to go; accompanied by the U.S. steamers *Currituck* and *Sachem,* she bore south for Hampton Roads.

I I

At 11:00 A.M. on Saturday, 8 March, *Virginia* set out to challenge the Federals. Captain Franklin Buchanan was saddled with a crew that had had no time to drill and a vessel whose faults were all too obvious (her draft was twenty-two feet, and her machinery could barely keep her at five knots). Still, the ironclad vessel tore easily through the Union squadron. Contemporary observers knew they had witnessed a revolution in naval warfare.

About nine in the evening, long after *Virginia* had retired to Norfolk, *Monitor* steamed into Hampton Roads. From her deck Worden was greeted by a sobering sight. It was the same sight enjoyed by an exultant Confederate, Brigadier General Raleigh E. Colston:

> The moon in her second quarter was just rising over the waters, but her silvery light was soon paled by the conflagration of the *Congress,* whose glare was reflected in the river. The burning frigate four miles away seemed much nearer. As the flames crept up the rigging, every mast, spar and rope glittered against the dark sky in dazzling lines of fire. The hull, aground

upon the shoal, was plainly visible, and upon its black surface each port-hole seemed the mouth of a fiery furnace. . . . At irregular intervals, loaded guns and shells, exploding as the fire reached them, sent forth their deep reverberations.[12]

Worden could see only half the carnage wrought by *Virginia*. Early in the battle she had rammed and sunk the frigate *Cumberland*, which now lay quietly beneath the calm waters of Hampton Roads. A third frigate, *Minnesota*, was hard aground and had been saved only by the onset of darkness and an ebbing tide, which had persuaded Buchanan to withdraw.

Within hours the news of *Virginia*'s appalling victory had reached the White House. Early on Sunday morning Welles was summoned to attend the president.

At the White House emotions were in high gear. The cabinet was shocked by *Virginia*'s easy devastation of the Union squadron. Clearly, nothing could stand in the ironclad's way. The secretary of war, Edwin Stanton (a man for whom Welles had little affection), was especially alarmed, according to Welles:

The Merrimac, he [Stanton] said, would destroy every vessel in the service, could lay every city on the coast under contribution, could take Fortress Monroe. . . . Likely the first movement of the Merrimac would be to come up the Potomac and disperse Congress, destroy the Capitol and public buildings; or she might go to New York and Boston and destroy those cities, or levy from them contributions sufficient to carry on the War.[13]

Taken aback by the style, if not the substance, of Stanton's remarks, Welles told the group that *Monitor* was already at Hampton Roads and would, he thought, put an end to *Virginia*'s rampage. Furthermore, the talk of *Virginia*'s bombarding Washington was nonsense, for her draft would not let her up the Potomac. New York and Boston could also rest easy. With her heavy armor and marginal freeboard, *Virginia* was hardly a blue water sailor. Despite Welles's reasoned response, Stanton continued to fulminate. Dahlgren was ordered to find sixty canalboats, fill them with stone, and sink them in the Potomac, to prevent *Virginia* from steaming upriver. Following the meeting, cooler heads prevailed, and Welles was able to prevent the sinking of the canalboats, which, unfortunately, had already been purchased.

On a later trip down the Potomac, an observer asked Lincoln about these canalboats, which still floated by the shore. " 'Oh,' " said the President, " 'that is Stanton's navy. Welles was incensed and opposed the scheme, and it has proved that Neptune was right. Stanton's navy is as useless as the paps of a man to a sucking child. There may be some show to amuse the child, but they are good for nothing for service.' "[14] While secretaries dueled in Washington, events were moving fast at Hampton Roads. Having been grounded during *Virginia*'s attack, *Minnesota* was in a perilous position. Through Saturday night and into Sunday morning her officers and crew, with the assistance of tugs, made every attempt to get her off, but nothing seemed to work. All knew that at dawn *Virginia* would be back to finish her job. Unless *Minnesota* could be freed and moved out of harm's way, she was doomed. Toward midnight the watch spotted a queer craft coming toward them from the direction of Hampton Roads: the *Monitor*. Worden placed his ship between *Minnesota* and Fortress Monroe, a location that hid him from the Rebels yet put him close enough to slip out and intercept *Virginia*.

At eight in the morning *Virginia* steamed toward *Minnesota* and *Monitor*. This time Franklin Buchanan was not in command, he had been injured during the previous day's battle. Reluctantly he had turned over command to his executive officer, Catesby ap Roger Jones.

By the morning light Jones could see *Monitor* lying close aboard *Minnesota*. She looked curious and small next to the towering frigate, but despite her diminutive size, it was clear she was there to defend her neighbor. To get the frigate, Jones knew that he must first destroy or drive away this odd iron craft.

Virginia's crew was called to an early breakfast, and at about eight o'clock Jones signaled engines ahead. *Virginia* could barely make five knots. Her great length and deep draft made her difficult to control, and she was imprisoned by the channel. At a fair distance Jones commenced fire from his forward gun, concentrating on *Minnesota*. He hoped to range close enough to be able to open with a full broadside against *Monitor*. But *Minnesota*'s grounding in shoal water kept *Virginia* at a distance. Jones's cautious pilots became more wary when *Virginia* struck bottom about a mile from the frigate. It took fifteen minutes of hard backing on the engines to free her. In the meantime, *Monitor* steamed close enough so that Jones was able to deliver broadsides against her, but they had little effect. At one point in the battle *Virginia*'s guns fell silent. Jones went below to find out why his batteries were quiet.

" 'Why are you not firing, Mr. Eggleston?' "

" 'Why, our powder is very precious,' " replied the lieutenant; " 'and after two hours incessant firing I find that I can do her about as much damage by snapping my thumb at her every two minutes and a half.' "[15]

That response convinced Jones to try ramming. It took nearly an hour of hard maneuvering for Jones to get into a position from which he could order full ahead to ram. Even then *Monitor*'s greater speed and maneuverability allowed her to avoid any serious damage.

For four hours these two ironclads slugged it out. With her two eleven-inch guns, *Monitor* fired in a fashion intended to breach her opponent's armor, while *Virginia* returned the favor with crashing broadsides. Never more than two hundred yards apart, and often as close as thirty yards from each other, neither ship seemed able to gain an advantage.

Then Jones ordered his gunners to concentrate on *Monitor*'s pilothouse. At about eleven thirty a shot struck close to the tiny slit in the armor through which Worden was peering. Small particles of paint and iron flew into the commander's eyes. Temporarily blinded, he turned command over to his executive officer, Lieutenant Samuel D. Greene. By then, however, the battle was nearly over. *Monitor* moved into shallow water to gain a moment of peace. By the time she moved back into deep water *Virginia* was on her way to Norfolk. The withdrawal of both vessels allowed each side to claim victory, although in fact, the battle was a draw.

Virginia's ten guns had allowed her to deliver a heavier volume of fire against *Monitor*. Her shot had struck Ericsson's armor more than twenty times, but not once had it penetrated. Jones's biggest problem had been the ungainliness of his vessel. She had become even more difficult to maneuver halfway through the battle, when he had lost his smokestack. Draft to the fires had been reduced, causing already low steam pressure to fall. Had *Virginia* been swifter and more agile, she might have been able to ram *Monitor* into submission. As it was, she was barely able to maneuver, let alone close on the enemy.

Monitor's turret-turning machinery had not worked smoothly, but Ericsson attributed that to the effect of shot striking the armor. Most important, *Monitor* had completed her mission of defending *Minnesota*. Washington, to the great relief of all, was safe from attack by the terror of Hampton Roads. For his heroic action, Worden was promoted to commander and given command of *New Ironsides*.

For the first time in history two-steam powered ironclads had slugged it out. To the officers and crew of these iron water beetles, it was an extraordinary experience. These men, as all seamen before them, had been trained in sailing vessels. Whether they were ships, brigs, sloops, or schooners, whether they were assisted by paddle wheels or screw propellers, the men sailed, lived, and worked in an open world exposed to the sea and air. They went aloft to set and trim sails; they were on their hands and knees holystoning the deck or standing watch. In battle, an experience that few of them had ever had, they might be stationed on a lower deck, where the smoke from exploding powder and the lack of sunlight made it a confined and gloomy scene. Even then they were able to catch glimpses of light through the ports and hatches, and they had the comfort of knowing that most of their shipmates were above them, fighting an enemy they could see.

All that was now changed. Both Confederates and Federals were locked in tight iron boxes. Officers on *Monitor* complained that when the vessel was battened down for battle in the stygian darkness, they lost their sense of direction. White lines had to be painted inside *Monitor*'s turret so that her men might know port from starboard.

Once the battle began, the ironclads were filled with noises unknown to sailing sailors: the chugging and clanking of steam machinery used to turn the turret and to run ventilators and pumps. Inside, the air turned hot and foul. Men responded to orders but had no idea what was going on. Only the pilot and captain could see, and even then very imperfectly. On *Monitor*, since the pilothouse was up forward, orders had to be passed back to the turret by means of runners. It was slow and inefficient. The battle was dominated no longer by sounds of cannon and small arms, but by muffled roars and the ringing sound of solid shot bouncing off thick iron plates.

Below the gundeck in the bowels of the engine compartment stokers heaved coal from the bunkers into the boilers. Engulfed in noise, heat, grime, and grit, this "black gang" knew virtually nothing of the battle above. Henceforth in battle men aboard ironclads would be more and more cogs in an industrial machine gone to sea. The age of Eugene O'Neill's play *The Hairy Ape*, a drama of sailors "caged in by steel from a sight of the sky," was close at hand.

Once back in Norfolk, *Virginia* went into dry dock to repair the damage done to her ram during the engagement with *Cumberland* and to strengthen her armor. Buchanan, still recovering from his wounds, was not able to resume command. On 25 March Mallory ordered Josiah Tattnall, whose futile but brave defense of Port Royal had impressed the secretary, to take over command. He was told by Mallory that *Virginia* had proved herself a powerful weapon and a great threat to the Union fleet. Tattnall nodded agreement to Mallory's enthusiastic remarks, but he also understood that when it came to *Virginia,* public perception and naval reality were far apart.

> I could scarcely be supposed insensible to the peril of reputation to which I became exposed from the extraordinary and extravagant expectations in the public mind, founded on ignorance of the character of the ship, and the recent brilliant success of Commodore Buchanan under circumstances which could not again be looked for . . . while it could not exalt him [Buchanan] too highly in public estimation, unfortunately produced a false estimate of the ship, dangerous to the reputation of his successor.[16]

On 4 April *Virginia* came out of dry dock; one week later she sortied out toward Hampton Roads. It was all a bit of anticlimactic. She fired a few desultory shots at *Monitor;* the only response was silence. Tiring of this cool reception, she returned to Norfolk. The truth of the matter was that while *Virginia* might puff back and forth across the roads, she could not defeat *Monitor.* The real battle for control of the area was being decided on land.

In mid-March General George B. McClellan had begun his Peninsula campaign, a movement designed to advance his army between the James and York rivers toward Richmond. In the weeks between mid-March and early April he landed a hundred thousand troops at Fort Monroe. They moved to invest Yorktown, and on 3 May, under cover of darkness, the Confederates withdrew. The fall of Yorktown outflanked the Confederates and made the situation in Norfolk hopeless. After some consultation with the military commanders, Tattnall agreed that *Virginia* would take up a position near Sewall Point and from there cover the Confederate forces as they evacuated Norfolk. Time for evacuation was placed at approximately two weeks, a period allowing for an orderly and complete removal of all personnel and stores. Tattnall left that meeting on 9 May concerned about the future of his ship. His concern was justified. The very next day, despite all their promises to the contrary, the Confederate land forces virtually fled from Norfolk, leaving Tattnall to fend for himself.[17]

Allowing *Virginia* to fall into enemy hands was unthinkable. Relying on information provided by local pilots, Tattnall decided to take her up the James toward Richmond, where she could help defend the city against McClellan's advance. If *Virginia* could reduce her draft to eighteen feet, she could be floated up to Westover, about forty miles from Richmond. Unfortunately the local pilots misjudged the vessel. By the time her draft was down to twenty feet six inches from her normal twenty-two feet, it was apparent that any further reduction could cause great instability. Nor had anyone taken the weather into account. A steady wind out of the west prevented water in the river from reaching a depth sufficient for *Virginia*. This forced the pilots to reverse their former position and argue against moving the ironclad toward Richmond. Tattnall had been poorly served, and now he faced an unhappy situation. He might have tried to move *Virginia* as far upriver as possible, take up a blocking position, and hope for the best; instead he decided to scuttle his ship. Early in the morning of 11 May, after evacuating the crew, Tattnall gave the command to set *Virginia* afire. At 4:58 A.M. the fire reached the magazine and blew the ironclad apart.

Virginia's demise left the James open to the Federal navy. *Monitor*, joined by two other ironclads of more conventional design, *Galena* and *Naugatuck*, proceeded up the river until they encountered obstructions and heavy fire at Drewrys Bluff (also referred to as Wards Bluff). Shots did not bounce off *Galena* as they had off *Monitor;* they holed her repeatedly, causing numerous casualties. *Monitor* moved close to provide support but found that she could not elevate her guns sufficiently to reach the emplacements on the bluff. A few hours of this punishment forced the Federals to retire.

In the following weeks *Monitor* and the Federal vessels remained in the James River and Hampton Roads area, providing support for McClellan. On land, however, McClellan's forces were checked in their advance toward Richmond. After a series of setbacks McClellan skillfully withdrew his troops from the peninsula. At least for the time being Richmond was secure.

By December it was clear to the Union navy that *Monitor* was no longer needed in Hampton Roads. She was ordered to Beaufort, North Carolina, to join the fleet then being organized for an attempt against Charleston.

Hampton Roads to Beaufort meant passing Cape Hatteras at the worst possible time of year. Since everyone knew what a poor sailer *Monitor* was, this seems an astonishing order. Her slight freeboard and low center of gravity gave her all the sailing qualities of a stone. So that she could make some speed, she was taken in tow by the powerful side-wheeler USS *Rhode Island*. According to J. P. Bankhead, *Monitor*'s commander, they passed Cape Henry at 6:00 P.M. on December 29, "wind light at S.W., weather clear and pleasant. . . ."[18] By the next morning a breaking sea was coming up from the southwest. The rolling and pitching loosened the oakum packed around the turret, and *Monitor* began to take water, but so small an amount that the bilge pumps could still dispose of it. About 7:30 in the evening the wind shifted to the south and began to pick up, bringing high seas with it. By now *Monitor* was towing very badly, "yawing very much." Every roll, pitch, and yaw worked the turret, opening seams and allowing more water to flood in. Bankhead ordered additional pumps put to work. By 8:00 P.M. *Monitor* was plunging heavily into steep seas, completely submerging her deck and pilothouse. Water came down through the blower pipes. Each time she fell, after being lifted by the waves, the flat underside of her armor struck the water with such force that more seams were opened. Several times Bankhead signaled *Rhode Island* to halt, hoping to find an easier riding position for *Mon-*

itor. But stopping only exaggerated the roll to such a degree that capsizing became a worry. About 10:30 Bankhead signaled his desire to abandon ship.

Rhode Island came as close as possible. This was risky, since any collision with *Monitor* was bound to do heavy damage to the wooden side-wheeler. *Monitor* was lying with her stern under the side-wheeler's port quarter when Bankhead signaled that he wished to take his crew off. Gingerly *Rhode Island's* crew lowered two small boats. Fortunately the night was clear and there was a half-moon. In the rough seas the boats came alongside *Monitor;* one was nearly crushed against the ironclad's side. Still, both were able to bear off a good number of men. While waiting for the boats to return, *Monitor's* engineer reported that both the engines and pumps had ceased to work. With no power, the ship fell off into the trough and was rolling so wildly that it was impossible to bring boats alongside her. Bankhead ordered the anchor let go to her full length of chain. Happily that brought *Monitor* up into the wind and allowed the boats from *Rhode Island* to take off more men. Some of *Monitor's* crew, fearful of being washed overboard, refused to come on deck. Bankhead, having done everything he could to save the crew and ship, left *Monitor*. A few minutes later *Monitor* slipped to a watery and unmarked grave. Sixteen men went down with her.[19]

Despite her ignominious end, *Monitor* had proved to be a remarkable vessel. The meeting between *Monitor* and *Virginia* might well be termed a stalemate, but still it was a stalemate in favor of the Federals. Now that both sides had ironclads, the advantage would go to the navy that could produce the greatest number. This was a race that the industrialized North could not lose.

5

Farragut

C losing the Atlantic ports was vital to the success of Welles's strategy. But it was also crucial—and in some ways more problematic—to control the vast expanse of the Gulf coast. Early on the Union had had a stroke of good fortune when Lieutenant Tunis Augustus MacDonough Craven, commanding USS *Crusader,* arrived at Key West on 25 March 1861. He found the town "filled by violent disunionists," but thanks to his determined show of force, the town stayed in Union hands.[1] By 19 April, when Lincoln proclaimed his blockade, Key West was the only secure port on the entire Gulf coast available to Union forces.[2] Craven's decisive action provided a toehold from which the navy could advance into the Gulf.

A quick glance at Bache's Coast Survey charts for the Gulf region was discouraging. It was more than fifteen hundred miles from Key West to Matamoros on the Mexican side of the Rio

Grande. Trying to blockade the entire coast seemed an impossible task; in fact, this measure proved unnecessary.

The two ends of the coast, Texas and Florida, had only minor importance. Although both had extensive coastlines, they had few good harbors.

Galveston in Texas and Tampa in Florida were among the most significant of these. Both remained in Confederate hands during most of the war, but they were so far from the scene of battle that they were virtually useless to the Rebels. Moving war matériel from Tampa up the Florida peninsula to the major armies, or across Texas from Galveston or Brownsville, was difficult and hazardous. Good inland roads were virtually nonexistent; both armies needed water and rail networks in order to move materials. In fact, between Key West and Matamoros only two ports were important: New Orleans and Mobile.

New Orleans was the South's greatest port. It was the region's largest city and the sixth-largest in the nation. Most of its wealth was due to its enviable position on the banks of the Mississippi. Like a queen, New Orleans ruled the river and took tribute from all the trade (cotton, wheat, sugar) that passed by. No one has described that great river and its role in American history better than a Mississippi river pilot turned author, Mark Twain.

> The Mississippi is not a commonplace river, but on the contrary is in all ways remarkable. Considering the Missouri its main branch, it is the longest river in the world—four thousand three hundred miles. It seems safe to say that it is also the crookedest river in the world, since in one part of its journey it uses up one thousand three hundred miles to cover the same ground that the crow would fly over in six hundred and seventy-five. . . . The area of its drainage is as great as the combined areas of England, Wales, Scotland, Ireland, France, Spain, Portugal, Germany, Austria, Italy and

Turkey; and almost all this wide region is fertile; the Mississippi valley, proper, is exceptionally so.[3]

The city of New Orleans was the key to control of the giant vital river.

Strangely enough, the South's chief port was a long way from salt water. After passing by New Orleans, the Mississippi flowed more than one hundred miles until it finally met the Gulf. Moving at a rate of two and a half to four miles an hour, the river looked like a broad brown ribbon threaded through inhospitable marshes and bayous. Many miles from the Gulf the river suddenly turned east. At this bend stood two forts: Fort Jackson on the south bank and Fort St. Philip on the north. From here the river widened to an average of two-thirds of a mile, with a depth of thirty-six to ninety feet. Twenty miles down from the forts the river changed suddenly again. At a place called the Head of the Passes it branched off into a triptych of navigable channels, Pass à l'Outre (leading to the east), South Pass, and Southwest Pass. Only Pass à l'Outre, with a depth over its bar of at least seventeen feet, was suitable for large vessels. South Pass could offer only six feet of clearance, and Southwest Pass about thirteen feet.[4]

Welles recognized the critical importance of showing force in the Gulf. Early in May he ordered Captain William Mervine to proceed to the navy yard at Boston. As soon as he arrived, Mervine hoisted his flag aboard the steam frigate *Mississippi* and made preparations to proceed to the Gulf. Welles's orders were explicit: "[Y]ou will establish and enforce a blockade at each and all of the ports in the States . . . south of Key West to the Rio Grande."[5]

Most of Mervine's squadron was already in the Gulf. It included the steam frigate *Niagara* along with the steamers *Brooklyn, Powhatan, Mohawk, Crusader, Huntsville, Wyandotte,* and *Water Witch* and the sloop of war *St. Louis.* At nine in the morning on 23 May *Mississippi* cast off her lines and steamed down

Boston Harbor bound for the Gulf and blockade duty. As she passed the granite walls of Boston Harbor's Fort Warren, something happened:

> [T]he port delivery pipe burst, which, when examined, was found to have been intentionally cut, and the division concealed by an envelope of gutta-percha and canvas. Upon further examination the other pipe was found to be in a like condition. Suspicion as to the perpetrator of this villainous deed points strongly to the late engineer, Michael Quinn, or to a man named Green, a Virginia machinist, who was . . . employed upon the engine at Norfolk. Perhaps both may have a hand in it.[6]

Crippled by this sabotage, *Mississippi* limped back to the navy yard. Four days later, in good repair, she set out again, and on 7 June she arrived at Key West.

From his new base Mervine set about enforcing the blockade. He sent vessels to Fort Pickens and Apalachicola. By the time of his arrival both Mobile and New Orleans were already under watch by the navy. David Dixon Porter in command of *Powhatan* was off Mobile, and *Brooklyn*, under Charles H. Poor, had taken up a position at Pass à l'Outre. In early July *South Carolina*, commanded by James Alden, blockaded Galveston.

The crews of the blockading squadron were beset by mosquitoes, flies, heat, and rotten food. They also had to combat boredom. Neither side was anxious to precipitate action, and indeed, there seemed to be a sort of de facto accord along the coast. Those onshore and those at sea were content to watch one another but do little else. With so few ships Mervine was severely limited in what he could do. It was no secret that despite all the threatening pronouncements from Washington, traffic continued to flow in and out of the Gulf ports.

II

The first fight came in August at Galveston. One of Alden's small boats had been down the coast on patrol. While returning to *South Carolina*, she was fired on by a battery in the town. Alden, according to his report, waited several hours, expecting someone to come out from the town with an explanation for this untoward action. When no one came forth, he decided to bring *South Carolina* within range just to see if the Confederates would "repeat such an act of aggression."[7] Sure enough, they did. As soon as he could see the shots falling near his ship, Alden opened fire.

Unfortunately the Confederate battery was located on the far side of Galveston. During the return fire some of *South Carolina*'s shot fell into a crowded part of the town, killing "an unoffending Portuguese and wounding boys and peacefully disposed persons."[8] Such "acts of inhumanity unrecognized in modern warfare" brought a stiff condemnation from the resident foreign consuls. Alden replied angrily, claiming that he had had no intention of harming civilians.

Alden had done as much as he could for the Union side. One ship could never blockade all the entrances and exits of the port, "and vessels were running in and out at night without interruption."[9]

The ineffectual nature of the blockade at Galveston was an embarrassment to the Federal navy, but not a danger. Galveston was, after all, a somewhat small and remote place. Even in its best prewar years it had been only a minor outpost. New Orleans, however, was an entirely different situation. And the weakness of its blockade was a matter of intense concern.

Mallory, too, recognized the importance of New Orleans, not only as a port but also as a source of ships. He hoped that somewhere in the South's largest port he might find steamers capable of being refitted as warships. He found two: the bark-rigged steamer *Habana*, built at Philadelphia in 1859, and *Mar-*

ques de la Habana, another bark-rigged steamer which had once been a pirate. Mallory bought both and renamed *Habana Sumter;* the *Marques* became *McRae.* Although he intended to refit both vessels as high-seas raiders, only *Sumter* actually got to sea. She went under command of Captain Raphael Semmes.

In selecting Semmes to command *Sumter,* Mallory could not have found a better officer. Like so many of the men to whom Mallory would turn, Semmes was a veteran officer of the United States Navy. He had entered the service in 1826, and by 1861 he was a commander in the navy and chairman of the Lighthouse Board. In mid-February Semmes received a telegram from the the Confederate government at Montgomery urging him to come south. As soon as *Sumter* had been purchased, Mallory offered her command to him.

Mallory had *Sumter* fitted out with one eight-inch pivot gun and four thirty-pounders in broadside.[10] Her mission was to get to sea and attack northern commerce. It was a task for which *Sumter* was ill suited, since she could barely carry eight days' supply of coal, was slow, and had a green crew aboard. Nevertheless, Semmes was anxious to get to sea.

After a brief shakedown run in mid-June he took his ship to the Head of the Passes. From his anchorage Semmes could make out in the distance *Brooklyn* and *Powhatan,* recently arrived from Mobile. They, too, were aware of Semmes's presence, but neither Poor nor Porter was willing to risk approaching *Sumter* for fear of running aground on one of the numerous unmarked sandbars. For the time being, all would watch and wait.

Semmes got his chance to act on 30 June. A local oysterman came alongside with the news that *Brooklyn* had gone off on a chase and left Pass à l'Outre uncovered. In less than ten minutes the crew had stowed their gear and steam was up. A young pilot came aboard, took his station on a horse block, and called over to Semmes, "Give her hell and let her go!"[11]

Brooklyn had left her station to chase down an unidentified vessel, which turned out to be the British bark *Augusta Jessie.* While the boarding party from *Brooklyn* was alongside, Poor sighted *Sumter* making for the open sea. As soon as he could get his men back, he turned to pursue. With a head start and light winds from the north and west, Semmes hoisted all his canvas and told the engineer to push for every possible pound of steam. After a three-and-a-half-hour chase Poor gave up. His pursuit of *Sumter* was taking him far from his station and showed little promise of success.

His decision to turn back was not a popular one; a *New York Times* account complained that Poor's choice had been ill founded.[12] Needless to say, the reaction in Washington was both embarrassment and anger. Mervine, Poor's superior, had the unhappy task of informing Secretary Welles of *Sumter*'s escape. Welles's response was succinct: "No more privateers must be permitted to make their way into the Gulf."[13] Perhaps, Welles suggested, the best way to close New Orleans was to seize a point of land above the Head of the Passes and mount a battery to cover the river.

Fortifying a position at the Head of the Passes made good sense. The secretary's suggestion was soon echoed by the Blockade Board, whose reports on the Gulf proposed just such a scheme. Mervine, under heavy pressure from Washington, decided to attend to the business himself. After consulting with army engineers and arranging for heavy ordnance to be shipped from Tortuga, he ordered Captain John Pope, commander of the steam sloop *Richmond,* to proceed to the Head of the Passes and construct a battery. Pope arrived on 13 September to await the arrival of supplies.[14]

Fully aware of the peril New Orleans was facing, the Confederates had not been idle. Since the city had facilities for both engine manufacture and ship construction, the Confederate Congress had looked there for vessels to defend not only New Orleans but the entire Mississippi. In the late summer of 1861 one million dollars were appropriated for defense of the city and the river. Unfortunately a good deal of the money was squandered as unscrupulous shipowners rushed to sell unfit vessels to credulous government buyers. At the same time Stephen Mallory anxiously dispatched naval officers to bring order out of this embarrassing confusion. According to one of the city's newspapers, "It was clear that there was much dangerously wrong." Among the officers sent was George Hollins, formerly of the United States Navy.[15]

At New Orleans Hollins took charge of one of the queerest craft of the entire war, the ram *Manassas*. Originally launched at Medford, Massachusetts, as the steamship *Enoch Train*, she had been cut down and converted to an iron-plated ram. In early September 1861 she was commissioned as a privateer.[16] *Manassas* was shaped like a whale. Her hull, only three feet of which were above water, was covered with one-and-one-half-inch iron plate laid over a convex surface. Armed with only a single gun up forward, she attacked mainly by ramming with her sharp iron prow. With *Manassas* and an odd assortment of other vessels under his command, Hollins decided to make a daring attack on the Federals at the Head of the Passes.

The boredom of blockade duty often bred sloppiness among commanders, and Captain Pope was no exception. At the Head of the Passes he had stationed four vessels: *Richmond, Vincennes, Preble,* and *Water Witch.* Before dawn on 12 October *Richmond* was taking on coal from the schooner *Joseph H. Toone.* Contrary to good sense and standard naval behavior, Pope had not bothered to post pickets. By the time his own lookouts spotted a strange-looking craft lumbering toward them, it was too late. Even as the alarm was sounded, *Manassas* plunged into *Richmond.* As the ram backed off, damage control parties rushed below to find several broken planks under the port fore channels, admitting a stream of water. The injury was not serious, and within moments the situation was under control. On deck, however, things were in a mess.

There was total confusion on board *Richmond.* Men fired guns at shadows, hoisted signal lights, set off rockets, and abandoned their posts. *Richmond,* with *Manassas* in sluggish pursuit, fled down Southwest Pass without informing her sister ships. Henry French, commander of *Preble,* noted with perceptible sarcasm that when he was told by his lookout that *Richmond* was taking off, "I could not and would not believe it possible until I ran aft and saw her astern and heading down."[17] Not wanting to be the last left on station, French wasted no time getting under way. The others joined in the flight, and as the four vessels moved down the pass, they came to a low-lying sandbar. *Water Witch* and *Preble* passed over the bar, but the two larger vessels were stuck. For several hours both sides exchanged fire, with little damage being done. At about nine in the evening it was reported to Pope that several boats could be seen leaving *Vincennes* and making for *Richmond*. A few minutes later a bizarre scene unfolded on board *Richmond*.

Commander Robert Handy, captain of *Vincennes*, came through the gangway and presented himself to Pope. Wrapped around his middle in large folds was an American flag, apparently the one he had taken down from *Vincennes*. Incredulous, Pope demanded to know why the captain had abandoned his ship. Handy shot back that it was in obedience to signal. Pope had indeed signaled Handy, but his message had been to get under way, not to abandon ship. Someone had either missent or misread the signal.

Pope ordered Handy back to his ship, but Handy replied that it was impossible. He had set a slow match in the magazine and any minute *Vincennes* would be blown to New Orleans. Fortunately incompetence saved the day. The fuse went out, the magazine did not blow, and Handy slunk back to his ship. The next day Handy lightened his vessel in every way he could to get her off the sandbar. Nothing worked. Finally, as a last resort, he heaved all the guns over. *Vincennes* was now afloat—and unarmed.[18]

Federal warships fleeing down the pass, misread signals, a captain abandoning his ship, and a Rebel ram striking terror into the Federal navy—all these images were scornfully reported by the northern press. The navy had been shamed again. Given its importance, New Orleans had to be sealed off. But with so many routes to the sea, it was hard to see how the small force that was currently available could stop the Confederates. If the port could not be blocked, then perhaps it must be seized.

This, as already noted, was not the conclusion reached by the Blockade Board in its 9 August report. At that time the "conquest" of New Orleans had been seen "as incompatible with the other nearer and more urgent naval and military operations. . . ."[19]

Since the report some of those "operations"—the Hatteras inlets and Port Royal—had taken place and in their completion the navy had learned some valuable lessons. One was that a naval force could stand alone against land fortifications. In the case of New Orleans, this was vital. The Union army could hardly be expected to spare large numbers of troops for an operation so distant from its main theaters in the West and northern Virginia, yet it was crucial to strangle southern commerce.

The exact sequence of the events leading to the attack on New Orleans is not known. It does seem, though, that in this expedition, as in so many others, Gustavus Fox played a key role. In his prewar career Fox had commanded merchantmen in and out of New Orleans, and he knew its waters well. What he did not know, however, was the size and power of the Confederate force in the city. Intelligence reports indicated that Forts Jackson and St. Philip had been strengthened, the former mounting seventy-five guns and the later armed with forty. Any naval force trying to steam up would have to pass close to these powerful positions. Fox devised a clever solution. First, Union success at Hatteras and Port Royal had shown that heavy naval gunfire could suppress hostile land fire. Secondly, steam-powered vessels enjoyed a mobility which could slip them quickly by enemy positions. Fox also suggested passing the forts at night. This would be a tricky operation, but he was confident that it could be accomplished.

Passing the forts, however, would not eliminate the serious threat posed by Confederate ironclads such as *Manassas* to any wooden-hulled warship. Fox's answer was simple. As bad as the danger might be now, it would only grow worse as the Confederates built more rams in New Orleans.

If the forts and the rams could be breached, the rest would be relatively easy, for the city itself had a soft underbelly. At the opening of the war strategists on both sides had envisioned an attack on New Orleans via the northern Mississippi. Most of the city's defenses were positioned to repel attacks from the North. If the Union navy could sweep aside the defenses on the southern perimeter, as Fox predicted, a small number of troops could march in via the back door and easily take the city.[20] It was an upending of previous strategy. Instead of using the ponderous Anaconda scheme, with its inexorable march south along the Mississippi, Fox would strike quickly and hard and in one stroke tie off the Confederacy's main artery.

Even Welles, the stodgy bureaucrat, was enthralled by the sheer magnitude and daring of the plan. But he was still uneasy. How could he be certain that his information on the situation below New Orleans was accurate? Bache's charts and Fox's experience were based on prewar data. One person who had up-to-date information was David Dixon Porter, who had just arrived at New York, after seventy-six days of Gulf blockading duty. As always, Porter was eager to put himself forward, and when he received orders to report to the secretary, he did so immediately. Porter arrived in Welles's anteroom on the morning of 12 November. While Porter's account of the meeting focuses characteristically on himself, it is nevertheless instructive:

> I had been waiting nearly all the morning at the door
> of his office when Senators Grimes and Hale came along
> and entered into conversation with me concerning my
> service on the Gulf Coast. During this interview I told
> the senators of a plan I had formed for the capture of
> New Orleans, and when I had explained to them how
> easily it could be accomplished, they expressed sur-

prise that no action had been taken in the matter, and took me in with them at once to see Secretary Welles. I then gave the Secretary, in as few words as possible, my opinion on the importance of capturing New Orleans, and my plan for doing so. Mr. Welles listened to me attentively, and when I had finished what I had to say he remarked that the matter should be laid before the President at once; and we all went forthwith to the Executive Mansion, where we were received by Mr. Lincoln.

My plan, which I then stated, was as follows: To fit out a fleet of vessels-of-war with which to attack the city, fast steamers drawing not more than 18 feet of water, and carrying about 250 heavy guns; also a flo-tilla of mortar-vessels, to be used in case it should be necessary to bombard Forts Jackson and St. Philip before the fleet should attempt to pass them. I also proposed that a body of troops should be sent along in transports to take possession of the city after it had been surrendered to the navy.[21]

What followed was predictable. Lincoln, according to Por-ter, asked the group why all this had not been thought of before. He told them to "go and see General McClellan" and led the way to McClellan's headquarters. McClellan, of course, thought it was a fine idea—as long as he did not have to supply any troops. After some discussion the general agreed that detach-ing a modest force would not endanger Washington. The troops would be ready to move no later than 15 January 1862.[22]

Always cautious, Welles felt a bit uneasy as events surged forward. Two points in particular troubled him. First was Por-ter's insistence that the attack on Forts Jackson and St. Philip be preceded by a mortar bombardment from mortar boats. Preparation for such an assault would take more time than Welles was willing to permit; furthermore, once the heavy mortars began hurling shells, all thought of surprise and the advantages it might bring was over. The second problem was that Porter wanted to go beyond New Orleans. Immediately after the fall of the city, he had decided, the navy should push upriver and seize Vicksburg. That part of the plan seemed to Welles like an overwhelming challenge. After all, Vicksburg was more than two hundred miles upstream from New Orleans. The enemy was in possession of every inch of riverbank between the two cities and could be expected to put up a ferocious resistance. With his usual exuberance Porter was pressing the grand plan.

One great question remained: Who could command such a daring expedition? The three most prominent names that came to mind were Samuel F. du Pont, L. M. Goldsborough, and Charles Wilkes. Unfortunately, all already had important commands from which they could not be spared. As Welles scanned farther down the list of potential leaders, his eye came to the familiar name of Captain David Glasgow Farragut.

Farragut was not an exciting prospect. Born in Tennessee, he had been in the naval service since 1810. His career had been respectable, but far from brilliant. yet it was more than a simple process of elimination that drew Welles to Farragut. As a southerner Farragut, like his shipmates, had faced the agonizing decision of loyalty. When war broke out, he and his wife, also southern-born, were living in Norfolk. He had never hesitated. He told those in the service who elected to join the Confederacy, "Mind what I tell you: You fellows will catch the devil before you get through with this business." With that he turned his back, left Virginia, and moved to New York.[23]

At a time when so many of his fellow officers went south, Farragut's loyalty drew notice. Something else about him also drew notice: He was David Dixon Porter's "stepbrother." The relationship was unusual and important in a service where family and political ties played so large a role.

Farragut's biological father, George Farragut, was a sailing master in the navy. A poor widower with a large family, he took his brood to New Orleans shortly after David's birth. At about the same time Commodore David Porter, father of David Dixon

Porter, was posted to the city as the senior naval officer. With the commodore was his father, the venerable David Porter, who had been appointed a sailing master in the American navy by George Washington. The elderly Porter, eighty-four years of age, enjoyed fishing, and one day, while angling on Lake Pontchartrain, he collapsed from sunstroke. Farragut's father discovered him lying prostrate in the boat. He took him home, but the old man was so weak he could not be moved. The elder Farragut cared for him until he died. At about the same time Mrs. Farragut also died of yellow fever. Grieving for their mutual loss and wishing to repay the kindness of the Farraguts, Commodore Porter offered to become the guardian of Farragut's young son David Glasgow. George Farragut agreed, and David went to live with the commodore and his family. Young David spent fewer than three years with the Porter family, for in 1810 the elder Porter managed to secure a midshipman's appointment for his young charge. Farragut improved on this good offing over the next half century and earned a reputation as a fine officer. That reputation, coupled with the recommendation of his "stepbrother" persuaded Welles that Farragut was the man to send to New Orleans.[24]

Welles wanted a Horatio Nelson, but Farragut hardly fitted the bill. He lacked dash, was not particularly eloquent, and was never a romantic figure. But his uninspiring appearance was misleading. Behind this drab mask was an officer who was to become the nation's first admiral and the modern American navy's first great commander.

To compare Farragut with Nelson would be unfair, but it is not amiss to measure him by standards that may be applied to all great naval commanders. Such standards may vary, but those articulated by the British officer and historian Admiral Sir William Milbourne James are perhaps the best.[25] James suggested that a great naval commander needed to possess at least four "aces": "Moral courage; endurance to resist strain and fatigue; imagination and creative powers for his strategical and tactical plans; and he must be a fine seaman." Farragut either had these qualities or developed them through the experience of wartime command.

Perhaps it was Welles, the politician, a man who had made a career of sizing up others, who sensed in this officer the potential for greatness. Porter would have us believe, of course, that it was his urgency in recommending Farragut that carried the day. That seems unlikely; others, including Fox, may had reason to suggest Farragut. In fact, Farragut had been highly recommended to Fox by Hiram Paulding, the distinguished naval officer and commandant of the New York Navy Yard.[26]

Nor is it correct to say that Welles chose Farragut simply because there were no others. As secretary Welles was not bound to follow a seniority list slavishly, and indeed, he often did not. It may well be that Welles was inclined to select Farragut to avoid selecting someone else—namely, John Dahlgren. It was no secret that Dahlgren was Lincoln's favorite—the president had often suggested that Welles find a suitable place for so talented an officer—but Welles may well have wished to avoid giving such a powerful command to the ever-ambitious Dahlgren, whose direct links to the president might undermine his own authority.

Farragut was first approached informally; Porter went to New York to sound him out. Porter telegraphed back, "Farragut accepts the command, as I was sure he would."[27] Still others remained to be persuaded. Farragut came to Washington and met at breakfast with Fox, who had already endorsed him, and Montgomery Blair, who was still uncertain. Over eggs and coffee Farragut declared his enthusiasm for the New Orleans plan and his conviction that he could actually carry it out with fewer vessels than proposed. Blair detected a bit of bluster, but Welles and Fox carried the day.

By the time Farragut took command, several key decisions had already been made. Welles's misgivings notwithstanding, Porter's suggestion for a mortar boat attack had been accepted, and he had been given command of the flotilla. It had also been agreed that after the capture of New Orleans the fleet would move on to Vicksburg.

At Welles's direction, Fox had already decided upon the size and composition of Farragut's squadron. Benjamin Butler was posted as commander of an army force of eighteen thousand whose task was to occupy the city. On 20 January 1862 orders were dispatched to Flag Officer William McKean, Mervine's successor as commander of the Gulf Blockading Squadron. His command was being divided in half. He would have charge of the coast from Cape Canaveral around Florida to St. Andrew Bay, about a hundred miles east of Pensacola. From his headquarters at Key West, McKean was expected to patrol and blockade the entire Florida coast as well as keep a careful eye on Cuba and the Bahamas. The remainder of the Gulf, St. Andrew to the Rio Grande, was now in Farragut's hands.[28]

Farragut's flagship was the new (1858) screw sloop USS *Hartford*. On 28 January Farragut dropped anchor at Hampton Roads. As he began to scrutinize his officers' reports, which described the status and numbers of ships, men, and material, his early blush of confidence began to fade.

One of the first matters that drew his attention was care of the wounded, for he knew there would be many. He decided to convert the frigate *Potomac* to a hospital ship. Wounded men would be transferred from her as soon as possible to shore facilities. He knew how important it was for morale that the men should know that good medical care was available. He told Fox, "It is a great gratification to *Jack* to see that his comforts are looked to, when he is sick." Farragut went on to ask for additional medical supplies, particularly tourniquets, "as more men lose their lives from bleeding to death from want of early attention, than from the severity of the wounds."[29]

Farragut's correspondence did not confine itself to requests for medical supplies. He asked for coal, ships, ammunition. It seemed that he wanted more of almost everything. Welles and Fox were taken aback. Fox wondered why Farragut, who had seemed satisfied with the department's allocations now thought them inadequate. Fox queried Porter on the matter, probably hoping for reassurance. He got none. The "stepbrother" told Fox that Farragut was old and that a man of his age was "not fit for important enterprises, they lack the vigor of youth."[30] This was indeed a bewildering change of tune!

After some delay at Key West, primarily because of the difficulty of finding adequate coal, Farragut got under way to his rendezvous at Ship Island. He arrived there on 20 February. Only about a hundred miles from the Mississippi delta, Ship Island was a perfect marshaling point for the expedition. Over the next several weeks other units of the squadron arrived, including Porter's mortar flotilla. By mid-March Farragut was ready to move on New Orleans.

6

New Orleans

For a little more than two weeks Farragut, engrossed in his plans for the new expedition, remained at Ship Island. He and McKean discussed the upcoming campaign as well as the continuing problems of the blockade. Undoubtedly McKean told his newly arrived colleague of the endless problems of monitoring so vast an area with so few ships. Even the vessels they had were in miserable shape, their boilers used up, their rigging worn, and their machinery ill cared for. Farragut commiserated with McKean and did as much as he could to shore up his end of the blockade. He bombarded the Navy Department with requests for more men and ships.[1] But this was a diversion, and Farragut never took his eyes off the real prize: New Orleans.

Although the overall strategy for the campaign had been worked out in Washington, Farragut still had to formulate precise instructions for his officers. The heart of the operation rested with Forts St. Philip and Jackson at the bend of the river. Even though it was risky, Farragut decided that he would pass the forts and drive on to New Orleans. It was a hazardous venture. Simply passing under the heavy fire of the Confederates was likely to exact a high price, and it would also mean leaving enemy strongholds in his rear. Success at New Orleans would, of course, cause Forts St. Philip and Jackson to wither and yield. On the other hand, failure at New Orleans, a prospect no one wished to contemplate, would mean a retreat downstream for a second pass in front of the forts. It was an all-or-nothing gamble.

Farragut was reminded of the high risk by Brigadier General J. G. Barnard, chief engineer of the Army of the Potomac, who forwarded a long and careful evaluation of the natural and man-made obstacles facing Farragut. In regard to the forts Barnard asked rhetorically:

> Would it be prudent, however, supposing these works to be all formidably armed, to force a passage, leaving them behind intact, while the fleet advanced on New Orleans? I think not, unless, perchance, in conjunction with an attack to be made on the city by a large land force from Lake Borgne or Pontchartrain; but it is as hard to get a land force from these lakes as to take Forts Jackson and [St.] Philip. A fleet can not maintain itself long above those works unless the city of New Orleans is captured and held by us. If it should meet with damage in passing, and serious reverses higher up, it would have to pass the gauntlet again in retiring and our loss become very great.[2]

Yet Barnard realized, as did Farragut, that if the risk was high, so, too, was the reward. Success would mean nothing less than control of the nation's most important waterway. If New Orleans were not taken from the sea, its conquest would have to wait for the painstakingly slow descent of Federal forces from the north.

While Farragut had good intelligence on the river, thanks

to the Coast Survey, and on the forts, thanks to the army engineers, he was less certain of what the Confederates were up to in the city itself.[3] Had he known what his enemy was doing in New Orleans, David Glasgow Farragut might well have felt a sensation of relief.

I I

Since New Orleans was vital to the Confederacy, it would have been logical for the southerners to take extraordinary measures for the city's defense. They should first and foremost have considered Napoleon's dictum that "nothing is so important in war as an undivided command." Unfortunately the Confederacy was a country that had as its political basis the doctrine of states' rights, a doctrine that mitigated against strong and unified leadership. During March and April 1862 New Orleans was a case in point.

General Mansfield Lovell commanded the defenses of the city. Born in the District of Columbia and a graduate of West Point, he had served in the Mexican War as an artillery officer. He resigned in 1854, became a New York businessman, and by 1861 was the city's deputy street commissioner. He was something of a late arrival in the Confederacy but was well received nevertheless. In October 1861, a newly minted major general, he was given command of New Orleans.[4]

While Lovell commanded New Orleans, his authority did not go beyond the city limits. The "external" defense, including Forts St. Philip and Jackson, was in the hands of another West Pointer, Major General Johnson Kelly Duncan. This division of authority, harmful in itself, was made worse by the fact that Lovell and Duncan had a fundamental disagreement about how the river should be defended. Lovell did not believe that the forts were strong enough to block the Union navy and urged Duncan to place obstructions in the river. Duncan, who, according to Lovell, "had undue confidence in the ability of forts to stop steamships of war," rejected Lovell's advice.[5] Later, perhaps too late, he did relent and had some obstructions put in place.

The command on land was not the only area of confusion. Between August 1861 and February 1862 four different Confederate naval officers were in charge at New Orleans: Lawrence Rousseau, George Hollins, William Whittle, and John K. Mitchell. All of them dutifully sat about building a strong base: building and converting ships and laying in supplies of ammunition and food. At no time did they receive precise instructions from Richmond, other than the usual carping admonitions that they were spending far too much money. What seemed ample to Richmond was paltry to New Orleans, and in February 1862 the governor of Louisiana, Thomas O. Moore, telegraphed a grim message to the Confederate capital: "The Navy Department here owes nearly a million. Its credit is stopped."[6] Moore was an alarmist but not by much. The navy could continue to function, and it was by no means bankrupt, as Moore seemed to suggest. The real financial problem was that the Treasury was forcing Mallory to pay bills with Confederate bonds. Anyone wishing to redeem these bonds for cash (everyone did) had to forward them to Richmond and await the Treasury's action. Mallory protested to the secretary of the treasury, Christopher Gustavus Memminger, and asked for additional cash. Although his response was cordial, Memminger was reluctant to invest scarce cash in the navy. (In this he reflected the general attitude at Richmond.) Mallory felt abused. After all, as he pointed out to Memminger, the War Department at New Orleans had been well supplied with cash. Why not the navy? Some cash was sent, but it was hardly enough to answer Mallory's needs.[7]

Throughout the gloom there was one glimmer of hope. Prewar New Orleans had been an important center for building rivercraft. Foundries existed for producing machinery, and across the river at Algiers were eight dry docks and a corps of skilled builders and mechanics. Already, with the conversion of

Sumter and *Manassas*, New Orleans had shown itself able to turn out capable ships.[8]

Still sitting on the stocks, however, were the city's, perhaps the South's, most ambitious efforts at shipbuilding—the iron-clads *Louisiana* and *Mississippi*.

Both ships were being built just north of New Orleans at Jefferson City, *Louisiana* in the yard of E. C. Murray and *Mississippi* at a facility operated by the Tift brothers. Keels for the two vessels were laid in October 1861, but because there were shortages of nearly every material, especially iron and machinery, construction was very slow. It was further slowed by a lack of proper supervision of the contractors. In the prewar navy the local commander had been obligated to supervise ship construction within his jurisdiction. Under new Confederate regulations, however, the local commander had no such authority. Not until March did Mallory order Mitchell to take control over *Louisiana*.[9] By then, of course, it was too late.

On February 6 *Louisiana* was launched. *Mississippi* went into the water on 20 April. Still, neither vessel was in a fit condition for combat. As New Orleans citizens anxiously awaited the Federal fleet's advance, workmen scurried to ready the two iron-clads for battle. It was hopeless. The workers could not find sufficient materials to complete them, but even if supplies had been forthcoming, it is doubtful that these two ships would have been effective. *Louisiana,* for example, had a serious design flaw: Her two paddle wheels were located amidships, on line with the keel. Even her chief engineer complained that "she was unmanageable in the Mississippi River."[10]

Mississippi was hardly an improvement over her sister. Her designer had never worked on a naval vessel before, and he came up with a most unusual plan. *Mississippi* looked like a floating house; she was propelled by triple screws powered by three engines and sixteen boilers. Since she did not survive very long, it is difficult to speculate on how she might have performed. One observer, Lieutenant Robert Minor, did note that the heavy weight of armor gave her a tendency to hog—that is, to droop at the ends. A recent historian has also noted that in light of *Mississippi*'s size and heavy armor, there is every reason to believe that handling her would have been hopeless in the current of the river.[11]

I I I

Although Butler had not yet arrived with his troops, Farragut decided to move up the river closer to the enemy. On 7 March *Hartford* and *Brooklyn* arrived at Pass à l'Outre. For three days Farragut labored to get his two deep-draft vessels across the bar. Both ships stuck for hours and could not be moved. Realizing it was hopeless, Farragut decided to try another route. He sent R. E. Halter, an assistant with the Coast Survey, to buoy the Southwest Passage. That worked, and despite some bumping and a one-hour grounding, *Brooklyn* floated across. *Hartford* followed, and both vessels steamed up to the Head of the Passes. Chastened by this experience, Farragut left *Hartford* and returned to Ship Island in order to supervise the lightening of his other large vessels so that they might pass the bar more easily. One, *Colorado*, was simply too large and drew so much water that she was finally detached from the squadron. She remained outside Southwest Pass to stand guard and act as a reserve ship from which men and material could be drawn.[12]

As the ships congregated at the Head of the Passes, Farragut, despite his sixty-one years, led his officers in energy and action. John Russell Bartlett, a young officer aboard *Brooklyn,* described what it was like at that anchorage with him: "Farragut was about the fleet from early dawn until dark, and if any officers or men had not spontaneous enthusiasm he certainly infused it into them. I have been on the morning watch, from 4 to 8, when he would row alongside the ship at 6 o'clock, either hailing to ask how we were getting along, or, perhaps, climbing over the side to see for himself."[13]

One of Farragut's principal concerns was to protect his ships as they passed close to the enemy guns. Since he had no armored vessels (it would be some time before he gave credence to such newfangled notions), the task was to get his wooden hulls by the enemy as quickly as possible. He took some field-expedient measures to improve his odds. He ordered anchor chain draped along the hull amidships to protect the boilers. This "chain mail" worked reasonably well, and other commanders later used it to protect vulnerable wooden hulls.

As was his wont, Farragut also took particular care of his men and saw to it that his commanders prepared their sick bays to accommodate casualties. *Brooklyn,* for example, rigged a cot over the main hatch by which the injured could be lowered to the sick bay, while in the surgeon's area itself everything not essential to medical work was cleared out to provide more room.

While readying his fleet, Farragut was pleased to hear that Porter had brought his mortar boats safely across the bar. Under tow from the steamers *Westfield, Clifton, Harriet Lane,* and *Owasco* they came up the river and took an anchorage in Southwest Pass. With the mortar boats safely at rest, *Westfield* and *Clifton* went back down to the bar to attempt to pull across the large steamers *Pensacola* and *Mississippi.* The crews took nearly every movable object off the ships, including most of their coal, and the officers carefully watched the currents and tides. By dint of fearsome tugging, both finally got across on 8 April and, to Farragut's delight, steamed up toward the Head of the Passes.

By mid-April Farragut was finally able to move toward his objective. In the meantime, the Confederates had done every-thing they could to strengthen their defenses. According to reconnaissance reports, they had fully manned the forts, with about seven hundred soldiers at each. As a harassment device, they had prepared fire rafts, which were tied alongshore ready to be loosed. Moored across the river were a series of wooden hulks chained together to block the Federals' passage. Neither the rafts nor the chain were particularly threatening. But some-thing else with far more potential for damage had arrived on the scene. The Confederates had brought down *Louisiana* and tied her up about a half mile north of Fort St. Philip. Farragut could not know that imposing as she looked, she was virtually impotent. Her engines were not working, and her battery was only partially operational. In addition to *Louisiana,* the Confederates had ordered the ram *Manassas,* along with the former tug *Jackson* and the steamer *McRae,* to assist in defense of the forts.[14] The Confederate force afloat was a piddling affair, but it looked very impressive.

Farragut's plan called for the attack to begin with a mortar bombardment aimed at demolishing the forts. On 13 April surveyors from the Coast Survey aboard the tug *Sachem* steamed upriver to fix locations. They then gave Porter and his mortarmen precise distances for ranging their guns. When the mortar boats moved in, they had charts that were accurate to the last detail.

On the morning of 18 April the boats opened fire, each aiming a shell every ten minutes at a range varying from approximately twenty-eight hundred to forty-five hundred yards. For six days, with only an occasional respite, the boats hurled their shells toward the forts. Thanks to the Coast Survey, their fire was accurate but not devastating, apparently. Of the seventy-five hundred shells tossed at Fort Jackson, more than forty-four hundred either landed in or exploded over the fortifications. The problem was not accuracy; it was fusing. Primitive fusing caused the shells either to explode prematurely (thus delivering an ineffectual shower of iron fragments) or, if the fuse was lengthened, to fire the charge only after it had landed. Since the ground in and around both forts was muddy, this often resulted in little more than a muffled roar, followed by a splattering of mud. Porter's ammunition began to run down. Farragut decided he could wait no longer; the time had come to attack.

Everything was in place. Butler had arrived on the nineteenth with his troops. On the night of 20 April a daring raid by the gunboats *Itasca* and *Pinola* had broken the chain across the river.[15] On that same day Farragut issued his general order. "Whatever is to be done will have to be done quickly," he told his men. He would "abide the result—to conquer or to be conquered."[16]

Farragut's first inclination was to put *Hartford* in the van. Fortunately his commanders persuaded him that by thus exposing himself, he might well lose control of the fleet. Farragut agreed to give up his shortsighted plan.

At two on the morning of 24 April two red lights were hoisted into *Hartford*'s rigging. At that signal, capstans turned and anchors were sucked from the mud. Farragut had divided his force into three divisions.[17] The leading, or red, division was under command of Captain Theodorus Bailey. Son of a United States senator, he sported a handlebar mustache and a full head of hair. Bailey was known throughout the fleet for his curious habit of striking his thigh whenever he was well pleased. He took the van on board the gunboat *Cayuga*, followed in column formation by *Pensacola, Mississippi, Oneida, Varuna, Katahdin, Kineo,* and *Wissahickon.* Bailey's division moved ahead and slightly to starboard, an evolution that brought his ships close to Fort St. Philip and at the same time gave the second division space to move into the stream. In the terse fashion common to the genre, *Cayuga*'s log recorded the moment:

> At 2 A.M. flagship made signal to get underway; weighed anchor and led the advance column toward the forts. At 3:30 crossed the barrier and stood upriver, close to Fort St. Philip. At 3:40 both forts opened fire on us. At 4 passed the line of fire of Fort St. Philip and encountered some eleven rebel gunboats; none of our supporting ships in sight engaged the gunboats alone. At 4:30 three of the rebel gunboats surrendered to us, when they were run ashore and burned. Same time the *Varuna* and *Oneida* engaged the other gunboats and sunk and burned them all. At 5 A.M. anchored off Camp

Lovell and received the submission of Colonel Szymansky and his command.[18]

Behind Bailey came the center or second division, composed of *Hartford, Brooklyn,* and *Richmond.* As they approached the forts, the din and smoke were incredible. With Porter's mortar boats pummeling Fort Jackson, and a hot fire pouring in from the ships, it was difficult for the Confederates to respond. Indeed, in all this confusion Farragut's great concern was the danger of being struck by friendly broadsides. Hoarsely he yelled at his gun crews to be sure of their targets lest they strike their own ships.

Farragut was shouting his orders from a perch high in the mizzen rigging. With utter disregard for his own safety, he had climbed the ratlines and braced himself against the shrouds. At that spot he was positioned above the dense, acrid smoke and could make out the forts and other ships. From the deck his signal clerk, B. S. Osbon, the former *New York Herald* reporter, implored his commander to come down to a safer position. Finally, Farragut returned to the quarterdeck. Seconds later a shell exploded near the spot where he had been viewing the battle.

As *Hartford* made her close approach to Fort St. Philip, she ran aground. While she lay in that parlous position, the Confederates pushed a fire raft under her port quarter. Flames licked up the side of the hull into the rigging. But thanks to *Hartford's* well-trained fire control party, the flames were extinguished. The flagship pushed off the mud and back into the battle.

While *Hartford* backed herself out of the mud, *Mississippi,* riding farther ahead, had her own share of problems. She was under attack by the nemesis of the Union squadron, the ram *Manassas.*

The ram's commander, Alexander Warley, knew his intended victim well. In his prewar career Warley had served on *Mississippi.* But there was no time for nostalgia now, and he ordered the helmsman to bear down on his former ship.

Mississippi's commanding officer was below on the gun deck and had left the con to his executive officer, the future hero of Manila Bay, George Dewey. In his *Autobiography* Dewey recalled that the alarm was shouted to deck by a newspaper artist who had gone aloft for a better view. What he saw was *Manassas*.

> Looking in the direction which he indicated I saw what appeared like the back of an enormous turtle painted lead color, which I identified as the ram *Manassas*. . . . There was no time in which to ask the advice of the captain. . . . I called to starboard the helm and turned the *Mississippi*'s bow toward the *Manassas* . . . but . . . Warley . . . wheeling in . . . managed to strike us a glancing blow abaft the port paddlewheel.[19]

Mississippi was tough and well built. She reeled from the blow, but *Manassas* glanced off. Gunners from the Union vessel fired a furious broadside, but *Mississippi*'s high profile and *Manassas*'s low humpback were a poor match. The shot flew harmlessly overhead, plowing up mud and undergrowth on the nearby riverbank.

Warley kept moving downstream, intending to attack and destroy Porter's mortar squadron. That plan was foiled when his own forts, amid the fog of battle, mistook *Manassas* for an enemy and fired on her. Warley came about and headed back up the river. Within a short distance he spotted a large steamer athwart the stream. It was *Brooklyn*. Immediately Warley ordered resin thrown in the fire to bring up steam. Valves were turned to full open, and *Manassas* slipped ahead as fast as her creaky engines would let her. The ram "struck *Brooklyn* fairly abreast of the mainmast with a tremendous crash."[20] The noise was misleading, for *Brooklyn* proved to be as stout as her sister *Mississippi*. Thanks to the chain draped along her hull, she suffered little damage from the impact. *Manassas* retreated upriver, only to come under heavy fire from other ships in the squadron. By now it was daylight. As she came up around Quarantine Point,

Farragut caught sight of her and hollered to his quartermaster, "Signal the *Mississippi* to sink that damned thing." With side-wheels churning the brown water, *Mississippi* dug in and moved toward *Manassas*. On her second encounter with the ram the steamer ran near and fired into her. It was all too much for *Manassas*. She was, in Warley's words, "shot through as though she had been of thin plank, both in the bow and broadside, her smokestack literally riddled."[21]

Having done all that he could, Warley ordered the helm to port and headed for the riverbank. As the bow hit, he ordered the crew ashore, leaving his ship to settle in the river. Her stern filled, she slid toward midstream and dropped to the bottom of deep water. As *Manassas* went to her final rest, Farragut began to receive damage reports from his commanders. The final assessment was unpleasant but acceptable.

One vessel, *Varuna*, had made it past the forts but had then been sunk by Rebel gunboats. Three vessels—*Itasca, Winona,* and *Kennebec,* all in the third division—had not made it by the forts. Although damaged, all three soon returned to service. There were 37 men dead and 147 wounded.

Farragut had passed the forts; however, he had not silenced them. And more trouble lurked nearby. *Louisiana, McRae,* and three smaller Confederate gunboats were still intact and ready to resist.

Downstream General Butler had watched the battle through thick clouds of cannon smoke. When he realized Farragut had passed the forts, he sent a jubilant message: "Allow me to congratulate you and your command upon the bold, daring, brilliant and successful passage of the Forts of your fleet this morning. A more gallant exploit it has never fallen to the lot of man to witness."[22]

Privately Butler was more restrained. He thought it a mistake to leave the forts in Confederate hands, but Farragut's error might well be to Butler's advantage. He asked Porter, who was left in command of the forces downriver, if he might borrow a steamer to bring a regiment around the back channels. He would try to take Fort St. Philip from the rear. Porter readily agreed, and the Twenty-sixth Massachusetts was packed aboard *Miami*. The soldiers were ferried around to a point in the bayous where the water shoaled to less than nine feet; there the men were put into thirty small boats. But even these small craft could not pass all the way through the swamp. For the last mile and a half Butler marched his men through the bayou mud until they reached the Quarantine Station just above Fort St. Philip.[23] Here he sent a few companies across the river to cut off Fort Jackson. No longer a simple spectator, Butler was in a position where he could claim a key role in the fall of the forts.

The general's arrival added to the hopelessness of the Confederate position. At midnight on the twenty-eighth a Confederate officer asked permission to come aboard *Harriet Lane* to speak with Porter. Once inside Porter's cabin, he asked what the terms of surrender might be. At daylight Porter ordered *Harriet Lane* up to the forts. Other officers came aboard to sign the surrender documents. Only then—to his astonishment—did Porter learn that the army officers had no authority over the Confederate vessels still lying along the bank. As he pondered this news, a call came from the deck that *Louisiana* appeared to be headed downstream.

The officers of *Louisiana* had decided on one last gesture of defiance. With guns shotted and combustibles left about, they had set fire to their ship, abandoned her, and cast her off down stream. It was a Wagnerian finale. *Louisiana* drifted down the river, with her guns exploding and flames leaping from every opening in her hull. Federal vessels shortened up on their anchor chains, and men rushed to battle stations, preparing to push aside the fiery intruder. But *Louisiana* never got close enough to worry about. With a blinding flash and a great roar she disappeared. "Not even a ripple showed where she had gone down."[24]

After passing Forts Jackson and St. Philip, Farragut quickly steamed up toward New Orleans. General Butler, who wanted desperately to be part of the surrender at New Orleans, had to scavenge for transportation and follow far in his wake.

Once off the city, Farragut drew up his ships with their broadsides trained over the levee. Since the river was high, Farragut's guns looked down on the city. It was a distressing sight. To prevent the enemy from seizing anything of value, the Confederates had set stores and cotton ablaze. It was, in Farragut's words, a "scene of desolation."[25]

Of particular concern to the Federals was the ironclad Confederate *Mississippi*. From their intelligence reports, they knew she was under construction at the Tift yard. Her exact condition, though, was unknown. Farragut sent *Oneida* upriver to find the ship. As it turned out, there was little need to worry. *Mississippi* was scarcely ready to defend herself, let alone challenge anyone else. Her captain, Arthur Sinclair, had tried unsuccessfully to move his unfinished command upstream to safety. Rather than face the humiliation of surrender, he gave standing orders that if the Federals heaved into view, *Mississippi* was to be scuttled. On the day Farragut arrived at New Orleans, 25 April, Sinclair was down in the city, looking for help to move his ship. When his lieutenant, James Iredell Waddell, saw the enemy, he carried out his captain's order. *Mississippi* went up in flames.

Back at the riverfront, Farragut charged his senior captain, Theodorus Bailey, with the task of going ashore to demand the surrender of New Orleans. Accompanied by Lieutenant George Perkins, Bailey went ashore, only to be greeted by an angry mob of citizens shouting catcalls and curses. Despite the surrender of their armed forces, the people of New Orleans showed no inclination to give up. Bailey and Perkins threw their shoulders back and marched unarmed and unescorted to city hall. Perkins later described that moment: "[A]mong the crowd were many women and children and the women were shaking rebel flags and being rude and noisy. As we advanced, the mob followed us in a very excited state. They gave three cheers for Jeff

Davis and Beauregard, and three groans for Lincoln. They then
began to throw things at us and shout 'Hang them! Hang
them!' "[26]

Despite the verbal assaults and threats of physical violence,
Bailey and Perkins made it to city hall. There the mayor, John
T. Monroe, and the city council met them. It was hardly an
unexpected visit, and the city fathers had rehearsed their greet-
ing. When asked to surrender, they replied that was not within
their power since the city was under martial law. The decision
would have to be made by General Lovell. When he appeared,
Lovell showed no more desire to take charge of the city's surrender than the civilian authorities. When Bailey asked him to
yield, he responded that he had evacuated all military personnel from the city and was about to leave himself.

Although he was distressed by the evasive conduct of the
mayor and general, there was little Farragut could do. Until
Butler's troops arrived, he had only a few hundred marines,
enough to anger the populace but not enough to control them.

The next two days, 26 and 27 April, were peaceful. Farragut made no attempt to land in the city; the people of New
Orleans gathered now and then on the levee to stare at their
conquerors. Symbolically, however, they defied the navy by flying
the state flag over both city hall and the United States customhouse. Farragut could have ignored the affront. On the other
hand, the idea of simply waiting for the army to arrive could
not have gone down well in the naval officers' mess. The outspoken General Butler, who had arrived in advance of his troops,
may even have scoffed at the navy's hesitations.

On 29 April Farragut decided to lower the flags and take
formal possession of the city. Under Captain Henry H. Bell, a
detachment of sailors, two boat howitzers, and a battalion of
marines landed and marched to the customhouse. Down came
the state flag; in its place the Stars and Stripes were raised. At
the city hall the mayor was asked if he wished to haul down the
state flag. It was an honor he gladly declined, and Bell's second-
in-command, Lieutenant Albert Kautz, climbed to the roof and

did the honors by slashing the halyard with his sword. In a gesture of goodwill and diplomacy, Farragut did not insist that the American flag be flown over city hall. It was enough, he said, that the flag be shown over the customhouse, which, after all, was federal property.

On 1 May, to Farragut's great relief, the transports carrying Butler's troops arrived. The next morning Farragut sent Lieutenant Kautz to Butler's headquarters at the St. Charles Hotel. His mission was to deliver to the general the keys to the New Orleans customhouse. That done, Farragut could turn his attention up the Mississippi toward his next objective, Vicksburg.[27]

Capturing New Orleans and closing the Mississippi may well have been the Union navy's most important achievement. With New Orleans in Federal hands, the Confederacy lost at one and the same time the South's largest city and its most important port. A crucial opening to the outside world was closed. Farragut's victory also made inevitable the seizure of the entire river by Union forces, which would split the Confederacy in two.

Just as important as the economic and strategic importance of the city's surrender was the psychological trauma it inflicted on the South. It was bad enough that New Orleans should fall, but that it should fall so easily was something few in the South could understand. Acrimony and accusations of cowardice and incompetence flooded into Richmond; a good deal of it was aimed at Stephen Mallory.

Mallory was understandably despondent. In a letter to his wife, he wrote that after the news of New Orleans he lay "awake night after night with my heart depressed and sore, and my eyes filled with tears." It was, he wrote, "a sad, sad blow."[28]

In the Confederate Congress depression over the fall of New Orleans was mixed with anger, a good deal of it directed at Mallory and by implication his commander, Jefferson Davis. Why, some members asked, had not *Louisiana* and *Mississippi* been sent upstream to safety? Indeed, why were they not finished? Had Mallory failed to push for their completion? Some even whispered that perhaps General Lovell, a northerner by birth, had not been loyal to his oath. Although a congressional investigation eventually exonerated both Mallory and Davis, the obvious confusion at New Orleans did little to enhance their reputations.

Thanks to muddled reporting and a good number of self-serving dispatches from junior officers, a few days passed before the North knew the heroism of David Glasgow Farragut. Some initial reports virtually ignored him and sang the praises of Porter and Butler. Upon reading one garbled account of the battle, Thomas Craven, captain of *Brooklyn*, wrote home to his wife:

> I see that the city of New Orleans surrendered to General Butler and to Porter's mortar boats. This is all as I suspected it would be, and I ventured to say more than six weeks ago to Captain Farragut, that it would be. . . . [O]ne of my remarks when in consultation one night upon the proper mode of attack was, "Should we be so fortunate as to succeed, it will appear in all of our journals as Commander Porter's victory; but should we unfortunately fail, it will be published as the defeat of the Gulf Squadron, under Flag-Officer Farragut.[29]

Thankfully the initial incorrect reports were soon corrected, and Farragut's fame spread across the North. This respectable middle-ranking officer had become a lionized leader. It would be nearly two years before President Lincoln found a commander on land who could equal his new commander at sea.

7

Gunboats

I

The Navy Department had never planned to rest content with the capture of New Orleans. Welles's orders were clear: "If the Mississippi expedition from Cairo [Illinois] shall not have descended the river, you will take advantage of the panic to push a strong force up the river to take all their defenses in the rear. You will also reduce the fortifications which defend Mobile Bay and turn them over to the army to hold."[1]

Farragut's original acquiescence to these orders had been predicated on the southward movement of Union river forces. That movement, however, had fallen far short of expectations. While the Union flag flew over New Orleans's city hall, the northern force was stalled at Fort Pillow, forty miles above Memphis and more than eight hundred miles upriver from New Orleans. The thought of steaming so far against a strong current through enemy territory was alarming, and Farragut began to have second thoughts. Perhaps Mobile might be a more tempting target.[2]

Compared with seizing the Mississippi, the capture of Mobile was of trifling consequence. The idea that the navy's new Nelson might move against such a strategically insignificant target alarmed Welles and Fox and certainly found no favor with Butler. After learning of Farragut's plan, Butler wrote to the secretary of war on 29 April that he was on his way to meet Farragut in the hope of persuading "the Flag Officer to pass up the River as far as the mouth of Red River if possible, so as to cut off the enemy's supplies and make there a landing and demonstration."[3] Fox was even more alarmed at the thought of abandoning a push up the river. Two weeks later he wrote to Porter: "Somebody has made a most serious blunder, in persuading the Flag Officer to go at Mobile instead of obeying his instructions to go up the Mississippi. . . . It seems extraordinary how Farragut could have committed this terrible mistake. . . . Mobile and the whole Gulf will fall at any time, but the Mississippi is a golden opportunity that I fear is fast slipping through our fingers."[4]

Fortunately Farragut changed his course. On 3 May he ordered Craven to proceed with *Brooklyn* to Baton Rouge and demand the surrender of the town.[5] That was easily accomplished, and on the ninth Farragut joined Craven at Baton Rouge. For the next three weeks his vessels patrolled the river between Natchez and New Orleans. At the same time he ordered *Oneida* to Vicksburg for reconnaissance. Early in June Farragut, under pressure on all sides, reluctantly agreed to move against Vicksburg and join up with the northern river force at Memphis. On 11 June he wrote to his old friend Theodorus Bailey:

> I am now up the Mississippi again, and when I will go down God only knows . . . the Department is under the impression that it is easier for me, with my dilapi-

dated vessels, to encounter the difficulties of the Mississippi and ascend a thousand miles against a strong current than it is for [Andrew H.] Foote or [Charles H.] Davis, with vessels peculiarly constructed for the river, to come down the stream, and therefore I am compelled to do it, at what sacrifice time will show.[6]

Farragut's misgivings were echoed by his staff. Henry Bell noted in his private journal: "Opinions in the fleet unanimously against the feasibility of the undertaking."[7] But whatever Farragut, Bell, and the other officers might think, their orders were clear. It was their duty to steam up the Mississippi and make contact with the northern river squadron.

River operations along the upper Mississippi and Ohio had gotten under way soon after the fall of Sumter. Early in May 1861 General Scott, as part of his Anaconda Plan, had suggested to George B. McClellan, commanding general of the Ohio Volunteers, that troop movement down the rivers needed to be supported by "from twelve to twenty seven steam gunboats."[8] At the same time some members of the cabinet were also urging action on the western rivers. Among the most vocal was the attorney general, Edward Bates. A Virginian by birth, Bates had become a successful lawyer and politician in Missouri. Having lived in river country, he understood the strategic importance of waterways.

Bates was a close friend of another native of river country: James Buchanan Eads, an expert salvager. During the 1840s river navigation was a hazardous business and wrecks were common. The young Eads, alert to opportunities, had started a salvage business. Although he had no formal training in engineering or design, he invented and patented a diving bell and a floating pump device. These ingenious new machines allowed him to lift apparently unsalvageable wrecks. By the mid-1840s James Eads was one of the best-known and wealthiest rivermen along the entire Mississippi.[9]

On 17 April Bates wrote to his friend from Washington:

"Be not surprised if you are called here suddenly by telegram. If called, come instantly. In a certain contingency it will be necessary to have the aid of the most thorough knowledge of our Western rivers and the use of steam on them, and in that event I have advised that you should be consulted."[10]

A telegram did follow, and Eads hurried to the capital, where he was introduced to both Welles and Fox. He had come prepared with a plan, and on 29 April he submitted to Welles a scheme for "effectually blockading the commerce of the rebelling States upon the Mississippi River."[11]

Quite correctly Eads saw that the key to control of the upper Mississippi was the town of Cairo, Illinois. As a place of habitation Cairo had little to recommend it; as a river base it was all-important. It was situated at the tip of a delta where the Ohio and the Mississippi joined. Any force that occupied the town could control passage on both rivers. Eads described its strategic possibilities in the strongest terms:

> The city of Cairo has a broad levee front on the Ohio
> River, raised about fourteen feet above the natural level
> of the city and extending for a distance of about three
> miles immediately along the river. On the Mississippi
> side extends a levee of the same height and about the
> same length, but removed from the bank of the river
> from 100 yards to half a mile distant, to be out of dan-
> ger from the caving in of the bank. From this levee,
> across from the Ohio River, a levee extends of the same
> height, by which the town is protected from the back-
> water, the whole forming a delta. These levees would
> afford admirable defenses upon which to plant batter-
> ies at proper points. The great Central Railroad of Illi-
> nois, in addition to the Ohio and Mississippi rivers,
> would afford means of supplying this point with great
> rapidity with troops, munitions of war, and provisions,
> and the place would be capable of accommodating a
> force on land of 50,000 men, if need be.[12]

Although Cairo was clearly in a commanding position, it had at least one serious drawback: The Mississippi channel swung very close to the Missouri shore, putting it nearly two miles from the Cairo shore. It meant that batteries in the town could not effectively cover that passage. Eads's solution was simple: a floating battery. And it just so happened that his Missouri Wrecking Company had a suitable vessel available for lease or purchase. His offer, however, was unwisely declined.

If the "tollgate" at Cairo were secured, Eads told Welles, that would leave the Confederacy only three outlets: "the Tennessee and Cumberland rivers and the railroads from Louisville to Nashville and Chattanooga." Each of these could, of course, be closed in turn. Once all were closed, "starvation is inevitable in less than six months."[13]

But Eads's astute observations and lucid proposals made little impression on the secretary of the navy. Preoccupied with saltwater matters, Welles was content to leave freshwater affairs to the army. On 14 May Eads's report was bundled off to Simon Cameron, secretary of war.[14] Cameron saw merit in the plan but wanted confirmation, so he forwarded it to McClellan. At almost the same time Welles, still reluctant to become too deeply involved in river operations but wishing nevertheless to be cooperative and helpful toward the army, ordered Commander John Rodgers to proceed to Cincinnati, where he was to help McClellan establish a naval armament on the Mississippi and Ohio rivers. Three days later naval constructor Samuel Pook was sent to Cairo to help Rodgers evaluate vessels.[15]

Rodgers was a splendid choice for the western assignment. His father had been a naval hero in the War of 1812. The younger Rodgers, who showed talent, too, had been given a variety of postings, including one which would give him special insight into the problems in the West. In 1844 he had been assigned to superintend the construction of a steam warship, *Allegheny*, in Pittsburgh. As a warship *Allegheny* was unusual in at least two respects. First, she was iron-hulled; secondly, she was powered by experimental Hunter wheels. The latter were steam-powered horizontal wheels, the invention of her prospective captain, William W. Hunter. The clever device proved impractical, and a few years after her launching *Allegheny* was converted to a screw-driven frigate. But the knowledge Rodgers gained from this experience later proved invaluable.

Aside from his technical expertise, Rodgers brought some political clout to his new job. His influence derived from both his distinguished name and a fortunate marriage. His sister was married to Montgomery Cunningham Meigs, quartermaster general of the Union army. Meigs and Rodgers were not only brothers-in-law but friends. As quartermaster general Meigs was the principal army officer responsible for procuring gunboats on the western rivers.[16]

Rodgers headed west as quickly as he could. He arrived in Cincinnati and took up lodgings at Burnett House. A few days later Pook joined him, and the two began to look for vessels. To their dismay, they soon learned that good riverboats made poor warships. Eads came forward to offer his boats, but Rodgers turned him down. The Eads boats, like all rivercraft, were shallow-draft, lightly built with high-pressure boilers exposed on deck. While such vessels were well suited for river navigation, they were sitting ducks against hostile fire.

But McClellan was growing impatient. He wanted gunboats, not excuses. With some reluctance, Rodgers and Pook chose three vessels (not owned by Eads) that could at least be converted: *A. O. Tyler, Lexington,* and *Conestoga.* Rodgers wrote Welles a letter which confided his concern:

> All the river boats are so different from war vessels in all their appliances that considerable alterations are necessary to fit them for use. They needed a good deal of strengthening, and because the crew would be liable to be picked off while passing along the banks of the river in places where no effectual return could be made to the fire of an individual, I decided upon putting bulwarks of oak plank 5 inches thick, which I found

by experiment a sufficient guard against small arms. The boiler and engines can not be defended against cannon shot. We must take our chances.[17]

The secretary's reply was quick and surprising. He made no comment on Rodgers's problems and instead told him that he had no authorization to buy vessels. Taken aback by this curt response, Rodgers sent a telegram; the cost of the vessels was being borne by only the War Department. Welles was pleased, for he had no desire to share either the worry or the expense of a western campaign.

Daniel Morton, a Cincinnati boatbuilder, won the contract to convert Rodgers's three boats. For a bid of forty-one thousand dollars Morton was expected to take three fragile river steamers and turn them into river warriors. On 12 August, after a difficult passage down the Ohio, the three timber clads arrived at Cairo.

No one had any grand illusions about the ability of these converted steamers to command the rivers. Converted merchant vessels, whether deepwater, or shoal-water, were only stopgap measures. The real battles would have to be fought by vessels built to fight. No one understood this principle better than John Lenthall, chief of the navy's Bureau of Construction, Equipment, and Repair, who on 1 June sent off a memo to General Joseph Totten, chief of the Army Engineers.

Lenthall's memo was somber. Personally he had serious doubts that it was even possible to design fighting craft for river service. It seemed impossible to fit out a vessel with proper protection and weapons while at the same time keeping her draft light. Furthermore, propulsion would have to be by paddle wheels since propellers would only aggravate the draft problem. Lenthall then provided a draft plan for a river gunboat which, when fitted out and armed, would draw about five feet of water. But Lenthall had had no experience in designing vessels for use in shallow water; he was wary of his own lack of expertise. In fact, he suggested to General Totten that he consult with men who knew more about river navigation.[18]

Totten forwarded Lenthall's memo and draft to General Scott. Scott endorsed it and recommended to the secretary of war that measures be undertaken quickly for the construction of sixteen gunboats, which would be ready for service on the Ohio by 20 September 1861. Scott also suggested that the navy appoint an officer to superintend the construction of each vessel. After launching, these same officers would command them as well.

Welles would have none of it. He had already shown how he felt about spending his department's money for western operations. At a moment when the navy was being pilloried in the press and Congress for its ineffectual blockade he could ill afford to pay attention to the western rivers. Furthermore, the rivers were an army responsibility and problem. Welles's political instincts told him that if there were victories out West, the army generals would receive the laurels no matter what role the navy played. The navy's strategic responsibilities and political fortunes were anchored on the coast. At this point the best Welles could do was to allow constructor Pook and Commander Rodgers to continue to act as liaison with the army.

Lenthall's plans went west, where Rodgers and Pook had a chance to review them. The result was a new design, Pook's work.

Both designs called for flat-bottomed steamboats, but the Pook and Lenthall versions shared little else. Pook's plan called for a boat five feet longer than Lenthall's, with nearly twice the beam. Instead of using vulnerable side-wheels, Pook brought the paddles inboard, slightly aft of midships, and covered them over. Because of the weight and draft relationship, Lenthall had provided no armored protection for the crew. Pook, on the other hand, had a partially armored casemate running nearly the whole length of the boat, ready to accommodate twenty guns.

Pook's plan met with approval from the army, and on 18

July Quartermaster General Meigs advertised for construction bids. When the bids were opened on 5 August, to the surprise of few, James Eads was low bidder. Two days later Eads signed an agreement to build seven vessels at eighty-nine thousand dollars each and to deliver them no later than 10 October. While the price was a bit higher than expected, the promise to deliver within sixty-five days was enticing.

Eads decided to divide the project. Four vessels were laid down at his yard in Carondelet, on the outskirts of St. Louis. The other three were put under construction at Mound City, Illinois, a few miles upriver from Cairo. Materials, including timber and machine parts, were brought to the yards by rail and water. Soon, however, it became apparent that the optimistic sixty-five-day schedule was impossible. Working extra shifts did not help.

Even the best-laid plans are almost always altered once construction gets under way. Pook's plans were no exception to the general rule. Some alterations were forced upon Eads. Rodgers insisted on more armor protection for the vessels, a demand that resulted in approximately sixty tons of additional weight. If no reductions were made elsewhere, Eads pointed out, this would add a great deal to draft. Running aground would be an even greater nightmare than it already was in river navigation. Although the records are not clear, it would seem that a compromise was struck by reducing armament. Instead of carrying twenty guns, the boats mounted thirteen.

A second reason for delay had to do with money. In July Congress had appropriated funds for the construction of "Gunboats on the western rivers." The vagueness of the appropriation had allowed the recently appointed commander of the Western Department, Major General John Charles Frémont, to use the money for his own waterborne projects rather than have it go to Eads.[19]

John Charles Frémont was an unusual man. One of the first four major generals appointed by Lincoln, he was easily the most famous. He was a powerful man: an explorer, the

"Pathfinder," the Republican presidential nominee in 1856. He was also the son-in-law of the legendary senator from Missouri Thomas Hart ("Bullion") Benton. Accustomed to wielding influence, Frémont was rarely constrained by the normal canons of behavior.[20]

When, in July, McClellan was given command of the Army of the Potomac, Frémont succeeded him as senior officer in the Western Department. Using his new authority, Frémont diverted funds from the Eads project to finance the construction of mortar boats and tugs for the general's own campaigns against Confederate forces in Missouri. Despite repeated requests from Eads and others, money for the gunboats was slow in coming. In a vain attempt to keep pace, Eads used his own considerable credit; but even that was not enough, and by the end of October he was threatening to halt construction altogether unless funds were sent forward. Quick to demand performance, the government was less eager to pay for it. Not until several months after completion did Eads receive full payment for his work.[21]

Eads was not the only person to suffer from Frémont's promotion. Shortly after the two officers met in early August, Frémont wrote to his friend the postmaster general Montgomery Blair: "It would subserve the public interest if Commander John Rodgers were removed and an officer directed to report to me to have command of the operations on the Mississippi. Show this to [the] President."[22]

Frémont had good reason not to like Rodgers. The general's own quartermaster was involved in a heated dispute with Quartermaster General Meigs over certain purchasing procedures. Meigs's unpopularity at Frémont's headquarters did nothing to enhance his brother-in-law's position. More important, however, than any family quarrel was the fact that the commander himself had challenged the general.

Back in June, Rodgers had rejected Eads's offer to sell the government his boat *Submarine 7* with good reason. The vessel was not well suited to naval purposes: She was underpowered and overpriced. But Frémont felt differently. He needed a gunboat, and now Eads offered *Submarine 7* to the general at a lower price. Over Rodgers's objections, Frémont bought *Submarine 7*, gave Eads the contract to convert her, and then renamed the craft *Benton* in honor of his father-in-law.[23]

Welles got the message. His political barometer told him that stormy times lay ahead if he did not placate Frémont. On 30 August he ordered Rodgers to turn his command over to Captain Andrew H. Foote. He offered Rodgers the option of remaining on station as Foote's second-in-command. Under the circumstances, Rodgers's pride prevented that, and he requested a command at sea.[24]

A deeply devout man, once described by a contemporary as an officer who "prays like a saint and fights like hell," Andrew Hull Foote was the son of a former governor and senator from Connecticut. He was also a school chum of Welles's from the Cheshire Academy. His early school days had been followed by a short stint at West Point before he accepted an appointment as a midshipman.[25] Known in the service as a reformer, he argued forcefully for temperance and against the slave trade. Although he was relatively unknown at the beginning of the war, those who knew him admired him for his technological acumen and his skill as an administrator.

Foote's position, like Rodgers's, was somewhat anomalous. Although appointed by the Navy Department, he reported through the army chain of command. Foote recognized the potential difficulties, but unlike Rodgers, he made every effort to accommodate himself. Indeed, his first important decision reflects his keen talent for policy. Where Rodgers had tended to remain in either Cairo or Cincinnati, Foote took up residence in St. Louis, closer to General Frémont.

On 6 September Foote took command. His inventory of vessels included the three wooden vessels already in service, the seven ironclads commissioned by Pook and Rodgers (still under construction), and two of Eads's conversions: *Benton* and *Essex*. In addition, General Frémont had made arrangements for the construction of thirty-eight mortar boats. These fifty vessels were

to become the core of Union naval strength on the western rivers.[26]

On 12 October the first of the Federal navy ironclads (*Monitor* was not launched until 30 January 1862) went into the water before a large and enthusiastic crowd at Carondelet. She was christened *St. Louis*[27]—thanks to Foote. Rodgers had intended to name the vessels after well-known Americans: Nathaniel Lyon, George B. McClellan, J. C. Frémont, John Rodgers (his own father), N. P. Banks, M. C. Meigs, and a seventh yet to be decided. But Foote proved himself a far abler diplomat. Rather than offend the many influential people for whom the vessels would not be named, he christened them after river towns. *St. Louis* was the first, then *Mound City, Cincinnati, Cairo, Carondelet, Louisville,* and *Pittsburgh.*

The boats were finally in the water; now they had to be manned. This was more easily said than done. Welles finally agreed to supply officers, but enlisted men were another matter. At first the secretary suggested that crews be recruited in the West, but the army had already absorbed a good deal of the region's manpower. So Welles was forced to send precious seamen to Foote. Still, in order to get his boats into commission, Foote also had to pluck men from the army. The resulting force was a medley of men: professional naval officers, amateur officers, rivermen, landlubbers, and farmers. This motley crew would have to man Foote's awkward new rivercraft.

I I

Across the Ohio the Rebels had not been idle. Facing Union forces was a Confederate army under the command of General Albert Sidney Johnston. Appointed to command on 10 September, Johnston was responsible for Confederate Department Number Two. This vast area stretched from the Appalachian Mountains westward into Missouri, and beyond it as far as the

Indian territories. On 14 September Johnston arrived at Nashville. His problem was as clear as it was difficult. Only a small force was available to him. Should he advance into Kentucky or husband his resources and prepare to defend Tennessee? He compromised by ordering Brigadier Simon Bolivar Buckner to march on Bowling Green, Kentucky. Buckner was to hold that advance line while Johnston held fast to his own. It was a classic bluff, and at least for a time it worked. By advancing, Johnston gave a false impression of great strength.[28]

The rivers were key to Johnston's plan. Three major streams—the Tennessee, Cumberland, and Mississippi—flowed through his territory. Each lay on a north-south axis, making them ideal paths for Union attack. Johnston's most vulnerable spot was located where the Cumberland and Tennessee both flowed northward into Union territory. In Tennessee, where the two rivers came within a few miles of each other, the state government had erected two forts: Henry on the Tennessee and Donelson on the Cumberland.

As soon as he arrived, Johnston pleaded with Richmond to send reinforcements. He knew that each day his enemy was growing stronger and that his offensive ruses would eventually fail. He also recognized that his river flanks were completely exposed. Unlike the Federals, the Confederates had no gunboats at hand on the Tennessee or Cumberland; indeed, they had very few available in the West.

The lack of gunboats sprang from the twin causes of Confederate weakness: lack of resources and poor coordination. Iron for armor cladding was in short supply, as was machinery to drive the vessels. Even more critical was the scarcity of skilled manpower. Ironically, to a great extent the shortage of men to build vessels was self-imposed. The South had numerous men skilled at the crafts necessary for building river gunboats. The problem was that most of them were in the army, and Mallory's frequent pleas to the army to release these men went unanswered.

Unable to build sufficient gunboats to block the Federal

advance, Mallory decided early that the best he could do was harass the enemy. For the rest, he would leave his vessels under the army's command. Mallory's resignation about river operations is understandable. With so few resources, there seemed to be little he could do. However, if he had been a cleverer strategist, he might have done a great deal more. Mallory failed to appreciate the real value of torpedoes (mines) to his defense on the rivers. Here, as in little else, he was too cautious, he avoided these relatively new and untried weapons. Properly employed, torpedoes would have done far more to slow the Federal advance than the small number of gunboats he mustered.

In November the Federals launched their attack when the Union commander Major General Henry Halleck ordered one of his brigadiers, Ulysses S. Grant, to move south along the Mississippi from his base at Cairo. Following his orders, Grant led a force toward Belmont, Missouri. Supported by the gunboats *Tyler* and *Lexington,* he drove the enemy back but had to withdraw when Confederate reinforcements arrived.

Despite the setback, Grant delivered a creditable performance. He also began to appreciate the usefulness of gunboats in support of land operations.

From reconnaissance conducted by Foote's gunboats, the Federals had a fair idea of the situation on the Cumberland and Tennessee rivers. After reviewing their information, Foote and Grant agreed that Fort Henry might "be carried with four ironclad gunboats and troops."[29] They informed Halleck of their conclusion and got his permission to attack. On 3 February 1862, with remarkable dispatch, the expedition got under way.

Foote was confident, perhaps too confident, that his squadron could take the fort. Now wearing the insignia of flag officer, he took command of the squadron and pushed upriver. Although only four of the new ironclads were with him, they were an impressive sight as the first American warships "to combine armor, steam propulsion, rifled cannon and shell guns. Each of these vessels—with her thick, rectangular wooden casemate squatting on a broad, shallow hull; her two high-pressure steam engines turning a single, stern-located paddle wheel; her iron plates meant to cover the most vulnerable surfaces; and her mixed battery of rifles, shell guns, and smoothbores— seemed, even before her trial by fire, to be a formidable weapon."[30]

On 4 February Grant asked William D. Porter, captain of the ironclad *Essex* and brother of David D. Porter, to take him upriver, as close as possible to Fort Henry. Grant needed to fix the range of the fort's guns as well as find a suitable place to land his troops. Porter steamed within about two miles of the fort, lobbed a few rounds at the Confederates, and, to his surprise, received accurate fire in return. One shot penetrated *Essex*'s unarmored upper deck, flew through the officers' quarters into the officers' pantry, and then exited out the stern via the captain's cabin. Grant decided to land his troops about three miles downriver, beyond range of Fort Henry's guns.

But Grant's reconnaissance had misled him. Despite the impressive hits on *Essex,* the Confederates were in a precarious situation. The commander of both Forts Henry and Donelson, Brigadier General Lloyd Tilghman, had pleaded for days with his own superior, Major General Leonidas Polk, for reinforcement, but to no avail. Tilghman had at his disposal barely five thousand men.

Manpower was not Tilghman's only problem. Although Fort Henry had a commanding view downstream, it was vulnerable on the back side. With only one road leading out toward the east, the fort could be easily cut off. From the earthworks fortification, twelve guns looked toward the river, while five covered the land approaches with a series of hastily dug rifle pits. Across the river was a still-unfinished position, Fort Heiman.

On the fourth Tilghman informed Johnston that the Federals were about to land and urged that troops be sent. When none arrived, Tilghman decided to cut his losses and move his men out of their trap. On the morning of the sixth he ordered the garrison to withdraw to Donelson. The general himself remained behind with about eighty men, just enough to delay Grant.

Unaware that their quarry had fled, Grant and Foote moved ahead with their own plan. Grant assigned the main force to move against Fort Henry, with a smaller force assaulting Heiman. The first objective was to move around Henry and isolate it from the east while Foote's gunboats pummeled it from the river. It was a simple, sound plan that went awry.

Nature confounded the Federals with heavy rains and swollen streams. Just before noon on the sixth Grant's troops began their slow trudge through the muck. While the soldiers inched ahead, Foote's squadron heaved into sight of the fort. The gunboats were in two divisions, the first composed of the four ironclads. With smoke belching from their stacks, *St. Louis, Carondelet, Cincinnati,* and *Essex* came head-on to the fort. Behind them, with their paddles churning, came the second division, composed of the three wooden sisters *Tyler, Lexington,* and *Conestoga.*[31]

Abreast, the ironclads moved to within range and opened fire. Slowly and steadily they kept up the barrage and closed the distance. At first Tilghman could return the favor with only his long-range guns, but as the Federals drew closer, all his weapons replied. To Tilghman's horror, one of his guns burst, injuring every man in the crew. A short time later a smoothbore forty-two-pounder blew up, killing two more men. Already short-handed, the Confederate gunners began to fear for their lives.

But they knew their business, and Foote soon found himself in a heavy battle. Fortunately the wind was with him. Although he had a stiff current against him, a favoring breeze blew away the smoke from both his stacks and guns, allowing his gunners to sight well. As the Federals found their range, Tilghman's position became hopeless. Still the Confederates fired on. *Cincinatti, Carondelet,* and *St. Louis* all were hit, the favorite target being the armored pilothouse. As iron shot bounced loudly off the armor plating, Foote's pilots stood their posts with ringing ears.

On board *Essex,* however, the damage was most deadly. She was starboard of the flagship when a Confederate shot found its way through the port casemate and into the center boiler.

Its plates ruptured, the boiler released a frenzy of live steam. *Essex*'s second master James Laning described a scene straight from the *Inferno:*

> In a very few minutes after the explosion our gallant ship ... was drifting slowly away from the scene of action; her commander badly wounded, a number of her officers and crew dead at their post, while many others were writhing in their last agony. ... The pilots, who were both in the pilothouse, were scalded to death. Marshall Ford, who was steering when the explosion took place, was found at his post at the wheel, standing erect, his left hand holding the spoke, and his right hand grasping the signal bell rope.[32]

Steam had added a new dimension to the horror of dying in battle; what happened on board *Essex* was only a ghastly prelude.

Essex's unhappy fate had no effect on the outcome of the battle. Further resistance was useless, and at one fifty-five in the afternoon Tilghman surrendered his forts. Fort Henry's capture had taken fewer than three hours, not enough time for Grant's troops to move close enough to be of any assistance. To everyone's amazement, Foote's included, the victory had been a naval one. When his forces finally did take possession of the Confederate emplacements, Grant ordered that Fort Henry be renamed Camp Foote.

For the Federals, the victory had not been costly. Despite the havoc on *Essex,* total casualties among the gunboats were relatively light: two men dead and nearly forty wounded. In addition to the sailors, four soldiers were killed and fifteen wounded. All of them were sharpshooters aboard the gunboats.

After Fort Henry's capitulation, Foote ordered his wood-clad boats to run up the Tennessee as far as the river was navigable. They steamed all the way to Florence, Alabama, where the Muscle Shoals prevented further passage. Along the way they destroyed several steamers, captured large quantities of military supplies, and destroyed a Confederate encampment. It was a powerful demonstration of what gunboats could accomplish when raiding the rivers.

Strategically Fort Henry was only half the package. If the Federals could take Fort Donelson, Johnston's center would crumple. The Federals could march on Nashville, and the Confederates would be forced to withdraw, abandoning Kentucky and imperiling Tennessee.

Buoyed by the ease of victory at Fort Henry, Grant and Foote laid plans for the move on Donelson. Although only eleven miles away by land, it was more than ten times that distance by water. Foote recalled his gunboats from their excursion up the Tennessee and regrouped for his next campaign. On the eleventh he embarked from Cairo with six vessels: the four iron-clads *St. Louis, Carondelet, Louisville,* and *Pittsburgh* and the woodclads *Tyler* and *Conestoga.*

Grant's force moved independently, in a quick cross-country march. The general was delayed leaving Fort Henry until the twelfth, but was outside Donelson the next day. By the fourteenth Foote had arrived, and the two commanders were ready to launch the attack.

Inside the Confederate fort there was much confusion. After the fall of Fort Henry, Johnston had wisely ordered the abandonment of Donelson in order to withdraw and consolidate somewhere south of the Tennessee River. It was a morally courageous decision, but one which was politically unacceptable to his superiors. The unfortunate Johnston was forced to reverse his plan. Against his better judgment, he threw additional forces under Brigadier Generals Gideon Pillow, John B. Floyd, and Simon Bolivar Buckner into Donelson.[33]

Tactically Donelson was in a strong position. The main breastwork stood on a height overlooking and commanding the river; it mounted at least fifteen heavy guns and two carronades. Along the storeline was a smaller shore battery. Landward the fort was protected by nearly three miles of earthworks defended by infantry. On each flank the earthworks were covered by small streams. Grant, reinforced by General Lew Wallace's division, had nearly twenty-seven thousand men facing twenty-one thousand inside the fort. Grant's troops took up positions on the land side; the plan was to trap the doomed Confederates.[34]

At 3:00 P.M. on the fourteenth, while the Union troops moved into position behind the fort, Foote signaled his gunboats to attack. Foote and Grant planned for the gunboats first to silence the water batteries, then to steam farther up to where they could shell the enemy's riverside entrenchments. First to open fire was the gunboat *St. Louis* at a range of about one mile. She was quickly joined by her sister ironclads *Pittsburgh, Carondelet,* and *Louisville.*

From the fort came no answer. Foote steamed closer and kept up his fusillade. The two woodclads remained to the rear, arching shells over the ironclads and into the fort. At four hundred yards, virtually point-blank range, the Confederates opened up. Forced to engage with only its bow guns, Foote's squadron was unable to bring its full firepower to bear, whereas the gunners in Fort Donelson fired with volume and effect.

Carondelet and *Pittsburgh* got the worst of it. Henry Walke, commander of *Carondelet,* reported four men killed and thirty-two wounded. Sadly some of the damage came from friendly fire. An eight-inch shell lobbed over by *Tyler* fell short and exploded off Walke's stern with fragments penetrating through his casement. As for *Pittsburgh,* she took hits forward near the waterline. Forced to withdraw, she kept afloat only by shifting guns to raise her bow.

St. Louis, the flagship, took fifty-nine hits. One struck the pilothouse, killing the pilot and injuring Foote himself. The boat became unmanageable, and she was left to drift downstream. The same thing happened to *Louisville,* which had had the tiller blown off.

In his report to Welles, Foote reported, "There were 54

killed and wounded in this attack, which we have reason to suppose would, in fifteen minutes more, could the action have been
continued, have resulted in the capture of the fort bearing upon
us."[35] Grant's observation, recorded many years later in his *Personal Memoirs,* seems more true: The "sun went down on the
night of the 14th of February, 1862, leaving the army confronting Fort Donelson anything but comforted over the prospects."[36] Foote had been firmly repulsed. His gunboats were
powerful weapons, but they were hardly omnipotent.

Despite the retreat on the river, timidity ruled inside the
fort. Floyd and Buckner were convinced that resistance was
useless and that their only hope lay in escape. On the fifteenth,
troops under Pillow and Buckner smashed a hole in the Federal
line, opening the road to Nashville. Buckner urged his fellow
brigadiers to march quickly through the gap, but to his astonishment they preferred to take their men back into the fort,
whence they telegraphed Johnston that they had won "victory
complete and glorious."[37] Gloom came with nightfall, when it
was learned Grant had received reinforcement. In one of the
strangest scenes of the war, Brigadier General Floyd turned to
Brigadier General Pillow and announced, "General Pillow, I turn
over my command." Pillow rejoined, "I pass it," leaving Buckner in command just long enough to surrender the fort.

When Buckner asked Grant for terms, he was told, "No
terms except an unconditional and immediate surrender can
be accepted."[38] They were accepted. Pillow, Floyd, and a relatively unknown cavalry commander, Nathan Bedford Forrest,
escaped with about three thousand men. Those who remained,
including General Buckner, surrendered to Grant.

Mallory had no good answer for the men in Richmond who
asked where the navy was. He had tried, he responded, to build
gunboats on the Mississippi but had thus far been very disappointed. Two, *Tennessee* and *Arkansas,* were under construction
at Memphis, but work on them lagged terribly. He had difficulty finding iron and machinery, and even when he did, he
could not find workmen to fit the vessels. For the latter he blamed

the army; in its quest for soldiers, it had taken skilled men from the yards in Memphis. If only he had the resources, iron, and men, he was certain that he could launch a gunboat that would "be worth more than an army of 20,000 men."[39] But the army continued to withhold the resources he desperately needed.

The fall of Donelson left the path to Nashville wide open. Johnston fell back and took up a new line with Memphis on the left and Chattanooga on the right. Columbus, Kentucky, on the Mississippi, was evacuated, and the Confederates on the river fell back to a line anchored by Island Number Ten opposite the border between Tennessee and Kentucky. The river navy now turned its attention to that island.

8

On to Memphis

I

From Cape Girardeau, Missouri, thirty miles north of Cairo, to the Gulf of Mexico, the Mississippi meanders nearly eleven hundred miles. At almost any point on the river the countryside is flat and low; in times of high water it is also wet. At rare moments bluffs rise up, but mostly the view is monotonously level. The Confederate defenders were hard pressed to find topographical features which might help them establish choke points to block the Union advance.

By mid-fall 1862 the Confederates had been forced to withdraw into southeastern Missouri. With that withdrawal went any hope of a serious offensive in the upper Mississippi Valley. The local Confederate commander, General Leonidas Polk, was inclined to husband his forces and withdraw to a fortified position along the river at Forts Pillow and Randolph on the Chickasaw Bluffs. Polk's instincts were sound, and he should have stood firm. Instead, he listened to Brigadier General Gideon

Pillow, who persuaded him that an advanced position at Columbus, Kentucky, was of "paramount military necessity," that it might even "close the door effectually against invasion of Tennessee or descent of the Mississippi." Unwisely Polk agreed, and Columbus was fortified.[1]

In making his decision to hold Columbus, Polk naturally assumed that Johnston would keep a steady hold on Forts Henry and Donelson. Once they fell, Columbus was outflanked. Trapped between an advancing Union force on the land side and a waterway open to Foote's gunboats, Polk had no choice but to abandon Columbus and fall down the river. Johnston also had to rethink his strategy. He decided to withdraw his forces south to a line running roughly from Chattanooga in the east to Memphis on the river. With this line, pivoting at Corinth, Mississippi, not far from Shiloh, Johnston sought to protect the vital Memphis and Charleston Railroad.[2]

On the river the Confederates took their position at Island Number Ten and the nearby town of New Madrid. The island was located about sixty miles south of Columbus where the Mississippi took a sharp turn from its southerly course and ran six miles west to New Madrid. On the Tennessee side of the river, Reelfoot Lake and a large number of connecting swamps made it almost impossible to take the island from the east.[3]

New Madrid, on the other hand, was not so easily protected. Although guarded on its eastern flank by these watery obstacles, the town lay wide open to a land approach along Sikeston Ridge, a rise that angled down from the northwest. In late February 1862 Union General John Pope marched his columns along this route. Rain, snow, and mud slowed the advance as his grumbling soldiers pushed, pulled, and cursed, moving heavy artillery through the Missouri mud. Finally, on 3 March, Pope's advance guard met up on the perimeter of the town with Confederate pickets, who were easily driven back as the Federals invested New Madrid.

On the night of 11 March, with a thunderstorm covering

their movement, the Confederates left New Madrid. It was something less than a model maneuver. Amid the darkness, rain, and thunder, the undisciplined Confederates scattered, leaving huge quantities of precious supplies behind. Fortunately for them, the Federals were almost equally inept. They failed to realize what was going on until daylight, when a white flag was borne toward them. Pope marched into a deserted town and took up positions covering the river.[4]

New Madrid was only half the battle. Island Number Ten, located at a critical bend in the Mississippi, was far more crucial to control of the river, and there the Confederates had been hurriedly improving their positions. In charge of the preparations was Captain A. B. Gray of the Confederate Engineers. Working with slaves and a construction unit of Irishmen, he had twenty-four pieces of heavy ordnance well placed on the eastern or Tennessee shore and nineteen additional guns in four locations on the island.

Still, though the Confederates were snugged down and well armed, their position was not enviable. The same swampy barriers that slowed their enemies made their own escape impossible. The only way to retreat was to cross over to the mainland and flee down the single road leading through the hamlet of Tiptonville. If Pope could move his forces along the west bank of the river and cross below Tiptonville, the men on Island Number Ten would be trapped. Pope wanted dearly to snare the Confederates by this maneuver, but to accomplish it, he needed gunboats to cover his crossing. For that support he looked to Commodore Foote.[5]

Pope and Foote were a poor match; the former was impatient and the latter cautious. Pope had been promised gunboat support, and he was angry that Foote's forces had arrived so late. Foote did not appear on the scene until 15 March, the day after the Confederates had evacuated New Madrid. He claimed that he had been held up at Cairo, as yard crews finished repairing the boats damaged at Forts Henry and Donelson. His own health, too, may have been a consideration. Foote had been wounded at Donelson, and the injury was not healing. He was hobbling about on crutches in a good deal of pain.

Finally, on the morning of 14 March, the flotilla got up steam and headed downriver. After a brief stop at Columbus to pick up additional troops, Foote arrived at the bend at about nine on the morning of the fifteenth. His force consisted of six gunboats and eleven mortars.[6] Foote was worried about how to move on the attack. Tactically the situation was far more difficult than the one he had faced on the Tennessee and Cumberland. In those engagements he was moving upstream to attack, so that if his vessels had been damaged, they could have drifted back away from enemy fire. Here the situation was reversed. Should anything untoward happen, the boats would be carried toward the Confederates and certain destruction. To make matters even worse, the river was running high and fast. Foote realized the situation all too well. He also understood his own special responsibility. Pope could afford to lose men. But if Foote lost his boats, Union operations on the entire river would imperiled.

Strategy, tactics, and ill health bore heavily on the commodore and led him to be even more wary than usual. Rather than steam ahead to attack, he took up a position "round the bend" and from there lobbed shells onto Confederates. The fire did little damage. Wisely the southern batteries remained quiet, preferring to await better targets. On the seventeenth, Foote decided to move closer.

Underpowered and awkwardly built, the gunboat *Benton* had to be lashed between *Cincinnati* and *St. Louis* so that she would not be swept into a hail of Confederate fire. Very slowly the flotilla moved forward, three gunboats rafted together and the others steaming independently. At two thousand yards they opened fire, and for nearly seven hours they kept that distant range, fearing the danger of being hit, disabled, and swept down by the current. *Benton* and her sisters concentrated their fire on

Battery One or the redan works located on the Tennessee side. Sloshing about in two feet of water from the swollen river, the Confederate defenders on land put up a good fight; only one was killed and seven were wounded. Union losses were higher, but not on account of Confederate rounds. A gun explosion aboard *St. Louis* killed two men and injured fifteen others.[7]

Darkness forced Foote to withdraw. He should have planned to resume the attack on the morning, but his dispatches hinted at something else. He told Welles that "this place is even stronger and better adapted for defense that Columbus" and finished the report by pleading, "From exhaustion, arising from continuous service and want of sleep, you will excuse this incoherent, discursive report."[8] Foote was having second thoughts. Moving in to attack was, in his judgment, too dangerous. The next day and for the remainder of the month he kept his mortars and gunboats upriver firing on the enemy but refraining from any close engagement. The commodore was convinced that putting his boats in harm's way was too risky. Perhaps he was right. At least General Halleck, Pope's superior, agreed: "I am very glad that you have not unnecessarily exposed your gunboats. If they had been disabled, it would have been a most serious loss to us in the future operations of the campaign, whereas the reduction of these batteries this week or next is a matter of very little importance indeed. I think it will turn out in the end that it is much better for us that they are not reduced till we can fully cut off the retreat of their troops."[9]

Although Pope could not have been pleased at Halleck's casual endorsement of delay, his suggestion of cutting off the enemy's retreat was well placed and fitted nicely with Pope's own emphasis on battlefield maneuver. Having already taken New Madrid by feint rather than assault, Pope now decided to outflank the Confederates again by crossing the river behind them and taking them from the rear. Pope asked Foote to run by the island with gunboats so that he could cover a cross-river assault. For the first time since leaving Cairo, Foote summoned a council of his officers. With the exception of Henry Walke, captain of *Carondelet,* all the officers present advised against the run.[10]

Frustrated, Pope ordered a canal dug north of New Madrid along a line marked by two shallow bayous, Wilson's and St. John's. If this worked, Pope could bring boats across and out of range of enemy guns, get them into the river beyond Island Number Ten, and position them to cover his downstream crossing. It took six hundred engineers nineteen days to cut a twelve-mile passage through muck, mire, and a never-ending maze of half-submerged stumps and roots. By the time it was all done, nature had dealt Pope another blow. The river level fell to a point where only the shallowest-draft vessels could float through.[11] Clearly the Mississippi was defending its own.

In the meantime, Foote continued his constant but relatively ineffectual bombardment. Even with the aid of an observation balloon to direct fire, Union shelling was still not strong enough to dislodge the Confederates. And then the commodore had a change of heart. It was common knowledge that Henry Walke wanted to run past the Confederates. On 30 March Foote issued orders to Walke that he was to "avail" himself "of the first fog or rainy night and drift your steamer down past the batteries, on the Tennessee shore, and Island No. 10, until you reach New Madrid."[12]

When he heard Foote's order, Pope was skeptical. He had already begun to make his own preparations for a river crossing without naval support. He told Halleck, "I have no hope of Commodore Foote. He has postponed trying to run any of his gunboats past Island No. 10 until some foggy or rainy night. The moon is beginning to make the nights light, and there is no prospect of fogs during this sort of weather. We must do without him."[13]

Pope's meteorological instincts were a bit off the mark. Although fogs were not common in the valley during these months, thunderstorms were. On the evening of 4 April, heavy clouds rolled in from the west, blocking out the moon and wrapping the river in darkness. Henry Walke was ready to take advantage of nature's gift. For several days he had been working on *Carondelet*. He had taken bales, boxes, and crates and piled them on the upper decks to absorb plunging fire. Along the port side he lashed a barge loaded with coal and hay to stand between his gunboat and the Confederate shore batteries. He had his engineers rig a steam line that carried escaping steam aft and around the stacks, so that any telltale puffing sound would be muffled. Finally, he took aboard twenty-three sharpshooters from the Forty-second Illinois, men whose orders were to remain silent unless the boat was spotted by the enemy. Then they were to fire at anything that moved on the Confederate shore.

Walke passed out pistols, cutlasses, muskets, boarding pikes, and hand grenades lest any Confederates try to board *Carondelet*. As added insurance he ran hose lines from the boilers, so that high-pressure steam and scalding water could be poured on any unwanted intruder.

At ten o'clock, after the moon had set, Walke ordered the lines cast off. It was a nervous time, and no one has ever described it better than Walke himself:

> Dark clouds now rose rapidly over us and enveloped us in almost total darkness, except when the sky was lighted up by the welcome flashes of vivid lightning, to show us the perilous way we were to take. Now and then the dim outline of the shore could be seen, and the forest bending under the roaring storm that came rushing up the river.
>
> With our bow pointing to the island, we passed the lowest point of land without being observed, it appears, by the enemy. All speed was given to the vessel to drive her through the tempest. The flashes of lightning continued with frightful brilliancy, and "almost every second," wrote a correspondent, "every brace, post, and outline could be seen with startling

Fort Sumter, South Carolina. After a heavy bombardment the Confederate flag replaced the Stars and Stripes. *Courtesy of National Archives, Washington, D.C.*

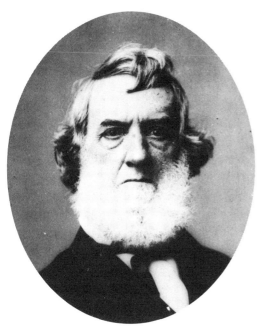

Secretary of the Navy Gideon Welles.
Courtesy of National Archives, Washington, D.C.

Secretary of the Confederate States Navy
Stephen R. Mallory.
Courtesy of National Archives, Washington, D.C.

Rear Admiral David Glasgow Farragut.
Courtesy of National Archives, Washington, D.C.

Rear Admiral David Dixon Porter.
Courtesy of National Archives, Washington, D.C.

The Blockade. Map of coastline

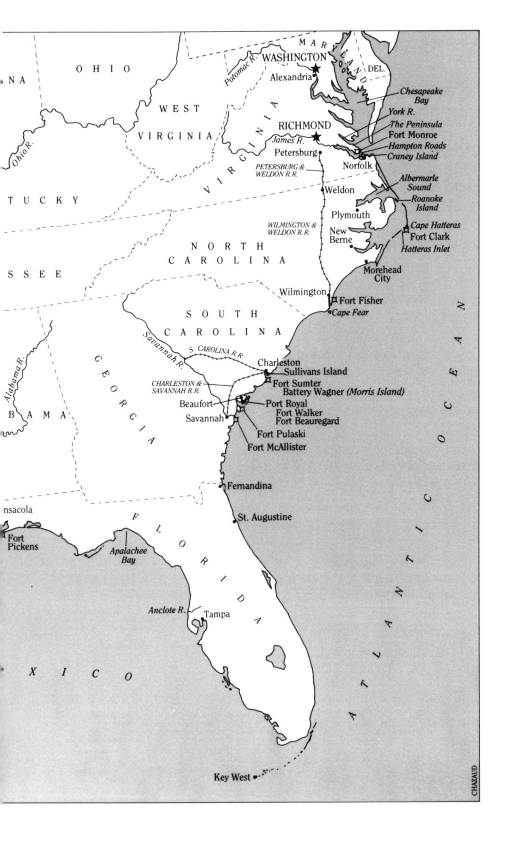

OHIO

WEST
VIRGINIA

Potomac R.
WASHINGTON ★
MARYLAND
DEL.
Alexandria

Chesapeake Bay
York R.
The Peninsula
Fort Monroe
Hampton Roads
Craney Island

RICHMOND ★
James R.
Petersburg
Norfolk

VIRGINIA

*PETERSBURG &
WELDON R.R.*

*Albemarle
Sound*
Weldon
*Roanoke
Island*

Plymouth
Cape Hatteras
Fort Clark
Hatteras Inlet

*WILMINGTON &
WELDON R.R.*
New
Berne

NORTH
CAROLINA

Morehead
City

Wilmington
Fort Fisher
Cape Fear

SOUTH
CAROLINA

Savannah R.
S. CAROLINA R.R.

Charleston
Sullivans Island
Fort Sumter
Battery Wagner *(Morris Island)*

GEORGIA

*CHARLESTON &
SAVANNAH R.R.*
Beaufort
Port Royal
Fort Walker
Fort Beauregard

Savannah
Fort Pulaski
Fort McAllister

Alabama R.

BAMA

Fernandina

St. Augustine

FLORIDA

nsacola
Fort
Pickens
*Apalachee
Bay*

Anclote R.
Tampa

XICO

ATLANTIC OCEAN

Key West

CHAZAUD

Alfred Waud, "Amphibious Landing of General Butler's Forces at Cape Hatteras, August 1861." This was the first combined amphibious operation of the war. *Courtesy of Franklin D. Roosevelt Library, Hyde Park, New York.*

"The Victorious Bombardment of Port Royal, S.C., November 7, 1861." The heavy and accurate fire from the Union fleet forced the Confederates to withdraw from the forts defending Port Royal. *Currier and Ives. Courtesy of Beverly R. Robinson Collection, United States Naval Academy Museum, Annapolis, Maryland.*

"The Great Fight Between the 'Merrimack' & 'Monitor,' March 9, 1862." This first battle between ironclads ushered in a new era in naval warfare. *Currier and Ives. Courtesy of Beverly R. Robinson Collection, United States Naval Academy Museum, Annapolis, Maryland.*

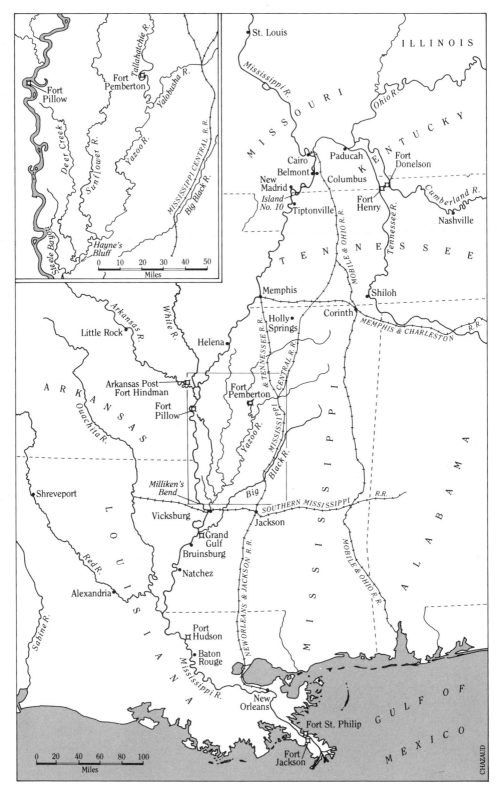

The River War

CCS *Manassas*. Her low profile made her a difficult target for Union gunners. *Drawn by R. G. Skerrett, 1904. Courtesy of National Archives, Washington, D.C.*

Mortar boats. These are typical of the type of vessel used by Union forces on the rivers. *James David Smillie (American, 1833–1909), pencil and neutral wash on board, 1862. M and M Karolik Collection of American watercolors and drawings, 1800–1875. Courtesy of Museum of Fine Arts, Boston.*

Sailors and marines on deck of the U.S. gunboat *Mendota*, 1864. Union vessels were heavily manned and often with racially mixed crews. *Courtesy of National Archives, Washington, D.C.*

Gun crew of a Dahlgren gun at drill aboard U.S. gunboat *Mendota*, 1864. It took a large number of men to handle each gun. *Courtesy of National Archives, Washington, D.C.*

"Bombardment and Capture of Fort Henry, TN." The fire from the gunboats under the command of Andrew Hull Foote forced the surrender of the fort. *Currier and Ives. Courtesy of Beverly R. Robinson Collection, United States Naval Academy Museum, Annapolis, Maryland.*

Battle of Memphis, Tennessee, 6 June 1862, showing at center, USS *Monarch* ramming CSS *General Beauregard*. At left are USS *Queen of the West*, CSS *General Sterling Price*, and CSS *Little Rebel*. *Engraving published in* Harper's Weekly. *Photograph courtesy of Naval Historical Center, Washington, D.C.*

Vicksburg before the Union siege. The large building in the center is the Warren County Courthouse. The city had a commanding view of the river below. *Courtesy of United States Army Military History Institute, Carlisle Barracks, Pennsylvania.*

Confederate ram *Arkansas* running through Federal fleet on Mississippi River, 1862. This was the most embarrassing day of the war for the Union navy. *Courtesy of Naval Historical Center, Washington, D.C.*

Admiral David Dixon Porter and General U. S. Grant plan joint army-navy campaign to capture Vicksburg, 1863. *Courtesy of Naval Historical Center, Washington, D.C.*

"The Great Naval Victory in Mobile Bay, August 5, 1874." CSS *Tennessee* is in the center surrounded by Union vessels. *Currier and Ives. Courtesy of Beverly R. Robinson Collection, United State Naval Academy Museum, Annapolis, Maryland.*

Submarine *H. L. Hunley,* the first submarine to sink an enemy vessel in combat. *Conrad Wise Chapman engraving. Courtesy of Boston Athenaeum, Boston.*

The interior of the northeastern salient of Fort Fisher during the attack of 13, 14, 15 January 1865. This assault resulted in the capture of the fort. *Frank Vizetelly watercolor. Courtesy of Houghton Library Harvard University, Cambridge, Massachusetts.*

Commander Raphael Semmes.
*Courtesy of Naval Historical Center,
Washington, D.C.*

CSS *Alabama*, the most formidable and most famous of the Confederate raiders. *Drawn by
Clary Ray. Courtesy of National Archives, Washington, D.C.*

distinctness, enshrouded by a bluish white glare of light, and then her form for the next minute would become emerged in the intense darkness." When opposite Battery No. 2, on the mainland, the smoke-stacks blazed up, but the fire was soon subdued. It was caused by the soot becoming dry, as the escape-steam, which usually kept the stacks wet, had been sent into the wheelhouse. . . . With such vivid lightning as prevailed during the whole passage, there was not prospect of escaping the vigilance of the enemy, but there was good reason to hope that he would be unable to point his guns accurately. Again, the smokestacks took fire, and were soon put out; and then the roar of the enemy's guns began, and from Batteries Nos. 2, 3, and 4 on the mainland came the continued crack and scream of their rifle-shells, which seemed to unite with the electric batteries of the clouds to annihilate us.

While nearing the island or some shoal point, during a few minutes of total darkness, we were startled by the order, "Hard a-port!" . . . We almost grazed the island, and it appears were not observed through the storm until we were close in, and the enemy, having no time to point his guns, fired at random. In fact, we ran so near that the enemy did not, probably could not, depress his guns sufficiently. While close under the lee of the island and during a lull in the storm and in the firing, one of our pilots heard a Confederate officer shout, "Elevate your guns!" It is probable that the muzzles of those guns had been depressed to keep the rain out, and that the officers ordered the guns elevated just in time to save us from the direct fire of the enemy's heaviest fort; and this, no doubt, was the cause of our remarkable escape.[14]

While the event seemed remarkable to Walke, in retrospect it seems less so. What *Carondelet* did at Island Number Ten in the years ahead became almost commonplace on the western rivers. Walke and naval officers like him serving under both flags had yet to realize how much technology had changed the rules. Trained on wooden vessels powered by sail and steam, these men did not appreciate the mobility and strength offered by steam and armor. Those behind the land parapets tended to overestimate their capacity to thwart a naval attack while those on board the attackers suffered from uncertainty bred from inexperience with the new devices at their disposal.

Two nights later a second gunboat, *Pittsburgh*, went the same route under similar conditions, sliding past the enemy guns. With two powerful gunboats at his disposal below the island, Pope moved his troops quickly and safely across the river to close on the enemy positions. Once over, he marched his men toward Tiptonville, where they overwhelmed a disorganized Confederate force. Understanding the hopelessness of their position, the Confederates on the island now opted to surrender to Foote. When the final count was taken, Pope and Foote tallied up prizes of five thousand prisoners, more than a hundred heavy guns, two dozen fieldpieces, and many thousand stands of small arms. In addition, Federal forces carried off large quantities of quartermaster supplies and hundreds of crates of ammunition. One small captured item of vital importance was a Confederate naval signal book, captured by Commander A. H. Kilty of *Mound City*. Foote would now be able to decipher intercepted messages from the enemy.[15]

I I

The fall of Henry and Donelson—followed in quick succession by Columbus, New Madrid, and Island Number Ten—foreboded evil. Confederate newspapers pictured a Union juggernaut making its way down the Mississippi. And calamity had struck in the East, too; the Confederate army had been pushed back at Shiloh and was now withdrawing toward Corinth.[16] One of the casualties of that battle was Albert Sidney Johnston, the architect of the western defense. His successor, Pierre G. T. Beauregard, tried to reassure the public and his superiors by downplaying these defeats. He dismissed Island Number Ten as of minimal importance. It was, according to Beauregard, simply one of the outguards for Fort Pillow; this fort was far more important and more easily defended.

Beauregard was right, at least about Fort Pillow. Located about forty miles north of Memphis, on the eastern bank of the Mississippi, it was the only important fortification standing between the Union gunboats and that city. Its entrenchments, located on high bluffs overlooking the river, stretched for several miles. Numerous batteries were placed on the crest of the bluffs at the water's edge. Since the debacle at New Madrid, more than a thousand slaves had been put to work improving the Confederate position.[17]

Foote wasted no time in pushing down the river, and on 12 April his flotilla began steaming toward Fort Pillow. By the evening they were at an anchorage just below the Arkansas line, fifty miles south of New Madrid. The next day Pope arrived with twenty thousand troops. The plan was not unlike the one the general and commodore had used at Island Number Ten. Pope would land his army five miles north of the Confederates and move on them from the rear, while Foote's gunboats and mortars attacked from the river. General Halleck, however, had a different idea. Wishing to concentrate against the Confederates under Beauregard, on 15 April he ordered Pope to come with his troops to Shiloh. At the same time he ordered Foote, who was still under army command, to remain at Fort Pillow, where he was to continue the bombardment and, if possible, with the few remaining troops left to him, occupy the enemy's position.[18]

Halleck's need for Pope's troops certainly outweighed any advantage the reduction of Fort Pillow might bring. Nevertheless, Foote felt abandoned. His health was still bad. The injury to his foot at Fort Donelson had not healed properly; he had never given it time or occasion to mend. On the day after he arrived off Fort Pillow he wrote to his old friend Welles that "my wound has quite a depressing effect upon me, from the increased inflammation and swelling of my foot and leg, which have induced a febrile action, depriving me of a good deal of sleep and energy. I can not give the wound that attention and rest it absolutely requires until this place is captured."[19] The next day a board of surgeons examined the injury and declared that in his present condition Foote would soon be "totally unfit" for duty. Foote forwarded the surgeons' report to Welles. If he was to be relieved, he asked that it be by Charles H. Davis. Welles agreed. Davis, dispatched on 22 April to Fort Pillow, reported to Foote on 9 May.[20] After briefing him, Foote left Davis in temporary command, expecting that after a short leave he would be able to resume his command. That afternoon, as his men cheered him, the commodore headed upriver.

Contrary to his own and Welles's hopes, Foote never returned to the river. After his health had improved somewhat, he was given a desk job in Washington. Then, in the spring of 1863, Welles asked his old friend to take charge of the squadron which was trying to reduce Charleston. On 11 June Foote left his family home in New Haven to assume his new command at Port Royal. He stopped overnight in New York, where he became seriously ill. On 26 June Commodore Andrew Hull Foote died in his room at the Astor Hotel.[21]

III

Foote's successor, Captain Charles Davis, was a Bostonian, a graduate of Harvard College, and an officer whom Welles and others held in high regard. He had served in a variety of posts since entering the service in 1824, many of them concerned with scientific work important to the navy. When war broke out, he was the officer in charge of the Office of Detail, a post Welles created, and he had served as du Pont's chief of staff during the Port Royal expedition. His posting to the Mississippi at such a critical moment was testimony to Welles's faith in him. On 17 June, recognizing that Foote was not likely to return, Welles made Davis "flag-officer in command of the U.S. naval forces employed on the Mississippi and its tributaries."[22]

Davis had hardly moved his gear into the commodore's cabin when he faced his first crisis. Foolishly the Union forces had settled into a very predictable pattern of behavior at Fort Pillow. Every morning, like clockwork, they towed a mortar boat downstream within range of the fort to hurl shot at the enemy. These mortar barrages alarmed the enemy but did little actual damage. Nevertheless, because it was virtually the only thing that could safely be done, every morning the same drill took place.

On the morning of 10 May, right on schedule, mortar boat number sixteen, with Second Master Thomas B. Gregory in command, was towed to a spot within range of Fort Pillow. Standing nearby was the gunboat *Cincinnati*. Number sixteen sent off her first round at six, and four more followed until Gregory spotted the belching stacks of Confederate gunboats up ahead, coming around Plum Point. Quickly he ordered his crew to range on them, a brave but futile move. *Cincinnati*, too, saw the boats approaching. Her commander, Roger Stembel, charged forward, followed by *Carondelet* and *Mound City*. The other boats farther upstream were less alert and slower to react.

This was Davis's introduction to the Confederate "River Defense Fleet." Facing him were eight gunboats: *General Bragg, General Sterling Price, General Earl Van Dorn, General Sumter, General M. Jeff Thompson, General Beauregard, Colonel Lovell,* and *Little Rebel.* Lightly armed and unarmored, they ought not to have posed a problem. However, with surprise on their side, they could be deadly. Aside from surprise, their chief weapon at Plum Point was speed. They could easily outrun and outmaneuver the heavily gunned iron-plated monsters under Davis's command. Their aim was to ram and sink the Federals.[23]

Bragg and *Sterling Price* made straight for *Cincinnati*. *Bragg* hit her first, followed by *Price,* which hit her just aft of midships. Reeling from those blows, *Cincinnati* swung into the stream, only to take a blow on the stern from *Sumter.* On deck Commander Stembel, ignoring his own safety, left shelter and came into the open to command better. He was struck down by a Confederate sharpshooter. Two tugs sent down by Davis pushed the sinking *Cincinnati* toward shore. She settled to the bottom in twelve feet of water, while her crew scrambled to the upper decks.

Mound City and *Carondelet* were the next to join in the fray. Steaming downstream directly at the enemy, the let go with their bow guns. *Van Dorn* took aim at *Mound City* and struck her a glancing blow on the starboard forward quarter. The contact opened a four-foot gash and sent *Mound City* scurrying to the nearest shoal water, where she, too, settled into the mud. By this time *Pittsburgh* and *Benton* were in the battle area and firing away. Having accomplished more than he had expected, the Confederate commander, J. E. Montgomery, signaled withdrawal. The Federals followed until they came within range of Fort Pillow, where the engagement was broken off.

Montgomery had two killed, one wounded, and no vessels lost. Davis counted two gunboats on the bottom and several men wounded. Try as he might to put the best light on the engagement, it was clear to all that the Federals had been found napping and had paid dearly for their carelessness.

At Plum Point the Confederates had their best ally in surprise, but it was a fickle friend. The Federals had a far more reliable companion: power. Although he was able to smite Davis, Montgomery could never have hoped to stop him, and in the end it was the Confederates who had to withdraw.

Fort Pillow's demise was not brought on by combat on the river. General Beauregard decided to make a strategic withdrawal from Corinth rather than risk losing his army against Halleck. On the night of 29–30 May he quietly moved his army out and toward a new defense line along the Tuscumbia River. Halleck, as was his custom, made a leisurely pursuit. He then decided not to march farther into Mississippi but to halt and consolidate his gains in Tennessee.

All this meant that Fort Pillow had been outflanked and was indefensible. Logic demanded evacuation. Memphis was now vulnerable, too. However, the city was too important to abandon blithely, so the decision was made to defend it. Since Memphis had little by way of fixed land defense, its survival rested almost entirely on Montgomery's ability to hold off Davis with his eight vessels. At 8:00 P.M. on 5 June Davis and his gunboats anchored "at the lower end of Island No. 45, about a mile and a half above the city of Memphis; the mortar boats, towboats, ordnance, commissary, and other vessels of the fleet tied up at Island No. 44 for the night."[24]

Davis's gunboats were not the only Union force on the river. Not too many miles above them, tied up against the Tennessee shore, was Charles Ellet and his ram fleet.

I V

Born in 1810, Charles Ellet was a highly successful engineer. He was particularly well known for his design and construction of suspension bridges and had to his credit the longest such bridge in the world, a 1,010-foot span over the Wheeling and Ohio rivers. Bridges, though, were only part of Ellet's career. He was one of those puttering geniuses who are curious about nearly everything. During the Crimean War he traveled to Russia and was present in Sevastopol during the allied siege of that great city. Here Ellet realized that technology might well be able to bring back an ancient device for modern naval war, the ram. Popular in the days of oared galleys, rams had lost favor when the sail-powered warship became dominant. A vessel under sail was at the mercy of the wind and as such made a poor ram. Steam, thought Ellet, had once more provided a method by which a ship could direct her own course, regardless of wind direction. He tried to convince the Russians that steam rams could break the allied blockade, but they refused to listen. Back in the United States, Ellet made the same plea to each secretary of the navy from James Dobbin to Gideon Welles. Each paid him no heed either. What elevated Ellet from fool to prophet was the Battle of Hampton Roads, where *Virginia* showed the world the potential of a steam ram. In the panicked aftermath of that battle, Secretary of War Stanton ordered Ellet to proceed to Pittsburgh, Cincinnati, and New Albany, Indiana, to "take measures to provide steam rams for defense against ironclad vessels on the Western waters."[25]

Stanton feared that the Confederates might be able to obtain an advantage on the rivers. He wanted immediate action from Ellet. There would be no time to build proper rams; Ellet would have to improvise. This made Ellet a little uneasy, but with his usual air of confidence, he deferred to Stanton. Although his rams would "be only off-hand contrivances at best, mere substitutes for rams," he could make them work.[26]

More bothersome than the matter of the boats was the issue of rank and command. Ellet was under command of the secretary of war, and as such he was outside naval authority. Technically, of course, all gunboats, although manned by the navy, were under army command. But that arrangement was proving troublesome. Naval officers disliked being part of the army chain of command and wanted more independence. Many in the Navy Department were pressing for greater control over riverine operations. Stanton insisted that Ellet hold rank and conferred upon him a full colonelcy. Ellet then asked that his younger brother Alfred of the Fifty-ninth Illinois, then a captain, be promoted to lieutenant colonel and placed in command of the troops on board the rams.[27] Stanton agreed, hardly realizing that this was only the beginning. Before he was through, Charles

Ellet managed to persuade the secretary to assign to his flotilla
four additional members of his family, including his nineteen-
year-old son, Charles Rivers Ellet.

Ellet selected seven riverboats for conversion, and in yards
at Pittsburgh, Cincinnati, and New Albany crews went to work
fashioning rams. Strength was essential to their purpose. Each
of the steamers had her hull reinforced and the forward end
filled as solidly as possible with hard oak. Three longitudinal
bulkheads were fitted and strengthened with iron stanchions;
when the bow crashed into an enemy, the whole weight of the
boat would be behind the impact. In the engine area the boilers
and driving mechanisms were battened down to prevent damage. Since the simple goal was to close with and batter the enemy,
Ellet emphasized speed and strength. With full throttle and heads
down being the tactic, there was little need for heavy weapons,
and indeed, Ellet's rams carried only light armament.[28]

On 25 May Ellet and six of his boats joined Davis just above
Fort Pillow. Ellet got a proper but cool reception. Davis had
little faith in the rams and was not enthusiastic about cooperat-
ing with this newly minted army colonel and his irrepressible
ram clan. After Fort Pillow's evacuation Ellet's rams followed
the gunboats down to Memphis.

The city was vulnerable, and with the forces at hand the
Confederates would be hard pressed to make a stand; but out
of bravery and necessity (his fleet lacked sufficient fuel to make
it to Vicksburg) Montgomery elected to fight. Victory was only
a distant hope, but on the morning of 6 June the citizens of
Memphis gathered on the levee to watch the battle that would
decide their fate. Near dawn Montgomery moved his eight boats
into the stream, where they opened fire on the Federals.

Davis, like Foote, was aware of the dangers of maneuvering awkward vessels in a strong downstream current. He, therefore, decided to back into the battle and headed his vessels
upstream, bow to the current. In this position, should the
engagement go badly, he would have a better chance of steaming away.

With bow guns blazing from the Confederates and stern guns answering from the Federals, the battle got under way. Twenty minutes into the action, Davis signaled "Follow my motions." With that, he turned *Benton* downstream and headed for the enemy. Thus far Ellet and his rams had been spectators. Indeed, Davis and Ellet had formulated no plans whatsoever. Since there was no plan, Ellet felt at liberty to do as he pleased.

At the first sound of guns Ellet was ready. On the hurricane deck of his flagship, *Queen of the West*, he ran to the rail, waving his hat to attract the attention of his brother Alfred, in command of *Monarch*. At the top of his lungs he called out, "Round out and follow me! Now is our chance!" Without hesitation the brothers charged ahead. The younger Ellet later described the scene of the battle:

> The morning was beautifully clear and perfectly still; a heavy wall of smoke was formed across the river, so that the position of our gun-boats could only be seen by the flashes of their guns. The *Queen* plunged forward, under a full head of steam, right into this wall of smoke and was lost sight of, her position being known only by her tall pipes which reached above the smoke. The *Monarch*, following, was greeted, while passing the gun-boats, with wild huzzas from our gallant tars.[29]

After passing through the gunboat line, *Monarch* and *Queen* made for the Confederate flotilla. It was a mad melee. From the hurricane deck, Ellet signaled his brother to make for the Confederate *General Price*, steaming on the right flank of the enemy line. As for himself, he made a dash for the middle of the line and the steamer *Colonel Lovell*. *Queen* and *Lovell* came on full steam, head to head, but at the last moment *Lovell* made for starboard. It was a fatal error. With all her momentum and speed, *Queen* slammed into *Lovell* broadside and sent her to the bottom. *Monarch*, too, found her mark. She struck a glancing blow at the *General Price* that sent her limping toward the nearest shore, but not before she exchanged fire with *Benton*. As Davis watched, his flagship sent a well-aimed shot into *Price*'s boiler, completely disabling her. In the space of a few minutes Montgomery had lost a quarter of his fleet.

While still recovering from her collision with *Lovell*, *Queen* found herself under attack from both port and starboard. *Sumter* and *Beauregard* brought Ellet under heavy fire. In his usual reckless manner, Ellet was hollering orders from the hurricane deck when he was cut down by an enemy sharpshooter. At the same time one of *Queen*'s wheels had been put out of action, and she sought the safety of the Arkansas shore. She was soon joined by *General Price*, which arrived in a sinking condition. Wounded but still in command, Ellet sent over boarders and took the vessel as his prize.

Thrown back by the unexpectedly bold Federal attack, the Confederates retreated down the river. Yankee rams and gunboats followed in pursuit. *Monarch* closed in on the fleeing *Beauregard* and rammed her broadside, sending her crew into near panic. With white flags waving, *Beauregard* edged toward the riverbank. *Monarch* kept steaming, this time toward the enemy flagship. *Little Rebel* had already suffered some injury from Davis's gunboats and was puffing toward the Arkansas side. She got unexpected help from *Monarch*, which hit her aft and drove her into the bank. Wasting little time, *Little Rebel*'s crew climbed over the side and took to the scrub-brush cover along the shore. *Monarch* steered around and headed back. She took the crippled *Beauregard* under tow and brought her onto a bar, where she settled in water up to her boilers.

It was a grand spectacle viewed by a silent audience on the levee. Years later Henry Walke, commander of *Carondelet*, recalled in dramatic terms the scene of battle: "The screaming, plunging shell crashed into the boats, blowing some of them and their crews into fragments, and the rams rushed upon each other like wild beasts in deadly conflict. Blinding smoke hovered about the scene of all this confusion and horror; and, as the battle progressed and the Confederate fleet was destroyed, all the cheering voices on shore were silenced."[30]

Near the end of the battle a white flag could be seen in the city. Ellet ordered his son, Charles Rivers Ellet, ashore with a small party. They delivered a summons for surrender to the mayor, who gave a predictably evasive reply. Young Ellet then marched boldly to the post office, where he raised the Stars and Stripes. Later in the day Davis sent his own representative to take official possession of the city.

While the Confederates paid a hefty price for their unsuccessful defense, the Federals got off very lightly. Montgomery lost, by either capture or destruction, seven of his eight vessels. The only one to escape was *General Van Dorn*. And casualties among the Confederate forces were heavy. On the Federal side there were few injuries and no deaths. Ironically, although it was not recognized at the time, the most serious injury was the one sustained by Ellet himself when he was struck in the leg. Ellet, sent upriver to Cairo for medical attention, died there on 21 June. He was succeeded in command by his brother Alfred.

Though the reports coming in from Memphis were melancholy, Mallory could at least take some pride in Montgomery's brave attempts to defend the city. But the loss of Memphis was a huge blow; along with New Orleans, it was the only place on the river with the resources to build gunboats. Both cities were now lost. Beside the smoldering ruins along the waterfront floated the remnants of the gunboat *Tennessee,* which had been put to the torch to avoid capture. Her sister, *Arkansas,* had managed to slip out of the town a few weeks before and been taken up the Yazoo, where it was hoped she could be completed. But even the generally optimistic Mallory knew that the few Confederate vessels left on the western waters could be no more than a slight nuisance to the powerful Federal flotilla. Henceforth Confederate rivermen would only snipe at Union forces, to little effect. Only one major obstacle stood in the way of Union control over the entire Mississippi: Vicksburg.

9

Vicksburg Resists

I

With Memphis secure, Flag Officer Davis turned his attention to salvage. His crews resurrected the remnants of the Confederate squadron from their watery grave and sent them up to Cairo for repair. Davis also pursued the lone escapee from the melee at Memphis, the steamer *General Earl Van Dorn,* and kept an eye out for any other vessels with which the Confederates might be planning mischief. He suspected that he might well find them in hiding on the White and Arkansas rivers.[1]

Meanwhile, across the river in Arkansas the Federals were in trouble. Major General Samuel Ryan Curtis, commander of the Department of Missouri, had advanced into northern Arkansas in early April. At first all went well, and his powerful force pushed the Confederates aside. However, as Curtis moved away from his supply depots, matters became worse. Unable to transport adequate supplies overland across the long distances from his base at St. Louis, Curtis tried supplying his army by local forage. Unhappily his foragers met heavy resistance. Faced with dwindling provisions, Curtis moved to the rear of the White River. Even there his situation was precarious, and he informed his headquarters at St. Louis that unless he received reinforcements, he would be forced to withdraw even farther east. When news of Curtis's predicament arrived at the War Department, Secretary Stanton quickly took up the matter with Welles. The naval secretary telegraphed Davis, instructing him to send gunboats immediately up the White River to open up a resupply route for Curtis's army.[2]

At first Davis saw the expedition as one in which his gunboats and Alfred Ellet's rams could move jointly. He proposed this to Ellet but was taken aback when the colonal insisted that his rams would not serve under navy command and must remain independent. Davis replied that such an arrangement would only "retard" the mission. The gunboats would go alone.[3]

On 13 June *Mound City, St. Louis,* and *Lexington* cast off from the Memphis wharf and headed downstream toward the White River. Two days later they were joined at the mouth of the river by the gunboat *Conestoga* and two transports carrying troops and supplies for Curtis. The next morning the squadron got under way and steamed up the river toward the Confederate position at St. Charles. As the squadron approached the town, *Mound City* was in the van, her guns firing on Confederate positions near the river. With little regard for her own safety, *Mound City* steamed to within six hundred yards of the enemy's guns. The lesson of gunboat vulnerability taught at Fort Donelson had not been sufficiently learned. *Mound Duty* had several gaps in her armor, and a well-directed Confederate shot tore into one. The round came through the casemate, killing three men instantly, and then ripped through a boiler. A wild hurricane of live steam escaped. The "howling of the wounded and the moaning of the dying" was beyond description. One hundred and twenty-five men died on the *Mound City;* it was one of the greatest single ship losses for the Federal navy in the entire war.[4]

St. Charles fell, but the victory was pointless. The horror aboard *Mound City* broke morale. The other gunboat commanders were reluctant to push farther upstream. Within a short time the lower level of the river made the issue moot. Without naval support the infantry could not advance, and both retreated down the river. Faced with little hope for resupply and reinforcement, Curtis retreated east. The White River expedition was almost a complete failure.

I I

It is a pity that Halleck and Davis allowed themselves to be distracted by the sideshow on the White River. This escapade served only to draw attention away from the real focus of the war in the West, Vicksburg.

Nowhere in its long course to the Gulf was the Mississippi more lazily serpentine than in its passage between Memphis and Vicksburg. Along the river's banks between the towns lay cotton land, low, muddy, and pestilential. A few miles above Vicksburg, at Milliken's Bend, the river slid past Pawpaw Island and was joined by the muddy waters of the Yazoo. Just beyond the Yazoo, at Tuscumbia Bend, the river took another sudden turn; it lurched nearly northward and then, just as quickly, south again, passing the village of De Soto to starboard and the towering brown bluffs of Vicksburg to port. Vicksburg hunched over the river, sullenly scrutinizing those who passed below.

Vicksburg's position was very nearly impregnable. The bluffs to which it was attached were part of the Walnut Hills, a long uprising of land that began at Memphis. These hills provided a sort of barrier, which enclosed a vast patchwork quilt of land laced by streams, bayous, and swamps. It was a place that was heaven for vegetation and hell for man.

Vicksburg's commanding presence over the river was only part of its importance for the Confederacy. It was also a choke point on the North-South axis and a link from the West to the East. Opposite Vicksburg in De Soto was the terminus of the Shreveport and Vicksburg Railroad; behind the town the Vicksburg and Jackson Railroad ran east. With the fall of New Orleans and then Memphis, Vicksburg became the only significant link between the Confederacy's bread basket in the West and its hungry armies in the East. Its capture, if achieved, would split the Confederacy and shorten rations in the Rebel army.

The first of many Federals to arrive at Vicksburg was Samuel Phillips Lee, in command of the gunboat *Oneida*. On 18 May 1862, fresh from the victory at New Orleans, he demanded the surrender of the town. Such effrontery naturally met a curt refusal. Within a day Farragut himself arrived with *Kennebec* and a few other vessels up from New Orleans. Accompanying him was General Thomas Williams with troops detached from Butler's command.[5]

As they surveyed the situation, Farragut and Williams agreed that Vicksburg could not be taken with the forces at hand. From their lofty position, the Confederates could rain fire down on the river, but Farragut's gunners could not elevate their weapons sufficiently to deliver fire up to the bluffs. Compounding the problem was the unhappy fact that the river squadron was now several hundred miles upstream from the nearest supply depot. Delivery of coal, food, and ammunition would be slow and difficult.

Even if Farragut had had a well-armed and better-supplied force, he would not have been able to take Vicksburg. Although naval force was critical to isolating the town, naval force alone would not capture it. Only a land army could breach the defenses and force a surrender.

Within two or three days of arriving Farragut decided to leave. Although the flag officer overestimated the enemy strength in the town, as well as its ability to reinforce, his essential judgment was correct. He wrote to Butler:

> It appears to be the general opinion here among the officers, General Williams included, that there is very little use in attacking Vicksburg, as the guns on the heights are so elevated that our fire will not be felt by them. As they have so large a force of soldiers here, several thousand in and about the town, and the facility of bringing in 20,000 in an hour by railroad from Jackson, altogether [I] think it would be useless to bombard it, as we could not hold it if we take it. Therefore we have determined to blockade it and occasionally harass them with fire until the battle of Corinth shall decide its fate. . . . I shall soon drop down the river again, as I consider my service indispensably necessary on the seaboard.[6]

By the twenty-eighth, Farragut was downriver at Baton Rouge, writing to Welles about his lamentable situation. He needed more vessels. Those that he had were in sad need of repair. Most had been aground at one time or another, several had been in collisions, and more anchors had been lost in the river bottom than Farragut had seen gone in a lifetime. All this was a result of sending deep-draft vessels under deepwater sailors into the shallow, tangled mess of river operations.[7]

The brief show of force against Vicksburg was not enough, and Farragut was soon informed that the president demanded more. Welles informed him that he was still bound by his orders given before the fall of New Orleans: "Open the river Mississippi." To do that he was to steam north, "effect a junction with Flag-Officer Davis," and capture Vicksburg. Reluctantly Farragut headed upriver again, taking with him the additional help of Porter's mortar boats.[8]

By 24 June Farragut was once again at Vicksburg. This time his squadron was stronger. In addition to Porter's mortar flotilla and his own flagship, *Hartford,* he was joined by *Iroquois, Oneida, Richmond, Wissahickon, Sciota, Winona, Pinola, Brooklyn, Kennebec,* and *Katahdin.* General Williams, with fifteen hundred men, was also there to assist. Altogether it was an imposing fleet, one that in terms of firepower greatly outweighed what the Confederate defenders could muster. Lincoln, Welles, and Fox thought naval gunfire with a small assist from the army could subdue the entrenched enemy at Vicksburg. This was Yankee hubris.[9]

Farragut was annoyed to drop anchor below the town and find himself alone. Davis, still recovering from the White River fiasco, was unaware of the extent of Farragut's advance and therefore had not sent anyone downriver to welcome the squadron.

This presented a wonderful opportunity for the irrepressible Alfred Ellet to move to center stage. Having succeeded to his brother's command, he informed Davis on 18 June that he was preparing to move downstream.[10] He brought his rams to a spot above Vicksburg, where he learned of Farragut's approach. Determined to make contact, Ellet called for volunteers to convey a message through enemy lines. Four men, including Ellet's son Edward and his nephew Charles Rivers Ellet, stepped forward. Through the night of 24 June the party pushed aside underbrush and slogged through swamps, and finally reached the river below Vicksburg on the morning of the twenty-fifth. At seven-thirty the men came aboard *Hartford* and delivered to Farragut the news that from Vicksburg north the river was under Federal control, the only close danger being Confederate gunboats downstream. Farragut's return message was a plea to Davis to get his squadron downstream.[11]

While Farragut dearly wanted Davis's help, he had no intention of standing idly by. On the twenty-fifth he issued a general order for the squadron to pass under the guns of Vicksburg. At four in the morning of 26 June Porter signaled his mortar boats to open fire. For two days the boats dropped mortar rounds on the enemy emplacements. It was a grand sound-and-light show but had little effect. In fact, it served only to telegraph Farragut's intentions to the enemy.

After a two-day bombardment, before dawn on the twenty-eighth Farragut signaled his squadron to get under way. With *Iroquois* in the lead, the squadron pushed upstream. At four the Federals opened fire and received shot from the enemy. To the background noise of Porter's boats delivering rhythmic mortar fire, the squadron, firing its own salvos, slowly made its way past the batteries of Vicksburg. Several of the vessels took hits; but none was serious, and the losses were minimal. By breakfast time the squadron was past the bluffs of Vicksburg and safely at anchor above the town.

It was a meaningless victory. Down below in *Hartford*'s wardroom Farragut and his officers were subdued. They understood that passing the batteries meant nothing. In fact, the squadrons' situation was made even more precarious by its new position upstream. The river was falling, and unless Farragut moved his deep-draft vessels back toward the Gulf, he was in danger of being trapped in the river, with the enemy between him and his main supply depots. Testy about what he viewed as the administration's ignorance of the situation on the river, the flag officer wrote to the navy secretary from his anchorage to report the passage, then commented that it was all "to no purpose."[12]

Farragut and Davis both understood that Vicksburg could be secured only by troops. Independently each of them informed Halleck of the situation and asked that he send additional forces. To this the general telegraphed a standard reply: "[The] scattered and weakened condition of my forces renders it impossible for me at the present to detach my troops to cooperate with you on Vicksburg."[13]

Halleck's depressing response made all the more poignant the first meeting between Farragut and Davis. On the morning of 1 July Davis's belching black gunboats, hunkered down in the water like "turtles," steamed into view. What a contrast they made with Farragut's lofty sailing vessels. After exchanging a few pleasantries, the two commanders sat down to talk. Both shared the opinion that without troops the situation was hopeless. As they talked, General Williams moved some of his troops ashore onto the peninsula opposite Vicksburg. His plan was to dig across this low-lying piece of land a canal that might allow the boats to pass from north to south without coming under the guns of the Confederates.

As the Union navy pondered and the army dug, the Confederates were not idle. Up the Yazoo, not far from Vicksburg, they were preparing a potent surprise: CSS *Arkansas*.

Having escaped Memphis in her unfinished condition, *Arkansas* had taken refuge in the Yazoo near Liverpool, where work on her continued. Short of proper materials, the Confederates had to make to do with whatever they could find. Isaac Brown, captain of *Arkansas,* reported that he had been unable to find the right equipment to bend iron around the stern and the pilothouse. Instead, he had used boiler plate iron, which was "imperfectly" tacked around.[14]

Despite the hasty expedients used to fit out *Arkansas*, she was still a formidable weapon. Her heavy ram could sink virtually anything the Federals had in the river, and her ten guns could wreak deadly damage. Her propellers were independent of one another, so that by reversing one screw, she could turn almost in her own length. This made her one of the most maneuverable vessels afloat.

As mid-July approached, the water in both the Yazoo and the Mississippi continued to fall. Brown was fearful. Unless he moved downstream within a few days, *Arkansas* would be snared in the shallow waters of the upper Yazoo. He ordered the ram moved closer to the Mississippi.[15]

Davis and Farragut were worried, too. Farragut made it no secret that he felt he was wasting his time up the river. Unless he moved his deep-draft vessel downstream, he was likely to be stuck there for months. Adding to his woes was the near-tropical climate. Most of the army troops were on sick call, down with everything from exhaustion to yellow fever. In July the lower Mississippi was a malarial trap.

In the midst of this misery Ellet reported that the Confederates were up to something on the Yazoo. Since his own boats could not navigate the twisting, shallow channels, Farragut asked Davis if he would send a few of his gunboats to take a look. Before dawn on the morning of 15 July *Queen of the West, Carondelet,* and *Tyler* made their way in line abreast up the river. Little did they realize what was in store for them.

About six miles ahead lay the *Arkansas,* anchored close to shore. Her chocolate-colored hull and low profile blended in nicely with the riverbanks and made her difficult to detect. In the first light of dawn *Carondelet's* lookout spotted the Rebel ram. The Federal fired first with her bow gun and then ranged closer, letting loose with her broadsides. Dabney Minor Scales, a younger officer aboard *Arkansas,* wrote to his father: "We were so close that our men were burnt by the powder from the enemy's guns."[16] *Queen of the West* and *Tyler* joined in the fray. The Federals were no match for *Arkansas,* and they knew it. Within a few minutes all three were trying to "skedaddle" back to the fleet. In the melee *Carondelet* took the brunt. Hit at least twenty times and severely injured, she headed for shore and safety. *Arkansas,* unable to follow into the shallow water, passed within forty feet. As she slid by, she let loose with a rollicking broadside. *Tyler* and *Queen of the West* continued their race to the river.

The sudden return of the gunboats, with *Arkansas* close on their stern, caught Farragut and Davis napping. For the comfort of the crew and as a measure to conserve fuel, engine room fires were usually kept low. At the sound of gunfire, coal heavers were sent to their stations, but getting up steam was a long process. By the time *Arkansas* made her appearance, the Federals still had no more mobility than the rocks in the riverbed.

In all of the Civil War this was probably the single most embarrassing moment for the Federal navy. *Arkansas* came charging out of the Yazoo with guns blazing. Like a participant in some grand naval review, the Confederate ironclad passed in front of the entire Federal squadron (*Hartford, Iroquois, Richmond, Sumter, Louisville, Oneida*, and many more), each of which poured a broadside at her. Behind the iron casemate, Brown was everywhere, urging gun crews to load, ram, and fire fast and true. In the engine room the temperature was at 130 and climbing. Smoke hung over the river, and it was dark as nightfall. For a time all that could be seen were muzzle flashes cutting through the dense, acrid clouds. For one hour *Arkansas* beat her way through the fleet; finally, she came to safe anchorage under the protective guns of Vicksburg. It was none too soon. Although her hull had not suffered critical injury, the smokestack had been holed so many times that the fires lacked draft, and pressure in the boilers had fallen to only twenty pounds. A few more minutes, and *Arkansas* would have been a helpless, drifting derelict. As it was, she was a battered heroine. Even Farragut, shamefaced and angry, had to admit in his official report that *Arkansas*'s feat was a "bold thing." Indeed, it was one of the grandest naval scenes of the entire war.[17]

Farragut and Davis boasted that the Rebel ram was severely injured, but they felt less certain than they seemed. Having such a potent devil loose below the city, where she might decimate the support and transport vessels at anchor there, was too horrible to contemplate. Almost as soon as he had steam up, Farragut headed down the river, hoping to be able to send *Arkansas* to the bottom. But *Arkansas* was already safely in the embrace of Vicksburg's guns.

In Vicksburg the Confederate commander General Earl Van Dorn had big plans for the heroic ram. It was his intention to repair her and send her south on a voyage of rampage that, if carried out properly, might well drive the Federals from the river. No one needed to be clairvoyant to divine Van Dorn's intention. Time was quickly running out for the Federals. Hurriedly the Union flag officers laid their plans.

David Dixon Porter, recently arrived in command of a rebuilt *Essex*, was central to the plan. While Farragut's squadron engaged the enemy batteries on the south, and Davis's guns hit them from the north, *Essex, Queen of the West,* and *Sumter* would charge *Arkansas,* then ram and sink her. At four in the morning on 22 July the attack got under way. It featured confusion, mis-communication, and just plain ineptitude. Most of the Federal shots missed. When the smoke cleared, *Arkansas* still floated proudly at the river's edge, watching as the Federal trio slunk away in retreat.

The situation was glum. With the river falling, as was usual for this time of year, Farragut saw no choice but to leave. Davis, too, was pessimistic. Of his 130 mortarmen, 100 were in sick bay. One-quarter of *Benton*'s men were down with fever, one-half of *Carondelet*'s crew were ill, and a third of *Louisville*'s sailors were infected. And the worst of the Mississippi summer was yet to come.[18]

Davis and Farragut concluded that to remain at Vicksburg would be madness. On 24 July Farragut took his squadron downriver. Within a few days Davis sailed back to Memphis. By the end of July the river in front of Vicksburg had been abandoned by Federal forces.

Privately Davis blamed Farragut for the failure at Vicksburg. In fact, the fault rests more with him. For two months he had dawdled in front of the town. Had he moved more quickly downriver and assaulted the town sooner, there is every reason to believe that it might have fallen. Indeed, if Halleck had been more prescient, he would have supplied enough troops to have guaranteed the fall of Vicksburg. Davis's lethargy and Halleck's lack of foresight provided the Confederates with ample time to reinforce Vicksburg. The place fell eventually, but at a far higher price than it might have fetched in the summer of 1862.[19]

Whatever Davis felt about the failure to capture Vicksburg, Farragut was more than happy to say good riddance. He was a saltwater sailor who had never wanted to go upriver in the first place. He was relieved to be steaming back toward deep water, his native habitat. His relief soon turned to joy. On 10 August, when *Hartford* dropped anchor off New Orleans, Farragut read the official dispatch announcing that he had been promoted to rear admiral, the first man ever to hold such rank in the United States Navy. He was never prouder than at the moment when the quartermaster broke out the admiral's square blue flag and hoisted it to the top of the foremast. He stood, visibly moved, as a cheer went up from the men of the squadron.

I I I

In Washington no one was cheering. Vicksburg stood stronger than ever. In June, when Farragut and Davis had joined forces, the Confederates had been squeezed into a stretch of the Mississippi not more than a few miles to either side of Vicksburg. Now, with the Union navy in retreat, they held several hundred miles of river from Helena, Arkansas, to Port Hudson, Louisiana. The junction of the Red River and the Mississippi—which provided access to the rich lands of the Trans-Mississippi—was solidly within their grasp. As for *Arkansas,* she had come to an unhappy end. Following the Federal withdrawal, she had gone down to Baton Rouge to aid in a Confederate attempt to retake the town. During the battle on 6 August her tired engines finally gave out. She ran aground, and to avoid capture, she was scuttled by her crew.[20]

In Richmond the news of *Arkansas*'s fate brought criticism of Mallory to new heights.

At the beginning of the war, knowing that the Confederacy could never match the Federal navy in sheer numbers, Mallory had decided to build only a few powerful vessels. Quality would compensate for a dearth of quantity; the invulnerability of his ironclads would compensate for their small numbers. Yet what had happened? *Virginia, Arkansas* and *Mississippi* all had been scuttled; *Louisiana* had been blown up. In just five months the South had lost its four most powerful ironclads.

The loss of these vessels—together with the navy's generally disappointing performance at Hatteras Inlet, Port Royal, and New Orleans—sparked some members of the Confederate Congress to levy accusations of stupidity and incompetence at the secretary of the navy. Wounded, Mallory confided to his diary: "I am as sick as I am disgusted with the carpings and complaints of ignorance and presumption, that I have not built a navy. I feel confident of having done my whole duty, of having done all that any man could have done with the means at hand. I have my own approbation at least."[21]

For Mallory, though, the loss of *Arkansas* seemed a final, discouraging blow. He had believed that *Virginia, Arkansas, Louisiana,* and *Mississippi* would revolutionize the "naval warfare of the world." Yet they were gone, and all that was left was the "rage of the ignorant, the rabble and the prejudiced."[22]

I V

Federal woes in the West were not confined to the river. Late in June Jefferson Davis, in a somewhat peremptory fashion, dismissed Beauregard from his command of the Army of the Tennessee and put Braxton Bragg in his place. Time proved Bragg an indifferent commander, but just now he was poised with his army to move north and invade Kentucky. The Federals were back on the defensive.

The Union's setbacks in the West were mirrored in the East. McClellan, the commander of the Army of the Potomac, had orders to capture Richmond. But for weeks now his Peninsula campaign had consisted of parading and maneuvering. Facing McClellan was Robert E. Lee, the newly appointed commander of the Army of Northern Virginia. After a series of battles, known collectively as the Seven Days, McClellan opted to withdraw his army to the banks of the James River, where he was covered by fire from Union gunboats. The Army of the Potomac remained at the river until, in a controversial decision, McClellan was ordered to remove his army back toward Washington. Exasperated at McClellan's perpetual slowness, Lincoln removed him from command and replaced him with John Pope. It was Pope who led the army to its disaster at the Second Battle of Bull Run. Left with no choice, Lincoln gave the army back to McClellan. True to form, the general husbanded his forces and led his army cautiously, moving slowly to block Lee's invasion of Maryland. At Antietam McClellan turned back the Army of Northern Virginia, but then, in his usual laborious manner, he failed to pursue the retreating Confederates and allowed Lee to escape with his army bloodied but intact. All in all the summer of 1862 was not the best of times for the Union forces.

Although the Confederates controlled a good deal of the land along the rivers, the Federals still held the rivers themselves, and their gunboats patrolled the Ohio, the Tennessee, the Cumberland, and the Mississippi. Steaming along in full view of the shore, these gunboats made wonderful targets for Confederate sharpshooters, as well as an occasional Rebel artillery battery. Angered by these acts, Union commanders sometimes retaliated in an indiscriminate and somewhat cruel fashion.

When one Union ship was hit by fire from the riverfront of Donaldsonville, Louisiana, Admiral Farragut shot up the wharves and buildings along the river and torched the home of a suspected guerrilla commander. He then told the inhabitants: "Every time my boats are fired upon I will burn a portion of your town."[23] Others followed Farragut's example. When William Porter (David's brother), in command of *Essex*, took a few hits from guerrillas hiding in Bayou Sara, Louisiana, he shelled the town. So it went along the river, with each side unable to gain any particular advantage but determined to torment the other. The Confederates hit and ran. The Federals, bound to the water, could not chase, so they simply struck whatever targets lay in range.

Sometimes petty sparring gave way to more organized ventures. In mid-August Union Lieutenant Commander S. Ledyard Phelps cast off from the wharf at Helena and headed downstream with three gunboats and four rams under Ellet's direction. Phelps had two regiments of infantry and a hundred cavalrymen on board. They proceeded down to the Yazoo and then thirty-five miles up that river. Along the way they went ashore to destroy Confederate supplies, cut telegraph lines, and in general harass Rebel forces. Phelps's violent raid reminded the Confederates of Federal power on the river and underscored the urgent need to reinforce Vicksburg.[24]

V

Vicksburg fell within the theater of Union operations controlled by the newly created Army of the Tennessee. In October that army received its first commander, Ulysses S. Grant. Grant had earned the sobriquet "Unconditional Surrender" for his memorable response at Fort Donelson, and his appointment brought new vigor to western operations.

Grant was not the only commander in the West. Passing over a number of more senior officers, Welles had appointed David Dixon Porter to lead a newly organized Mississippi squadron. Unlike his predecessors, Porter was given full authority. His chain of command ran directly to the secretary of the navy, not to the local army commander; Welles and Fox had had to lobby Congress to order the change. The shift made sense, and Stanton offered little objection. Congress enacted the law in July, and on 1 October 1862, by order of the adjutant general, the Western Gunboat Fleet was transferred from the War to the Navy Department. Welles informed Porter of the transfer, at the same time notifying him of his command of the fleet with the rank of acting rear admiral.[25] Porter was expected to cooperate fully with Grant. Ironically, as it turned out, these two independent commanders cooperated more fully and with greater success than any of their predecessors who were, at least on paper, intimately linked.

As Grant planned his strategy in Memphis, Porter went to work in Cairo, altering and adding to his gunboat fleet. His energy and his expenses were a bit overwhelming, and from Washington came inquiries about the size of his bills. Welles was temperate in his queries, however, for he had no wish to antagonize an officer with such zeal and drive.

Now that he had complete authority, Porter planned to rein in Alfred Ellet and his free-floating rams. Ever since their first appearance on the river, the rams' relationship to the navy had been problematical. In the new circumstances of command, the situation was intolerable. Porter's ego was every bit the equal of Ellet's, and there was no way that the acting rear admiral would tolerate this irrepressibly independent soldier. Porter made his sentiments known to both Ellet and Fox. He told them he had no intention of suffering two commands on the river. As expected, Ellet resisted, but Porter was firm. As far as he was concerned, unless Ellet gave in, he could "cool his shins, and lie at the bank."[26]

They struck a bargain. Porter needed an amphibious force to help suppress the enemy fire that tormented him from shore. Why not assign Ellet, who was, after all, a military officer, to command such a "marine brigade"? After a good deal of cabinet-level discussion Lincoln agreed and assigned Ellet to Porter's command. It turned out to be a less than inspired idea. Though Porter now had his amphibious force, the "marine brigade" proved impetuous and ill disciplined. The scheme's only saving grace was that it made Porter the undisputed commander of river forces.

Once fully in charge, Porter lost no time pushing ahead. Before he left Washington, Lincoln had told him that General John McClernand had been authorized to raise a force in the Northwest to move against Vicksburg. The president asked that Porter cooperate with him. Porter was polite in his response, but secretly he opposed Lincoln's wishes. McClernand was a political hack with very little military experience. Depending on him to take Vicksburg was, in the admiral's estimation, a foolish idea.

According to Porter, late in November he and Grant had dinner together at Cairo, and they discussed the Vicksburg campaign. Unfortunately, Porter's postwar recollections are not always reliable, and there is some question whether or not such a dinner did take place. Nevertheless, he and Grant were in touch, and on 22 November the general telegraphed Admiral Porter that the move toward Vicksburg had begun. William Tecumseh Sherman was to move from his headquarters at Memphis and march to Holly Springs, Mississippi. A second force under General Frederick Steele was en route from Helena to Grenada, Mississippi. Would the admiral lend his services?[27]

Grant was urgent. He was in a race against McClernand, and the prize was Vicksburg.

Porter was anxious to cooperate. While he suspected that Grant wanted to take Vicksburg on his own hook and leave the navy out of it, or at least confine it to a distant secondary role, he also understood that this general could fight. McClernand, in Porter's eyes, was hopeless.

Plans were made for Porter to rendezvous with Sherman's army at Memphis and then ferry it to Vicksburg. In the meantime, Grant's move on Vicksburg would be the bait to draw the Confederates out of town and into a battle at Grenada. With the city weakened by the Confederate withdrawal, Sherman ought to be able to capture it.

While Sherman assembled his troops at Memphis, Porter ordered Captain Henry Walke to take a large squadron of gunboats and ascend the Yazoo. His goal was to prevent the Confederates from holding positions along the river that might interfere with land operations against Vicksburg's right flank. In addition, Walke was told that a number of Confederate boats had taken refuge up the Yazoo and ought to be captured. If all went well, and the water was high enough, Walke was to continue pushing upstream and penetrating into enemy territory, threatening Confederate lines of communication and drawing off forces that might otherwise oppose Grant's advance on Grenada.[28]

On board *Carondelet,* Walke arrived at the mouth of the Yazoo. Already the lightly armored and shallow-draft "tinclad" *Marmora* had gone up the river to reconnoiter. She had encountered harassing fire from Confederate infantry but nothing that would stop her progress. Then, twenty miles from the mouth, she took fire from a series of artillery positions. *Marmora*'s report persuaded Walke that he ought to wait a few days until the arrival of the rest of his squadron, including the ironclad *Cairo,* which dropped anchor at the river's mouth on 8 December. For the next two days the squadron busied itself coaling and resupplying. On the eleventh *Marmora,* in company with another tinclad *Signal,* went back up the river on reconnaissance.[29]

As the tinclads steamed forward, lookouts spotted an "unaccountable number of small scows and stationary floats of various kinds along the channel." Suddenly one of these floats blew up near *Signal.* The harmless-looking floats were torpedoes or, in more modern parlance, mines.

The Confederates, unlike the Federals, were adept at mines. Some Federal officers, including Alfred Thayer Mahan, even saw these "weapons that wait" as inhumane, barbarous, and totally uncivilized. Such righteousness was only slightly harmful to the Union cause. Mines were not essential to Union strategy since it was the task of the Federal navy to intrude into enemy waters rather than defend its own. One wonders, however, why these weapons were not utilized more fully in blockading southern ports.

For the Confederates, mines made a great deal of sense. They sank vessels, of course, but even when they were not present, the mere suspicion of mines caused engines to slow or stop. Certainly this was the case on the Yazoo as the captains of

Marmora and *Signal* called below to the engine room for slow ahead and posted lookouts forward.[30]

When the tinclads returned to the squadron's anchorage, the captains reported to Walke what they had seen. They also proposed a method for removing the mines. At seven-thirty the next morning Walke ordered *Marmora* and *Signal* back up the river. Accompanied and protected by the gunboats *Cairo* and *Pittsburgh* and the ram *Queen of the West,* the tinclads were embarking, perhaps for the first time in American naval history, on a mission as minesweepers.

Operating from *Marmora* and *Signal,* small boats went ahead, scouring the shoreline and channel for any suspicious objects. Confederate sharpshooters lurked in the heavy cover along the river, and it was a risky business. The tinclads covered their men in the boats. Just behind them came the ram, followed by heavily armed gunboats. Walke was explicit: Under no circumstances were the larger vessels to proceed until the mined areas had been swept clean.

Walke's orders were reasonable; unfortunately they were not carried out. As *Marmora* rounded a bend in the river, she was partially screened from *Cairo*'s view. At the same moment *Cairo*'s captain, Thomas Selfridge, heard heavy gunfire ahead. A prudent commander would have reacted cautiously, but Selfridge ordered full steam and came up on *Marmora,* only to discover *Marmora*'s crew firing at a suspected mine. Just as Selfridge realized this, the current swung his bow toward the shore. He backed out and then ordered slow ahead to bring his bow back into the stream. *Cairo* had barely moved ahead half a length when two quick explosions lifted first her port quarter, then her port bow. The powerful second explosion threw her guns into the air. Twelve minutes later *Cairo* went to the bottom, with her funnel barely showing above the river. Thanks to quick action by the captain and crew, no one was killed, but that was cold comfort to Selfridge.

Notwithstanding the loss of *Cairo,* Porter did not reprimand Selfridge. The captain had shown a little too much zeal, but that was preferable to caution. A bold man himself, Porter could only applaud Selfridge's initiative while lamenting its result. In the coming months Porter was to lose other vessels to mines; altogether the Union navy eventually tallied up forty casualties to this hidden menace. The Confederates' deployment of mines was clever and effective.[31]

Porter's presence on the Yazoo was vital, for it was there that Sherman intended to land his army for the assault on Vicksburg. On 20 December he and Porter met at Helena, ready for the movement toward Vicksburg. The Union plan seemed sound enough. General Nathaniel Banks had arrived at New Orleans with a large force; he would begin moving up the river with Farragut. Sherman, acting as Grant's right wing, would proceed down the river covered by the navy. Grant himself, with the Thirteenth Corps, would march southward, hoping to find and smash the main Confederate force somewhere near Jackson, Mississippi. The third attack on Vicksburg was about to get under way.

10

Vicksburg Falls

I

On 20 December 1862, the very day that Sherman and Porter were preparing to steam down to the Yazoo, disaster struck. General Grant had left Colonel R. C. Murphy of the Eighth Wisconsin to guard the army's supply base at Holly Springs. Such a target was too tempting to ignore, and General Earl Van Dorn, with a force of thirty-five hundred Confederate cavalry, outwitted the Federals, got behind their lines, and swept in on Murphy and his men, many of whom were asleep. After stuffing their pockets and saddlebags with everything they could carry, the Confederates put the rest of their booty to the torch. While clouds of smoke wafted up from Holly Springs, Nathan Bedford Forrest's men were tearing up track on the railroad line. The Confederates destroyed Grant's depot, and by attacking the railroad, they made it impossible to send down more supplies. Grant had no choice. He abandoned the campaign and retreated back to Memphis.[1]

Unaware that Grant was falling back, Sherman and Porter made their way toward the Yazoo. Porter had under his command the largest number of American naval vessels ever assembled. In fact, his squadron was larger than the entire navy had been at the outbreak of the war. On Christmas Day it arrived at the mouth of the Yazoo. Minesweeping began again, and as usual, the Confederates did all they could to harass the boats with both artillery and small-arms fire. Among those hit was Lieutenant Commander William Gwin, the captain of *Benton*, who refused to take refuge in the pilothouse and eventually took a mortal wound through the breast.[2]

Porter's gunboats did what they could to soften up the landing sites and draw the enemy's fire. The day after arriving, Sherman put his men ashore at three locations near Chickasaw Bayou, five miles northeast of Vicksburg. A swamp with virtually no cover, it was a poor choice. The plan was to move across the lowlands and seize a position on the bluffs a short distance inland. Unfortunately the Confederates had already taken the high ground, and from their protected position they could easily sight down on the advancing Federals. After two days of fighting, Sherman was repulsed. The Union troops suffered losses of nearly two thousand, while the defenders counted only two hundred casualties.

Grant's withdrawal to Memphis had allowed the Confederate commander Lieutenant General John C. Pemberton to concentrate his forces against Sherman. Vicksburg stood and was in fact becoming stronger every day. Under the direction of the chief engineer, Brigadier General S. H. Lockett, bombproof magazines were built and new batteries were put in place. The work was made easier by the marvelous geography of Vicksburg. The whole area consisted of irregular hills, bluffs, and ridges, all of which made excellent fortifications. Where nature had not been kind enough to provide natural defensive features, she had at least laid down a fine calcareous silt easily moved by engineers to be fashioned into safe refuges for soldiers and civilians. It was futile to continue the campaign, and after some brief discussion Sherman and Porter withdrew down the Yazoo.[3] Vicksburg's right flank was secure.

As they were coming down the river, they met General McClernand. He bore fresh orders from Grant, which gave him command of the army. Already depressed by what had happened up stream, Porter and Sherman were devastated by this unexpected news. In general, Porter had little faith in army officers, and McClernand's politicking increased Porter's already considerable cynicism about the breed.

For his part, Sherman was determined not to go home without something to show for his efforts. Despite the humiliation at Chickasaw Bayou, his army and Porter's fleet were still ready to do battle. What they needed was a target. Not too far away Sherman found one.

About halfway between the Yazoo and Memphis, the Arkansas River joined the Mississippi. Although the river was nominally under Confederate control, there was little to prevent Union forces from moving into its waters until about fifty miles upstream. At Arkansas Post a very strong bastion, Fort Hindman, had been constructed. As fearsome as it was, Fort Hindman posed no threat to Union forces, unless of course, they tired to pass it. But the only reason to attempt a passage would be to invade Arkansas, perhaps to cut off the railroad and take Little Rock. When informed of the idea by McClernand, Grant opposed the idea and told him so, but before his message arrived, the expedition was well under way. Sherman and Porter were determined to salvage their reputations, and Fort Hindman provided the opportunity.[4]

Late in the morning of 10 January the army landed about four miles south of the fort. Its task was to march on the fort and invest it, while the gunboats attacked from the river. Hindman itself was most impressive and by far the best-built fortification yet encountered on the western rivers. The bastion was well engineered. It was four-sided, with roughly one hundred yards to a side, and mounted thirteen heavy guns, two of them snug behind four layers of railroad iron.

Commanding this impressive bastion was Colonel John W. Dunnington. Dunnington had begun the war as a lieutenant in the Confederate States navy. But since the navy had far more officers than ships, this lieutenant, like so many of his naval peers, was put ashore to lend a hand. Since naval officers generally knew ordnance, it made sense to put them into places with heavy guns.

In preparation for his defense, Dunnington had marked the channel with buoys on which to range his guns. His mistake, however, was in placing the buoys at twelve hundred yards, for Porter, eager to close with the enemy, ordered his vessels to near point-blank range. It was a classic slugfest. There was no clever maneuvering, just plain muzzle-to-muzzle belching of fire and shot.

Porter's overwhelming firepower smothered the defenders, and within an hour Hindman's guns had fallen silent. As night covered the river, Porter withdrew, and Dunnington put his men to work repairing the damage. It was a massive job, and all through the evening, loud noises of men heaving and hauling, hammers striking metal, and soldiers digging could be heard across the water. By daylight Sherman had been able to move his troops into position on the land side. Dunnington was surrounded, but he showed no sign of wavering. Porter's boats came in even closer this time and once more hammered Hindman. It was futile to resist. Within a short time the guns had gone silent again and a white flag was raised from the ramparts.[5]

Despite the usual self-congratulatory rhetoric, it is difficult to see the strategic importance of Fort Hindman's fall. It was never a threat to Union forces. This victory did, nevertheless, provide a lift for the seamen and soldiers who had been thrown back at Vicksburg. It might also have helped Grant, who had first termed the expedition a "wild goose chase" but then thought better of it.[6] Confederate confusion on the west bank of the Mississippi would be useful to him as he prepared his army for a fourth assault on Vicksburg. And Union troops that had been tied down watching the Confederates in Arkansas were now released.

Three times Federal forces had assaulted Vicksburg (Farragut twice, Sherman at Chickasaw Bluffs), and three times they had failed. Grant was determined not to repeat their experiences. In mid-January he gave up any idea of a two-pronged approach to the city. He would attack with a single army and would personally lead them. On 16 January Grant left his headquarters at Memphis on his way downstream to meet with Porter, McClernand, and Sherman. He caught up with them at Napoleon, near the mouth of the Arkansas. At this meeting it was decided that McClernand and Sherman would proceed to Milliken's Bend and make preparations for a long siege. At the same time Grant instructed them to stand ready to cooperate with Nathaniel Banks, who was due to appear soon with his army from the south. It would take Porter some time to gather up his gunboat flock, but he, too, should report as soon as possible to Milliken's Bend. On 30 January Grant himself arrived at Milliken's Bend to take command.[7]

Grant's army numbered approximately forty-five thousand divided into three corps under Sherman, McClernand, and James B. McPherson. To assist Grant, Porter had marshaled an impressive river force of eleven ironclads, thirty-eight wooden and tinclad boats, and a host of transports and auxiliary craft. Altogether Porter had under his command three hundred guns and a force of fifty-five hundred men. Porter's naval firepower and mobility were essential to the operation.

While Vicksburg might be attacked from any point on the compass, it could be taken only from the east. Grant's problem was how to flank the city's defenses to get his army behind Vicksburg. He might land his army to the north and move from that direction, but such an operation would put him into some of the worst topography imaginable; bayous, swamps, snakes, and disease. Approach from the south might be better, but to do that, he would have to move his army past the guns of Vicksburg. Grant opted to try the northern route. Thus began four months of frustration and failure.

For better or worse, U. S. Grant's military reputation is largely based on his northern Virginia campaigns against Lee. Those were battles where gains were measured in small distances and horrendous casualties, a style of warfare often characterized as a prelude to the horror of World War I. That was not the case at Vicksburg. At Vicksburg Grant undertook a war of maneuver, and the early months of 1863 typify this strategy. Porter and his gunboats were a key part of his plan.

Early in 1863 the Mississippi River rose higher and higher. On the western bank it was difficult for a bird to find a dry place to land. In order to bivouac on high, dryish ground, Grant's army had to encamp on a line sixty miles long. On the east side the situation was even worse. As the river rose, the entire countryside flooded. The soldiers' problem, however, was the sailors' blessing. Cresting at a near record of seventeen feet, the Mississippi sent water into long-dry parts of the country. Bayous that were ordinarily as shallow as mud troughs were now deep rivers penetrating into the countryside. Much of the region was now accessible to Porter's gunboats.

Recognizing the possibilities this high water offered them, Grant and Porter made several attempts to use these bloated streams to outflank Vicksburg. First, Grant decided to follow Williams's example. He would cut a canal bisecting the peninsula opposite the city, so that vessels could be floated through without having to pass Confederate guns. Digging began in January and lasted until March, when a sudden rise in the Mississippi flooded the area. The troops were forced to retreat behind levees, and their work washed back into the river. Ironically, although the project failed as a canal, it did at least serve one good purpose. Idle soldiers in a prolonged siege are the bane of any commander, and digging kept "Billy Yank" occupied.

Two other attempts were made to flank Vicksburg by canal.

The shorter of the two was the Duckport Canal, a passageway that began at Milliken's Bend and wound its way through a maze of bayous to reenter the river about twenty miles south of Vicksburg. One small vessel actually made it through, but it was the first and last. The fickle Mississippi fell again, and the Duckport route turned to mud.

The Lake Providence canal, the last of this trio, was in some ways the most ambitious. Crescent-shaped, the lake was typical of the dozens of small, shallow bodies of water "Ol' Miss" had recently created. The soldiers cut a canal from the river to the lake, about seventy-five miles upstream from Vicksburg. There army engineers laid out a course which, after meandering four hundred miles through swamps and bayous, landed the Federals on the banks of the Mississippi considerably south of Vicksburg. Despite the distances involved, the plan was sound, and by March the soldiers had made great progress. They might even have finished the job, but by the time they neared the river, other, more promising approaches had become apparent. The last canal was abandoned.

I I

On Tuesday evening, 3 February, a loud explosion on the east bank of the Mississippi opposite Helena sent a large column of mud, dirt, and brown water spewing into the air. At the order of Rear Admiral Porter, Acting Master George Brown had just blown a hole in the levee. A torrent of water rushed through the gap, tearing away at the embankment. By dawn the passageway was fifty yards wide and growing wider. Within a few days, as the water levels equalized, the rush subsided. In place of a raging stream, Union officers looked over the remnants of the levee at a gentle stream leading east. It was the beginning, they hoped, of a route that could carry them to the upper Yazoo, where they might finally get behind Vicksburg.

Porter ordered Lieutenant Commander Watson Smith to take charge and move his flotilla through the levee toward the Yazoo. Originally the attack was designed to catch the enemy off guard. That proved impossible. High water and caution kept Smith from pushing through until 20 February. By that time all hope of surprise was gone. The Confederates were well aware of the Federal plan and had one of their own prepared to surprise the invaders.

Smith steamed forward with seven gunboats, a towboat, three barges loaded with coal, and thirteen transports, with forty-five hundred troops aboard under the command of General Leonard Ross. Commander Smith was one of fortune's favorites, with friends in very high places, including Charles Wilkes and Gustavus Fox. Porter himself, in an uncharacteristically affectionate moment, called Smith "my Pet of all the young officers of the Navy."[8] In view of the way in which Smith mishandled the expedition, it is hard to understand the general admiration he seemed to inspire. Perhaps Smith, a capable officer, was so ill with fever during February and March that his judgment and fitness of command were temporarily impaired.

Almost as soon as it had the levee over its sterns, Smith's squadron ran into trouble.[9] The enemy sniped and dropped trees in the channel to block its passage, but the natural obstacles it encountered were even worse. Overhanging trees became tangled in superstructures and carried away smokestacks; drifting branches imperiled paddle wheels. The heat, the insects, and the endless hours of backbreaking chopping, hacking, and sawing took their toll on the men.

Ten days of tough going brought them finally to the Tallahatchie. Ten more days brought them within striking distance of the point where the Tallahatchie and Yalobusha joined to form the Yazoo. There were only a few more miles to their target.

They never made it. In the time since he had left the Mississippi, Smith had shown great caution and reluctance to hazard anything. Now, as he neared the Yazoo, he heard disturbing news: The Confederates were waiting.

Even before Smith passed through the levee, Pemberton had begun preparations to defend the Yazoo. On 21 February General William Loring came down the Yalobusha from Grenada to find work already under way. The next day Loring went up the Tallahatchie and picked out a place to take his stand, calling it Fort Pemberton. His choice was good: a high spot, flanked by obstacles and commanding a view up the river. Indeed, the position was so well covered that Ross could never land his troops to get at the fort. It would be up to Smith's gunboats to subdue Fort Pemberton.

It was a situation that was by now a near classic on the western rivers: gunboats versus fort. As before at Henry, Donelson, and Arkansas Post, the boats had the advantage in firepower. What Smith needed—but what he lacked—was the boldness to move in close to his target and blast it into submission.

On 11 March Smith's advance gunboat came around a bend on the Tallahatchie and passed right into Loring's sights. Fort Pemberton opened first. Within minutes its gunners had found the range and were firing for effect. Other boats came forward, and the engagement became general. According to the lore, General Loring in the midst of the fray leaped onto the cotton bale parapet and shouted at his gunners, "Give them blizzards, boys! Give them blizzards!" Thenceforth Loring was always known as Old Blizzards.

The day ended with Smith retiring to repair damage and plan a new attack. The next day was spent strengthening the gunboats. On the thirteenth Smith attacked but was "severely handled" and once more retreated. Two lay days followed, and not until the sixteenth did Smith engage again. Within fifteen minutes one of his boats had been disabled, and he withdrew once more.

Now Smith's health, which had faltered from the beginning of the expedition, failed entirely. At the advice of his medical officer he reported himself "unfit for duty" and turned his command over to the next senior officer, Lieutenant Commander James P. Foster.[10] On 18 March Foster ordered a general withdrawal back to the Mississippi, then reversed the order when fresh troops arrived. The next day the gunboats moved within range again and fired a few rounds. That was the end of it. Foster kept the boats in the neighborhood, waiting for the army to do what he could not do: take Fort Pemberton. Finally, when the army began to withdraw, the navy followed suit, leaving the Confederates in charge.

Porter blamed Smith's "aberration of mind" and the army's lack of "hearty cooperation" for the failure at Yazoo Pass.[11] It is no surprise, then, that for the next (and thankfully last) plunge into the bayous, Porter decided to take the helm in person. As with the Yazoo attempt, this was a venture intended to sweep around Vicksburg's right flank and, if successful, make a lodging behind the bastion. The route was a northerly one up Steele's Bayou via Black Bayou to a smaller stream called Deer Creek. It then continued roughly north to an even tinier body of water (Rolling Fork) then east via the fork to the Big Sunflower River. From there it was clear sailing south to the Yazoo, bringing the Federals to the rear of the enemy.

Grant thought Porter's plan a good one. On the first day of the expedition, 15 March, he actually joined Porter as the navy cruised up Steele's Bayou. Grant returned back the same night and instructed Sherman to prepare to march to assist Porter's boats. From the very first, Grant and Porter recognized the vulnerability of gunboats in such narrow waterways. Without infantry to clear the banks, the boats were sitting ducks. By dropping trees into the channel, the enemy could trap its prey and then move in on it. Although heavily armed, Porter's boats would have a tough time fending off attack, since they could not raise guns enough to be able to fire over the embankments. Most worrisome of all was the realization that with each advance, the situation became even more precarious. Behind them, sailors could hear trees being felled into the water, preventing retreat. Without troops to guard the route, Porter could well find himself swallowed up by the bayous and left to the mercy of his foe.

Porter's worst fears were realized. Early in the afternoon of 19 March, as his advance boats closed in on Rolling Fork, alarming reports arrived. Large numbers of Confederate infantry were marching closer. The reports were quickly confirmed by the sound of minié balls ricocheting off the gunboats' armor. Porter sent Sherman an urgent message for help, while he and his men did their best to defend themselves. The squadron was trapped in a vise; unless troops came quickly to pry it open, the admiral and his fleet would soon be no more.

With no room to come about, Porter had to unship rudders so that his boats could drift backward with the current, bouncing off trees as they moved along. It was slow going, with willows snagging the hulls, overhanging branches sweeping the decks, and minié balls pinging incessantly off metal. The strain on the men confined in these iron boxes was close to intolerable.

On the morning of the twentieth one of the accompanying coal barges sank in the channel, completely blocking any movement. Raising the barge proved impossible since the salvage team made perfect targets for Confederate sharpshooters. The men sensed doom. Porter put the crews on half rations; he told them to sleep by their guns and stand ready to repel boarders. Should all this fail, they were to blow up the boats, arm themselves, and take to the swamps.

While Porter made preparations for his Armageddon, Sherman, responding to the admiral's pleas, had sent several regiments forward. In the night they marched with lighted candles, slogging through the swamp. Finally, at about four in the afternoon, they reached the imperiled river force. Now able to cover his salvage teams, Porter wasted no time removing the barge. By late in the evening his flotilla was once more moving freely. By the twenty-fourth the expedition was back to Hill's Plantation, from which they had set out with such high hopes fewer than two weeks before.

Dejected by the repeated failures of his boats, on 26 March Porter wrote confidentially to Welles that it was all over. As far as he was concerned, Grant should retreat to Memphis and then move southward via Grenada with an army of 150,000 men fully equipped to take Vicksburg. Clearly this was Porter's lowest point of the entire war. Temporarily bowed down by depression, he had lost his sense of judgment. Having invested so much in the Vicksburg campaign, Lincoln or Halleck could never permit Grant to abandon the project. The administration was already besieged by criticism of failures in the eastern theater; such a move in the West might bring it toppling down. Grant understood the problem and had no intention of leaving.[12]

From the very beginning Grant had seen that his best chance lay in moving his army south of the city and then marching north. Of course, he could do this only by moving the army along the west side of the river through Louisiana. Until now high water had made that impossible. But as spring approached and the river began to fall, Grant made plans to move.

Over the previous months Grant had been in touch with Farragut, whose fleet controlled the river from the Gulf to Port Hudson. Farragut had long suggested that it would be useful if Porter sent some of his gunboats south of the city. Although Porter had allowed some smaller vessels to scoot past the enemy's batteries, he had not permitted any of his powerful gunboats to attempt the same.[13] His reasons were sound. As he told Grant, even if the gunboats made it downstream, their speed against the current was so slow that they could never return. There was another, more political reason, which he left unsaid. Porter had no intention of dividing his own force unless he was certain that the outcome would redound to his reputation and the navy's glory. His strength in the partnership with Grant depended on the number of guns he could deliver. Dividing his force would not suit his personal or professional interests.

Despite opposition from several of his division commanders, Grant ordered the operation begun. He would march south along the west shore to New Carthage, Louisiana. A straight pass across the river at that point would place his army midway between Confederate forces at Grand Gulf to the south and Warrenton, Mississippi, to the north. On 27 March the Sixty-ninth Indiana Infantry shouldered arms and led the way to New Carthage.

It was critical to the strategy, of course, to move the army across the river, and Grant needed Porter's boats to cover his flanks. There was only one way for these deep-draft ironclads to get there: They would have to run the Vicksburg batteries. Porter was persuaded, and at nine in the evening of 16 April he signaled his squadron to move into the stream and head south. *Benton* was in the van, with the tug *Ivy* lashed to her starboard side, followed at fifty-yard intervals by *Lafayette, General Price, Louisville, Mound City, Pittsburgh, Carondelet,* three army transports, and finally, bringing up the rear, the tug *Tuscumbia.*

By maintaining a silent routine and allowing the boats to drift, they managed to avoid detection until they were abreast of the enemy's first battery. At eleven-sixteen the guns opened up. All along the shoreline tar barrels were set ablaze, casting an eerie, flickering glow across the river. Silhouetted by the light, Porter's boats made fine targets. But heavy and rapid fire from the boats forced the Confederates to keep their heads down, so despite the size of their targets, southern gunners had a hard time finding their range. Even when they did, mounds of logs and cotton bales stacked on deck deflected a good number of shots. In the meantime, Porter's civilian pilots kept their boats moving rapidly and in formation. Altogether they endured enemy fire for more than two hours. Remarkably little damage was done, and despite the din of battle, even Porter had to admit that "the danger to the vessels was more apparent than real."[14]

Only one vessel, the transport *Henry Clay,* was lost. The rest of the squadron arrived at New Carthage early on the morning of 17 April, ready to guard Grant's crossing.

As he contemplated crossing the river, Grant had to contend with the town of Grand Gulf on the east bank. Pemberton, correctly divining that Grant planned a move south of Vicksburg, had taken care to fortify Grand Gulf with seven to eight thousand men under the command of Major General J. S. Bowen. The town now stood as a southern guard to Vicksburg and posed a formidable obstacle to any advance.

Porter favored maneuver against the town. He had witnessed Sherman's debacle at Chickasaw Bayou and had no desire to see troops sent up against an entrenched enemy. Grant, on the other hand, true to his rising reputation, was more inclined to favor the direct approach. The general's plan was adopted. Porter's boats would come as close as they could to the upper and lower works flanking the town and silence those batteries. Once that was accomplished, troops would land and push a final assault.

On the morning of 29 April Porter's boats moved into position. The force was nearly evenly split: Half attended to the upper works, and the rest fired on the lower works. It was a fierce and bloody battle. Confederate heavy ordnance wreaked havoc with the gunboats. Although Porter's forces were superior in the number and weight of guns, they could not bring them all to bear simultaneously. A six-knot current made keeping station problematical, while at the same time a swirling eddy actually spun the boats around. These revolving gunboats became delighful targets for Confederate gunners. After five and half hours of some of the fiercest fighting Porter had yet seen, his boats withdrew. Conflicting damage reports filtered back, but it was clear that for the time being at least, the Federals had withdrawn and the Confederates were still in possession.

Since the batteries had not been eliminated, Grant decided to do much as Porter had originally suggested. He would land south of the town and flank it. On the morning of 30 April

several divisions of Grant's army landed unopposed at Bruins-
burg, a few miles to the south of Grand Gulf. When Bowen
realized he was in danger of being outflanked, he boldly marched
his army to meet the enemy. Outnumbered, he was routed and
forced to retreat with the remnants of his army toward Vicksburg. He paused only to blow up the munitions and guns he
had left at Grand Gulf. Grant now had a secure base on the east
side of the river.

Grant's new position spelled doom for Vicksburg. Had
Pemberton quickly united his forces and struck at the Federals
before they had had a chance to consolidate, he might still have
driven them back. Joe Johnston wired him: "If Grant's army
crosses, unite all your troops to beat him; success will give you
back what was abandoned to win it." But Pemberton, a cautious
commander, ignored Johnston's bold advice. Unwisely he elected
to remain at Vicksburg and to await the enemy.[15]

Pemberton, after all, was not entirely sure of his enemy's
intentions. Control of the river would provide Grant with
mobility. With Porter's assistance, the Union army could strike
almost anywhere along a two-hundred-mile front from Vicksburg to Port Hudson. On 30 April, the same day that Porter's
gunboats were bombarding Grand Gulf, Sherman, with the aid
of several vessels under the command of Lieutenant K. R. Breese,
launched an elaborate feint against Haynes Bluff on the Yazoo.
While Pemberton was trying to determine whether Sherman's
or Grant's was the real attack, he had also to cope with other
Union forces maneuvering to his rear. What he lacked was good
intelligence. Aware of his ignorance, he did what he thought
best: He stayed in place.

At dawn on 17 April Colonel Benjamin H. Grierson had
left La Grange near Memphis with seventeen hundred cavalrymen and several pieces of light artillery. His mission was to
sweep to the east of Vicksburg and distract the Confederates,
hoping to draw off forces that might be sent against Grant. In
what Grant himself later described as "one of the most brilliant
cavalry exploits of the war," Grierson and his men rode six

hundred miles in sixteen days behind enemy lines, raiding towns, tearing up railroad track, and in general terrorizing the countryside. They managed to confuse the Confederates and force them to disperse their own forces in a hopeless chase across the state of Mississippi.[16]

Puzzled and wary, Pemberton remained passive. Meanwhile, Grant made one of the boldest decisions of the war. He had at first planned to move south and link up with Nathaniel Banks, then move with Banks against Port Hudson. But Banks was delayed and could not march in time. Rather than wait, Grant elected to strike from Grand Gulf toward Vicksburg, thus putting his entire army between Pemberton and Joe Johnston. If the Confederates joined forces, Grant would be outnumbered. Unfortunately for the South, its forces were scattered, and Grant was gambling that they would not be able to unite against him. It was a high-stakes game. By moving inland away from the river, the Federals were severing their lines of communication. Everything they needed must be either in their own supply train or available in the countryside. After making preparations on 7 May, the army set out.

For eighteen days Grant campaigned against the Confederates. It was a brilliant exercise. Plunging deep into Mississippi, the Federals defeated the Confederates five times. By 18 May Pemberton's army had withdrawn behind the defenses of the city, preparing to hold its position until relieved by Johnston and his army. On the very same day that Pemberton withdrew into the city, he received a dispatch from Johnston advising him to evacuate Vicksburg. To remain there, wrote Johnston, was only to invite defeat and lose both the town and the troops. It was better to sacrifice the town and save the army. Pemberton thought differently. He summoned a council of war and laid the proposition before it. Should they defend or evacuate? Unanimously the officers declared that it would be "impossible to withdraw the army from this position with such morale as to be of further service to the Confederacy." Pride ruled, and Pemberton stayed.

While Grant tightened the noose on Pemberton, Porter reluctantly attended to business downriver. In mid-May he had received orders from Welles to proceed south and rendezvous with Farragut.

David Glasgow Farragut was never happy in freshwater. He preferred to be posted at sea, and the Mississippi maneuvers had taken their toll. Bowing to Farragut's insistence, Welles finally ordered a reluctant Porter to proceed downriver and relieve the admiral from his riverine responsibilities. High among these obligations was blockading the Red River.

The Red River was the Confederacy's chief supply route from the West. Tucked in between the Confederate strongholds of Port Hudson and Vicksburg, it was relatively secure from Union forces. Porter had tried to remedy that situation in February. He ran two vessels (*Indianola* and *Queen of the West*) past Vicksburg, but both were captured before they could seriously threaten the Red River route. Having replenished their naval arsenal with these potent weapons, the Confederates now represented a real danger. Admiral Farragut had to repair the damage done by Porter's daring. Within two weeks of Porter's exploit, he was bound up the Mississippi toward the Red River.

To get to the Red River, he needed to pass Port Hudson, and on 14 March 1863 he made a daring attempt to pass those formidable batteries with seven ships. Only *Hartford* and the smaller *Albatross* succeeded. With only two vessels, Farragut could effectively impede river traffic but could not control the Red River. For all of April he remained impatiently on station. It was with unconcealed joy that he welcomed Porter on 5 May. Three days later Farragut bade farewell and steamed away to New Orleans.

Porter dearly wanted to be with Grant back upriver, where the great events of the war were taking place. With characteristic energy, he made every effort to complete his business on the Red as quickly as possible. He secured the mouth of the river, then steamed up to Fort De Russey near Marksville, Louisiana. After partially destroying the enemy fortifications there, he ordered his boats farther upstream to Alexandria, which surrendered without a whimper. The next day General Nathaniel Banks arrived. Porter turned over command to him and hurried back up the Mississippi to join Grant.

By the fifteenth of May Porter was back on station off the Yazoo. On the sixteenth he heard firing, and through his binoculars he saw Sherman's troops storming up the bluffs along the Yazoo. This time they made it, and the Stars and Stripes rose over the river's bank. With the Yazoo now free, Union boats could pass up and assist the army as the siege of Vicksburg tightened.

Porter's gunboats were essential to forging the iron ring around Vicksburg. Divided now into two divisions, one stationed above and one below the city, they blocked any attempt at reinforcing Pemberton with troops from west of the river. At the same time their guns helped make life perilous in the city itself. Porter, a believer in mortars, could now demonstrate the force of his weapons. Thousands of shells from these squat monsters were dropped on the Vicksburg defenders. The volume of the bombardment was probably greater than the actual physical damage. As usual, primitive fusing and questionable accuracy did much to soften the rain of ordnance. Nevertheless, the Union shells were psychologically devastating to the troops and civilians holed up in the city. Some retreated to their cellars, while others dug caves in the hillsides. Food ran short, troops were put on reduced ration, and others scrounged for whatever they could find. Dogs and cats became endangered species. The incessant shelling frayed Confederate nerves. Still, Pemberton held out, clinging to the hope that Johnston would march to his relief.[17]

Each day Pemberton's forces grew weaker. At its strongest, his garrison numbered fewer than thirty thousand, and by early July ten thousand of those men were so ill and weak that they were unable to report for duty. Grant's siege was relentless. From the city's ramparts the clanking of shovels was heard, as Union engineers moved their trenches closer to the Confederate works.

The besieged in Vicksburg grew demoralized, believing that they had been forgotten by Johnston—indeed, by the whole of the Confederacy. In his diary Henry Ginder, one of Pemberton's engineers (referring to the Gettysburg campaign then under way in the East), complained that he was "almost sorry to hear of Lee's progress Northward; for it looks as if the importance of Vicksburg were not understood. What is Phalada [Philadelphia] to us if the Miss. be lost."[18]

Pemberton had only two choices: to surrender or to break out. The former would be humiliating, but the latter was suicidal. On 3 July he met with Grant to discuss terms. The next day, July Fourth, the official surrender took place. Four days later the garrison at Port Hudson, learning of Vicksburg's fall, surrendered to General Nathaniel Banks.

From its source to its mouth the Mississippi was now in Union hands. The river could, in Lincoln's words, flow "unvexed" to the sea. Thenceforth the western part of the Confederacy was cut off, no longer able to provide either men or arms to the main theater of operations in the East. Geographically the South was now surrounded. Scott's Anaconda was tightening its coils.

I I I

Although the war still held some hard fighting ahead for the river navy, it involved brief and violent encounters rather than grand strategy. In the year and a half remaining in the war the most serious effort was directed up the Red River, which, in the spring of 1864, Porter revisited with General Banks.

It was Henry Halleck who conceived the idea of an expedition up the Red. Uppermost in his mind was extending Union control into northern Louisiana and thus opening a route into Texas. Thus far in the war Union forces had been notably unsuccessful in venturing into the Lone Star State. Halleck also hoped that this thrust into Louisiana might induce large numbers of the state's silent Union loyalists to rally to the flag.

Finally, there was cotton to consider. The Red River was a rich cotton area, and up to two million bales of the stuff were said to be stacked up in warehouses near the river. At exorbitant wartime prices, that was a financial incentive that could hardly be sniffed at since according to the rules of war, 50 percent of the value of the prize went to its captors.

All these considerations led to one of the largest Union fiascos of the entire war.[19]

With Porter in command of the river forces, providing transportation and artillery support, and Banks in charge of the land element, the expedition proceeded up the river in early March. At first all went well. Banks advanced, the enemy retreated, and Porter steamed along, but then nature and incompetence came to the fore. Never a very deep stream, the Red began to fall. The depths announced by the leadsmen's calls were barely enough to float the squadron. On land the situation was even more difficult. Banks met the enemy at Mansfield, about forty miles south of Shreveport, and was soundly beaten. He pulled back, fought again at Pleasant Hill, Louisiana, and won but decided to continue to retreat anyway. It proved to be easier to pull the troops out than the gunboats, for the falling river threatened to snare the fleeing vessels. By the time Porter was back at Alexandria, he had already been forced to scuttle the steamer *Eastport,* which, after a torpedo injury, had run hard aground in the increasingly shallow water. Just above the falls at Alexandria, the water dropped to a level of three feet, less than half the depth necessary to flat some of the deeper-draft gunboats. Porter gave serious thought to scuttling the entire fleet. That action would have dealt a heavy blow to Union prestige and would seriously have imperiled northern control of the river. Porter's naval career would have ended on an exceedingly somber note.

Lieutenant Colonel Joseph Bailey, a former Wisconsin lumberman, stepped forward with an idea. Perhaps they should build a dam to back up the river to a depth of seven feet over the falls. With no other alternative, Porter agreed, and on 30 April the work got under way. It took thousands of men and hundreds of teams of mules, but the scheme worked after a fashion. Eight days later the dam was nearly completed, but then current and pressure won: The dam burst. Porter, watching his last hope wash away, was willing to try anything. He ordered four nearby boats to go forward at full steam with the flood. They took a banging, but all four made it. When Bailey saw the proof of his scheme go by, he asked to be allowed to rebuild the dam. With the enemy closing in, there was not enough time to build a complete span across the river, so a series of smaller wing dams were put in place. After three days of work the first vessel went by. Within two days all the other gunboats had made it to safety. Porter could not say enough in praise of Bailey.[20]

Porter went back to the Mississippi, where he continued to patrol the rivers and their surrounding areas aggressively. But coping with guerrillas and protecting commerce must have seemed anticlimactic after what he had already endured. In the fall, when orders to take up command of the station off Wilmington, North Carolina, arrived, Porter wasted no time in obeying. The heady days of the river war were over.

11

Galveston
to Mobile

I

For the North the Fourth of July 1863 was a glorious day. Vicksburg was in Union hands. Farther east, Lee's army had failed to push through Meade's lines at Gettysburg and was now in slow retreat toward the South. The tide of the war seemed to be finally turning in favor of the Union.

On 1 August 1863 a triumphal David Porter presented himself to Farragut aboard *Hartford,* anchored in the stream at New Orleans. At sixty-two Farragut felt too old for this business of war. He looked wan and tired. In private, he admitted, "I am growing old fast, and need rest."[1] For more than a year he had not enjoyed a single day off duty. He had silenced Forts St. Philip and Jackson, taken New Orleans, twice assaulted Vicksburg, and passed Port Hudson. It was with unfeigned relief that he now turned command over the entire Mississippi to his younger "brother." He left the next day, bound for New York for ease and relaxation.

Farragut knew that his sojourn would be only temporary, for there was still a good deal left to do in the Gulf. The blockade needed attention badly. There had been grand victories along the river, but trouble was brewing on the coast of Texas. Farragut's command along that low, sandy shore stretched from the Sabine River to the Rio Grande, altogether a distance of several hundred miles. To cover this coast, the admiral had only a small number of vessels (some of them sailing ships woefully inadequate to the task) and few troops. Indeed, the lack of troops was the Union's most pressing problem. Unless they actually occupied the ports, the blockaders would always find their task difficult, dangerous, and unrewarding.

Galveston and Sabine City in January 1863 were cases in point. In October 1862 a small Federal squadron (composed of the steamers *Westfield, Harriet Lane, Owasco,* and *Clifton* and the schooner *Henry Janes*), under the command of William Renshaw, captured Galveston after only token resistance from the Confederates.[2] But taking the city proved far easier than holding it. Renshaw soon discovered that his area of control was limited to the range of his squadron's guns. Aside from his squadron, Renshaw depended on fewer than three hundred men from the Forty-second Massachusetts Volunteers.[3] At night Confederate cavalrymen entered Galveston and roamed freely through all the town save the waterfront.

This nocturnal/diurnal change of command lasted several weeks, and by late December the routine had been well established. Toward the end of the month additional indications of enemy movement were detected, but Renshaw and Colonel Isaac Burrell, who commanded the Union troops, made no special effort to prepare for attack. They were confident that the big guns of the navy would protect them.

Early on the morning of 1 January, with smooth water below and a bright moon shining above, one of *Clifton*'s lookouts called out the alarm. Four Rebel gunboats were coming down the bay. The Confederates knew their almanac, and as the gunboats steamed ahead, the moon went down and the bright evening turned into murky darkness. The moon's setting was the signal for the land attack to begin, and soon the noise of heavy fire came from ashore. *Harriet Lane* took the brunt of the attack. The Confederate steamers moved on her, and after a fierce exchange, southern sailors managed to grapple and board her. Jonathan Wainwright, the captain of *Harriet Lane*, defended the deck but was finally cut down. The Confederates seized *Harriet Lane*, and a momentary truce was declared. The Confederates demanded that all the Federal vessels surrender, or they would proceed down the bay with their steamers and *Harriet Lane* to take the squadron forcibly. If the Federals agreed to leave, the Confederate commander warranted their safety and would provide a vessel for transport.

Renshaw refused the proposition. His situation, though, was critical, for his own command, *Westfield*, was hard aground. Believing he had no other choice, Renshaw ordered his vessels away from Galveston and at the same time set charges on *Westfield* to scuttle her. The charges exploded prematurely, killing Renshaw and those crewmen who had remained behind with him. With *Westfield* gone and *Harriet Lane* flying the Stars and Bars, command of the squadron devolved on Commander Richard Law of *Clifton*. He ordered the remaining vessels out of the bay in a hasty retreat, leaving the Confederates in possession of a fine warship, one schooner, two coal barks, a considerable quantity of stores, and several hundred prisoners. Farragut opined that there was "no justification" for the fiasco and quickly dispatched Henry Bell, then with him at New Orleans, with a small squadron to retake the place.[4]

January was not a good month for the Federals in the Gulf. Ten days after the glum reports from Galveston came more unnerving news. Since her commissioning at Terceira on 24 August 1862, the notorious Confederate raider *Alabama* and her equally famous captain, Raphael Semmes, had been at sea, terrorizing Union shipping. In January Semmes came into the Gulf.[5] Although Farragut did not know the raider's precise location, intelligence reports put her in his area, so he informed his captains, including Bell, to be alert.[6]

Semmes knew from newspaper accounts that the Federals were operating off the Texas coast. With his usual combination of cunning and courage, he decided to strike. On 11 January, as *Alabama* drew near Galveston, her lookout spotted Bell's squadron shelling the town. *Alabama,* too, was seen, and Bell sent the gunboat *Hatteras* to inquire of the stranger. He should have been more cautious than to send a small gunboat after a strange sail, especially since he knew that *Alabama* might be in the area. Having set his trap, Semmes drew the quarry in. He came about and headed offshore with *Hatteras* in hot pursuit. About twenty miles from the coast, they were within hailing distance of each other. By now night had set in, and in the darkness *Hatteras* challenged. *Alabama* responded that she was Her Majesty's ship *Petrel.* The Federals then announced they were sending a boarding party. As the party passed between the two ships, *Alabama's* first officer, John McIntosh Kell, called through the speaking trumpet that *Hatteras* was not interrogating *Petrel* but rather the Confederate States steamer *Alabama.* As the last syllable came out, Semmes let loose a broadside, and the fight was on. After thirteen minutes of hot exchange *Hatteras* was sinking. She struck her flag and transferred her men to *Alabama,* from which both crews watched the Union gunboat slide beneath the waters of the Gulf.[7]

Hatteras was iron-hulled and should have defended herself better against the wooden-hulled *Alabama.* But the latter had a better crew and a superior commander and was faster. *Hatteras's* defeat marked the only time a Confederate raider ever bested a Union warship. Coming so soon after the pusillanimous action at Galveston, the news had a devastating effect on the North. Matters grew worse four days later, when the Rebel raider *Florida* slipped past the Federal squadron off Mobile and disappeared over the horizon. Farragut was alarmed, for now the Confederates had two raiders at large in the Gulf, and they would have a third if they used the *Harriet Lane.* Still, the dreadful month of January was not over yet.

On the twenty-first two Confederate "cotton clads" (vessels using cotton bales as protection from enemy fire), *Josiah Bell* and *Uncle Ben,* charged out of Sabine City (several miles east of Galveston) to attack two Federal vessels which had been blockading the port. Crammed with army sharpshooters, the two steamers overtook the Federal ships, *Morning Light* and *Velocity.* After a fierce fight, lasting more than an hour, both surrendered to their attackers.[8]

The Federal navy's ill fortune on the coast of Texas was partly the fault of inept commanders and partly the result of inadequate resources. Only by securing the ports themselves could the navy maintain control, and without troops that was impossible. Farragut had never been given sufficient forces to accomplish his mission. This had been demonstrated twice at Vicksburg. In May 1862, when Farragut was alone, then again in July, when he was joined by Davis, the town might have been taken if the War Department, particularly General Halleck, had sent sufficient troops. In private Welles had nothing but contempt for Halleck. To his diary (and perhaps to a few close associates) he confided that the general "was good for nothing." What particularly irked Welles was that in his judgment, the withdrawals at Vicksburg and the donnybrook at Galveston were really the fault of the army, yet it was the navy that took the lashing in the press and congress.

Naturally Welles, the politician, was sensitive to his critics. After all, it was he who had to sit at cabinet meetings and explain to the president and his colleagues what had happened at Vicksburg and Galveston. It was he who had to answer questions posed by visiting senators and congressmen who were also urgent on the topics. It did no good to tell any of these gentlemen that the army was to blame. That sort of "buck-passing" would only anger Secretary Stanton and his generals, people upon whom, like it or not, Welles depended. The naval secretary restrained his public utterances for the sake of domestic tranquillity.

Despite the embarrassment at Galveston, Welles steered a steady course. He did not overreact to the emotional outcries and send heavy reinforcements to the western Gulf, for he realized that control of the Texas coast was not actually vital. As head of the navy Welles exercised his Yankee thrift, and in this case his parsimoniousness was wise. The Texas ports were far away from the main theater of war. Even when supplies for the Confederacy were successfully smuggled ashore, it was difficult to transport them east of the Mississippi to the areas where they were needed. It became virtually impossible to do so when Vicksburg fell and the Mississippi Valley came under firm northern control. Although considerable quantities of supplies continued to find their way into Texas, primarily from Mexico, their impact on the war was minimal. Psychologically all this was of small comfort to the western navy, whose reputation was suffering badly. But east of the Mississippi delta the tale was more pleasant.[9]

Federal operations in the Gulf between New Orleans and Key West were made considerably easier when, on 10 May 1862, the Confederates abandoned Pensacola. Their withdrawal was not caused by Union pressure. President Davis had decided to use units from the Florida coast to reinforce the Confederate forces that were being pushed back in Tennessee. Defending Pensacola from the strong Federal forces that had just seized New Orleans, was not, in his judgment, a good use of scarce manpower.

Thanks to their new base in Pensacola, the Federals were able to keep a steady presence along the coast. To the east and south, they patrolled the Florida coast, sailing down along the low, flat shore past such sleepy places as Cedar Key, Crystal River, Clearwater, and Tampa. Florida, like Texas, was isolated from the rest of the Confederacy without good access north. That, plus the shallowness of most of its ports, made it an inconvenient destination for blockade-runners.

But Florida's shallow harbors served it well in another venture. Lots of sun and shallow saltwater estuaries made the Florida coast a natural place for salt production. Although not ordinarily considered a strategic resource, salt, in an age without refrigeration, was vital, for it provided the chief means by which beef and pork were preserved for shipment to the army. Florida's contribution to the Confederacy grew more and more important as the war wore on. Once the Mississippi link was severed, Florida's beef production became essential. Florida emerged as one of the South's chief suppliers of beef and of salt.

Virtually the entire coast, from St. Augustine around to Apalachee Bay, was well suited to salt making. But the prime area was located on the Gulf Coast between Tampa and Choctawhatchee Bay, especially in the lowlands fronting St. Andrew Bay. The Federals began raiding saltworks as early as September 1862 and continued throughout the war. To protect themselves, the salt makers often moved inland, forcing the Federals to land and mount raids in the interior. While these naval raids virtually wiped out saltworks on the coast, they did not destroy the industry, which, thanks to the simplicity of its operation, could easily move to another location and set up even before the Federal raiders were hull down on the horizon.[10]

Far more problematical to Farragut was the continuing embarrassment of Mobile. Situated at the head of Mobile Bay, about thirty miles from the Gulf, the city was a southern jewel. In prewar days it had been one of the South's chief cotton ports. Cosmopolitan Mobile had a population of nearly thirty thousand, including a large number of foreign nationals. Proud of its Spanish and French heritage, Mobile presented the image of a sophisticated and cultured society.[11]

As a port, however, Mobile was not a seaman's dream. Although the harbor was well protected, the passage from open water up to the town was difficult. Ships entered the bay through a three-mile-wide gut, with Dauphin Island (hosting Fort Gaines) to port and Mobile Point with Fort Morgan on the starboard side. Most of the three-mile span was extremely shallow; the only navigable passage was on the starboard side close to Mobile Point. Farther up the bay, the depth remained relatively shallow, finally reaching an east-west obstruction called Dog River Bar, where the sounding was ten feet or less.[12] A good deal of

Mobile's peacetime commerce had been handled by lighters loading at the city wharves and carrying cargo to deep-draft vessels riding at anchor closer to the Gulf.

Behind the city, geography had been kinder. Built on the banks of the Mobile River, the city had excellent access to the rich agricultural interior of Alabama and Mississippi. The Tombigbee and Alabama rivers joined only thirty miles above the city to form the Mobile, and via this river system, steamboats and other craft brought huge quantities of cotton to the wharves of the town. There was also the Mobile and Ohio Railroad, one of the South's longest lines, running all the way north to Columbus, Kentucky.

According to Lincoln's Proclamation of 19 April 1861, Mobile was under blockade, and on 26 May David D. Porter arrived with *Powhatan* to enforce the president's orders. The ship's log recorded: "Observed on Fort Morgan the American ensign, union down, under the Confederate flat." Both Forts Morgan and Gaines had been surrendered to the state of Alabama in January 1861.[13]

For the remainder of 1861 the Federals kept up a somewhat loose blockade of Mobile. Since they were short of vessels, there was little else they could do. It was the usual tale of chasing down blockade-runners, sometimes catching the quarry, other times watching it scoot past into the safety of Mobile Bay. On 24 December the routine was enlivened when the Confederate gunboat *Florida* (not to be confused with the high-seas Confederate raider *Florida*) sortied out and fired on the blockader USS *Huntsville*. This was not *Florida*'s first appearance against the Federals. She was a coastwise packet built at Mobile and converted to a potent little warship at the same port. Her six-inch rifle gave her a sting that the Federals had learned to respect. She and *Huntsville* exchanged fire for slightly more than an hour before the latter retired. Neither had been hit, but it was clear that *Florida* was a vessel with which to be reckoned. Thenceforth the smaller blockaders kept a respectful distance.

Mobile's security, however, did not depend on *Florida*'s six-inch rifle or even the guns at Forts Gaines and Morgan. Chiefly the town owed its current safety to Federal indifference. Mobile was not on either Lincoln's or Welles's list of priorities. After the capture of Vicksburg, however, Grant suggested that Mobile ought to be taken. No one in Washington took much notice. Only after the Mississippi had been thoroughly secured, and even then only after Farragut insisted, did Mobile become a serious target.[14]

While the Confederate defenders may well have been grateful for the Union's indifference, they knew they could not rely on it, so they spent the year preparing for an attack. Aside from the usual array of batteries and underwater obstacles guarding the port's approaches, Mobile had one very special protective measure: Franklin Buchanan.

No Confederate naval officer was more admired than Franklin Buchanan.[15] Still showing signs of his wounds from the battle with *Monitor,* Buchanan arrived in August 1862 to take command of Confederate naval forces at Mobile. He had been sent by Secretary Mallory to relieve his unfortunate predecessor, Victor Randolph, who had been in charge since February.

A native of Alabama, Randolph had joined the navy during the War of 1812; at the time of his resignation he was one of the Union's most senior naval officers. It was Randolph who had led a bank of insurgents to the gates of the Pensacola Navy Yard on 12 January 1861 and demanded its surrender. For that he was deemed a hero in the South and a villain in the North.

As a former senior officer Randolph expected a high command from the new nation he was to serve. His failure to gain influence in Richmond made him bitter. Blaming Mallory for conspiring against him, Randolph alleged that the secretary was disloyal. More than likely Mallory posted Randolph to Mobile because it was far away from Richmond, not just because he was an Alabamian.

Mallory's hopes proved illusory, and Randolph got along

no better in Mobile than he had in Richmond. His greatest weakness was his failure to seize the initiative and move to the attack. Early in 1862, with the force he had at hand, he might well have given a rough time to the Federal squadron, which was almost entirely made up of sailing ships. But aside from a halfhearted sortie in April, he did little, if anything, to threaten the enemy. Instead, he concentrated on watching the blockade and asking for ironclads. Because of his ineptitude, Mallory removed him and ordered a court-martial.[16]

Buchanan wasted no time in taking charge. He reviewed his vessels and found them "in a state of efficiency, highly creditable to their officers and the service."[17] If nothing else, at least Randolph had maintained a good squadron. Still, not even Buchanan was willing to risk precious vessels against an enemy that seemed to grow stronger each day. Instead, he bided his time and waited for a reinforcement which he hoped would finally tip the scales in his favor: several new ironclads currently under construction along the Alabama and Tombigbee rivers.

When Buchanan arrived in Mobile, these ironclads were at varying stages of construction in Alabama, but problems abounded. Raw materials were available; but skilled workmen were scarce, and engines had to be salvaged from other steamers. Cannons and iron, too, were difficult to find, and transporting them was a chore. Despite the obstacles, Buchanan told the hagridden local contractors that he was determined to have his ships.

On 7 February 1863, amid cheering and boastful toasts, two of the vessels—*Huntsville* and *Tuscaloosa*—were launched at Selma. Neither was completely ready for service, and the plan was to bring them down to Mobile for final fitting out and commissioning. Some days later a third vessel, *Tennessee*, slid into the waters at Selma. She, too, was brought down to Mobile for the finishing touches.[18]

Having these vessels at his own wharf gave Buchanan daily doses of hope and despair. At last it actually seemed possible to challenge the Federal squadron, but he despaired at the endless delays in their final fitting out. Buchanan spared no one, including himself, in his efforts to find guns, armor, and sailors. Tirelessly he pushed, prodded, demanded, and threatened.

In the spring of 1863 *Huntsville* and *Tuscaloosa* chugged out onto Mobile Bay for their trial runs. But the runs did not go as smoothly as Buchanan had hoped. Weak engines were the main problem. With such low steam pressure, neither vessel, burdened with a massive weight of armor and guns, could do much better than three knots in a flat calm. Sea slugs like that would be welcome targets for the fast Federal fleet. About all that could be expected of the two Confederates was that they might serve as floating batteries with a little mobility.

Buchanan now pinned his hopes on two other vessels moving to completion: *Nashville* and *Tennessee*. *Nashville*, laid down at Montgomery and then brought down to Mobile, was by far the larger of the two. Her very size, though, turned out to be a problem. Without enough material to finish both *Nashville* and *Tennessee*, Buchanan opted to do only one at a time. Since *Tennessee*'s requirements were fewer, the decision was made to complete her first. By the time attention could be paid to *Nashville*, it was too late. In fact, she was never finished at all and played no part in defending Mobile.

Tennessee's story is quite different from that of the rest of her Alabama sisters, for she was completed and did fight. Nearly as long as Farragut's own flagship, *Hartford, Tennessee* was by any standard of the time a large and powerful warship. Well armed with two 7-inch Brooke rifles and four 6.4-inch Brooke rifles, she had a potent battery. Like her sister, though, she was gravely flawed. Her speed at roughly four knots was barely enough for headway, let alone sufficient for charging an enemy. Even more serious was the fact that chains connecting the steering mechanism in the wheelhouse ran aft to the rudder along the top of the afterdeck; they were almost fully exposed to enemy fire. Still, *Tennessee* presented a formidable threat. At the very least she frightened the Federal officers, who were credulous enough to believe the false reports about her marvelous strength.[19]

In addition to finishing his ships, Buchanan had to find crews for them. Buchanan was something of a martinet, cut from the same cloth as the old masters of the sailing navy. Strict, unswerving, and quick to censor, he was far from an ideal recruiting officer. In the end he had to depend upon the army, which sent him about 150 artillerymen from a Tennessee unit to man his batteries. It was hardly perfect, but it would have to do.

At his office in the Mechanics Institute Mallory read the dispatches from Buchanan. "Old Buck" needed more men, more guns, more ships, more of everything. The secretary was sympathetic. He knew and trusted the admiral. He never questioned his judgment, but the truth was that Mobile was the most expendable of the four major ports remaining in Confederate hands. (Charleston, Wilmington, and Savannah were the others.) Mobile had ceased to be useful as a port for blockade-running, while the other three continued to link the South to the outside world. With what little he had left, Mallory would help defend those ports. Mobile would have to defend itself.

While Buchanan was preparing to defend Mobile, his adversary and former brother officer Farragut was bathing in adoration. Feted, toasted, and celebrated, Farragut was the new lion of the northern navy.[20] To the chagrin of many of his peers, including John Dahlgren, the press and politicians made of him what he truly was: the Union's greatest naval hero. After celebrating the New Year with his family on 6 January, Farragut departed New York on board *Hartford* to resume command of the Gulf blockade.

Although far away, Farragut had been kept fully informed. After a conference with his officers on station, his own opinion was confirmed. Though it was embarrassing to allow the Confederates to hold so much of the Texas coast, it was really of no strategic import since the capture of the Mississippi Valley left Texas isolated. What was important was maintaining the blockade at and around Mobile.

On the very day that Farragut returned, Captain Thornton A. Jenkins, the senior Federal officer off Mobile, sent a somber report on the blockade that highlighted serious problems. He noted the weakness of his own squadron. Of the nine vessels assigned to him, from one to three were always absent seeking coal and provisions. Three were so lightly armed as to be virtually useless, and two were well armed but in dire need of refitting. Two days later Jenkins furnished another report, this time from a New Hampshire mechanic who had been working in Mobile but had recently escaped. His account, which Jenkins apparently accepted at face value, represented the Confederates as truly formidable, with sufficient force afloat to blow the Federals out of the water.[21]

I I

Ever the deepwater sailor (though his fame was won in shallow water), Farragut had an instinctive dislike of ironclads. He thought them ugly, clumsy, and lacking in firepower. Nevertheless, he had come to respect them, and he decided that they would be essential to the force at Mobile. He knew Franklin Buchanan. If *Tennessee* were indeed as formidable as the reports indicated, in Buchanan's hands she might well destroy the Federal squadron. To go up against *Tennessee*, Farragut realized that he must have his own ironclads.

On 17 January he wrote to Porter, who was still in command on the Mississippi, that he intended to push past the enemy's forts and into Mobile Bay. To do that, however, he needed ironclads to hold the enemy vessels in check. He asked Porter if he could spare at least two of his river monitors for the occasion. Three days later he wrote to Welles, asking for two monitors to be sent down from the Atlantic coast as well.[22] For the time being, however, neither Porter nor Welles could offer much in the way of support. The former believed he needed every vessel under his command for river operations, while the secretary was unwilling to divert his monsters from duty at Charleston. Farragut would have to wait for monitors.

In February he undertook a bombardment of Fort Powell, which guarded Grant's Pass, one of the smaller entrances into Mobile Bay. It was pointless. Percival Drayton commented: "We are hammering away at the fort here, which minds us about as much as if we did not fire."[23] As Farragut had learned elsewhere, ships could bombard forts, but they could not capture them. That was a task for infantry. The admiral now added to the list of his needs a force of soldiers to capture the forts at the entrance to the bay. The response to his new request was the same: Nothing was available.

Through the early months of 1864 and into the spring Farragut shuttled between Pensacola and New Orleans, with frequent visits to the ships off Mobile. He sent repeated requests to Welles for more of everything: ships, men, and coal. In the meantime, though, neither the Navy Department nor the War Department was willing to send him what he really needed: monitors and soldiers.

Toward the end of May rumors began to circulate that *Tennessee* was ready for battle, *Nashville* was on her way, and that "Buck" might come out at any moment. This was enough to move the men in Washington.

In June Welles ordered two monitors from the Atlantic coast, *Manhattan* and *Tecumseh*, to proceed immediately to the Gulf. On 1 July Porter, also feeling the pressure, ordered two of his monitors, *Chickasaw* and *Winnebago*, to steam to the admiral's assistance.[24] As the navy cooperated, so too did the army. General Sherman, in command of all western troops since Grant's departure for the East in March, saw advantages he could gain by sending troops to aid Farragut against Mobile. Sherman, planning his own upcoming drive into Georgia, knew that an attack on Mobile might well draw off Confederate troops to defend the city.

With demands coming from other quarters, though, it proved impossible for the army to release enough men. On 8 July Generals Edward Canby and Gordon Granger sat down with Farragut in his cabin aboard *Hartford*. They brought disappointing news. Because of a lack of troops, Mobile could not be assaulted. Could they invest Forts Gaines and Morgan? There were only enough troops to attack one at a time. Which would it be? Farragut recommended Gaines, and the generals agreed.[25]

Right on schedule, Granger arrived with his regiments on 1 August. To his embarrassment, Farragut had now to delay the operation since *Tecumseh* had yet to appear. Granger put his troops ashore on the third while Farragut waited impatiently. On the evening of the fourth *Tecumseh* heaved into view. Everything was now in place for the attack.

No one in the Union navy had more experience attacking forts than Farragut. From Forts St. Philip and Jackson to Port Hudson and Vicksburg, he survived violent fire from enemy guns. And he had learned a good deal from those ventures. Attacking at night was out; failures of control and communication in the dark might well invite catastrophe. Nor would he allow his vessels to proceed in single column. One hit in a vulnerable place would put a vessel dead in the water. To ensure survival, vessels would steam in pairs lashed to each other, with the smaller hugging the side away from the enemy guns.

On the Coast Survey charts, and with his own reconnaissance reports, Farragut examined the obstacles which nature had placed in his way. The initial course for the squadron would be north by east, passing close aboard Fort Morgan on the starboard side. Although Farragut was loath to bring his vessels this close to the fort, he had no choice. Buoyed out in the channel off to port were dozens of torpedoes (mines), placed so as to constrict the channel and force a close passing of the fort. Just ahead of the fort, Buchanan had anchored his own squadron on a roughly northwest-southeast axis. As Farragut's ships came up bow on, they would be exposed in a raking position to Buchanan and would be able to respond with only a limited number of forward guns. The charts further told Farragut that as he came parallel to Fort Morgan, he would have to alter course toward the northwest. This would allow him to train his guns at Buchanan, but it would also expose his stern to Fort Morgan; he could return its fire only with a small number of stern guns. All in all, it promised to be a tough passage.

While Farragut had had a great deal of experience in passing forts, he had rarely confronted an ironclad the size of *Tennessee* or maneuvered through a minefield.

Farragut's General Order 10 was explicit:

> Strip your vessels and prepare for the conflict. Send down all your superfluous spars and rigging. Trice up or remove the whiskers. Put up the splinter nets on the starboard side, and barricade the wheel and steersmen with sails and hammocks. Lay chains or sand bags on the deck over the machinery, to resist a plunging fire. Hang the sheet chains over the side, or make any other arrangement for security that your ingenuity may suggest. Land your starboard boats or lower and tow them on the port side, and lower the port boats down to the water's edge. Place a leadsman and the pilot in the port quarter boat, or the one most convenient to the commander.
>
> The vessels will run past the forts in couples, lashed side by side, as hereinafter designated. The flagship will lead and steer . . , and the others, as designated in the drawing, will follow in due order until ordered to anchor.[26]

After conferring with his officers, Farragut was persuaded to amend one very critical detail. Contrary to his original plan, *Hartford* would not take the lead passing the forts. His captains insisted, as they had more than two years before during the passage up the Mississippi, that in the van the admiral would have difficulty controlling the squadron. At the same time he and his ship would be in an exposed and dangerous position. Why not send *Brooklyn* ahead? In addition to all else, she carried under her bow a device intended to sweep mines. Farragut agreed to the new plan. *Brooklyn* would lead, and *Hartford* would follow.

On the morning of 4 August the wind was light from the south. The sky was overcast, and the humidity, as usual, was climbing. At five forty-five the fleet got under way. The four ironclads *Tecumseh, Manhattan, Winnebago,* and *Chickasaw* were slightly ahead and to starboard. Arranged on a parallel line on the port side of the ironclads were the fourteen wooden steamers of the squadron. Paired together, they were, in order: *Brooklyn* and *Octorara; Hartford* and *Metacomet; Richmond* and *Port Royal; Lackawanna* and *Seminole; Monongahela* and *Kennebec; Ossipee* and *Itasca;* and, bringing up the rear, *Oneida* and *Galena.* At six forty-seven *Tecumseh* opened with two shots at Fort Morgan. Within minutes the fort answered, and a lively action was under way. As the fleet ranged in with their bow guns, Buchanan's gunboats, including *Tennessee,* steamed out from behind the fort and brought their broadsides to bear, enfilading the Federal line. With so little breeze, the black smoke belching out of the cannons, combined with the soot-laden discharge from the squadron's funnels, soon settled down and hugged the ships. Farragut could barely see beyond *Hartford*'s bulwarks, so as he was wont to do, the admiral went aloft. He climbed up the ratlines on the port side to a point from which he could holler over to the captain of *Metacomet* and at the same time communicate with the *Hartford*'s pilot, who by this time was up in the maintop. As the thick smoke bellied up, Farragut climbed higher, until he was braced against the futtock shrouds at a point nearly level with the pilot. One of his arms wrapped around the shrouds, and his other hand clutched his binoculars. Fearing that even a close miss might send the admiral over the side, Percival Drayton, *Hartford*'s captain, ordered a seaman aloft to lash him to the rigging.[27]

Glancing ahead, Farragut saw something that alarmed him. Instead of pushing forward, *Brooklyn* was backing down, and as she did, her bow swung toward the fort. Disaster loomed. If the other ships in the column slowed, they would not be able to make steerageway, let alone hold their positions. They would collide and throw the whole effort into absolute chaos. While watching *Brooklyn* falter, Farragut observed *Tecumseh*, just to her starboard side, changing her course. Instead of passing inboard of a marker buoy, as had been planned, she moved farther into the channel, leaving the buoy to starboard.

Farragut was stunned. On their new course the line of monitors would cut directly across the main line of battle. On his own, *Tecumseh*'s captain, Tunis Augustus MacDonough Craven, had decided that if he held to the admiral's plan, it would mean running aground and possibly allowing *Tennessee* to escape. Craven brought his ship onto a new and fatal course. Within minutes of coming around, *Tecumseh* lurched side to side, stopped dead in the water, and then settled down by the head. Her stern came up, and her screw turned aimlessly, like a rogue windmill. The steamship had struck a torpedo; within minutes she sank out of sight.

Tecumseh's fate was precisely what *Brooklyn* was trying to avoid. Her lookouts had spotted the buoys in the water which they knew marked torpedoes. It was this sighting that had induced her captain to back down. Once he saw *Tecumseh* go down, Farragut knew the problem. He was in a desperate situation; but he had no choice, and with little hesitation he decided to steam ahead. As he passed *Brooklyn*, he called to Captain Alden, "What's the trouble?" Back came the reply "Torpedoes!" An angry Farragut hollered, "Damn the torpedoes! Four bells, Captain Drayton, go ahead!"[28]

The flagship moved past *Brooklyn*, leaving her and the others to follow in her wake, the crew believing, in the hyperbolic rhetoric of the admiral's after-action report, "that they were going to a noble death with their commander in chief."[29] Thankfully that expectation was not realized. Either because they were faulty to begin with or because salt water had corroded the contacts, the torpedoes did not explode. Farragut's men listened in horror to a succession of dull thuds along the hull, but that was the sum of the damage. By eight o'clock the entire squadron, minus poor *Tecumseh*, was in Mobile Bay.

As Farragut looked about, he rejoiced that his ships had come through. *Tecumseh* was gone, and *Oneida*, steaming in the most exposed position at the end of the column, had been handled severely and was limping along with *Galena*'s help. What had brought them through was Farragut's commitment, the belief that had served him so well in the past that "the safest way to prevent injury from an enemy is to strike hard yourself."[30] Heavy Federal fire had indeed sent the gunners at Fort Morgan scurrying for cover. Now past the forts, Farragut had to confront Franklin Buchanan.

Buchanan and his small flotilla had not been idle. As the Federals approached, the smaller gunboats, *Selma, Morgan,* and *Gaines,* had stayed ahead of the Federal column by about a thousand yards and fired on them from the oblique with telling effect. *Tennessee,* far too ungainly to engage in this arabesque, made straight for *Hartford* in an attempt to ram and sink the flagship. With fair ease, *Hartford* slid by the ram. Later the admiral remarked, "I took no further notice of her than to return her fire."[31]

The rest of the line, however, took notice. Buchanan steamed past them, blazing away with his broadsides and attempting to ram. It was a bloody run, and while neither side was able to inflict any fatal blows, both were hammered and dazed. By the time the squadron came to anchor near *Hartford,* their hulls were holed. Their rigging was torn, and the surgeons were busy tending to the wounded and dying.

While Buchanan moved down the line, Farragut steamed forward. He signaled the smaller gunboats to cast off from their sisters and pursue the Rebel boats. *Hartford's* partner, *Metacomet*, wasted no time getting away. She set after *Selma* and within an hour had captured her. The other Federal gunboats were not so spry. Their slowness gave *Morgan* and *Gaines* time to find cover under the frowning guns of Fort Morgan.

Damaged but hardly beaten, *Tennessee* was rounding up the bay, after having gone down the Federal line. Most expected that she, too, would take cover at the fort, but that was hardly Buchanan's intention. As it became apparent that "Old Buck" had no mind to run, one of his officers turned to him. "Are you going into that fleet, Admiral?" he asked, and Buchanan shot back, "I am, Sir."[32]

It was probably no surprise to Farragut when *Hartford's* lookout called to the deck that *Tennessee* was coming up the bay. Slowly the mass of dark iron approached. Farragut signaled that all monitors and those wooden ships able to fight were to attack and ram if possible. What followed was one of the closest and most heavily fought battles of the war. In quick succession *Monongahela, Lackawanna,* and *Hartford* rammed *Tennessee,* shaking her from stack to keel but accomplishing little else. What really hurt was the murderous shot from the eleven- and fifteen-inch guns of the monitors. Each time their rounds slammed into *Tennessee's* sheathing, there was violent noise and concussion; it was like being trapped inside a clanging bell.

There was also great danger from fragments of wood and metal torn loose by the impact. They flew around inside the ships like so many pieces of shrapnel. Among those wounded was Buchanan himself, whose leg was shattered by a ricocheting iron fragment. With so many hits along her side, hits which had bent her plates beyond repair, *Tennessee's* crew was having difficulty opening her gunports. Many of them were simply jammed shut. At the same time, on the open deck, the chains running from the pilothouse to the rudder had been hit, and relieving tackle had to be rigged. Unable to return fire, her steering crippled, *Tennessee* was in a woeful and hopeless situation. Her captain, James D. Johnston, ordered a white flag hoisted. As soon as the firing ceased, he came aboard *Hartford* and offered both his and Buchanan's swords to Farragut.

Morgan and *Gaines* were the only two Confederate survivors. *Morgan*'s plucky crew darted out from the safety of Fort Morgan and dashed through the Federal gauntlet up the bay toward Mobile. The Federals chased her for nearly twenty-five miles, but she fled to the safe haven of Mobile. She remained there for the remainder of the war and was finally surrendered in May 1865.

Her sister vessel *Gaines* was not so lucky; she was too badly damaged to make a run of it. Her captain decided to put her aground and then and there destroy her to prevent capture.

Ashore the Confederates were also defeated. *Conemaugh*, *J. P. Jackson*, *Estrella*, *Narcissus*, and *Stockdale* fired on Fort Powell early in the morning of the fifth "at easy rifle range." Four hours of close-in fire forced the garrison to evacuate its positions. By noon all was quiet and the Federal vessels came to anchor off the fort. Before they could land, however, a small party of Confederate soldiers managed to place explosive charges. At eleven that night they blew up the fort.

Fort Morgan was the last Confederate position to surrender. In the face of a tremendous Federal bombardment, its garrison managed to hold out for more than two weeks. On the twenty-third the fort's commander, Brigadier General R. L. Page, realized that the fort was near collapse and the enemy was drawing closer. As Page put it, "The only question was: Hold it for a time, gain the eclat, and sustain the loss of life . . . or save life and capitulate?"[33] Reason prevailed, and Page surrendered.

The Union operation had closed Mobile Bay, and that was that. Now the Federals were content to leave Mobile to wither. No move was made against the city itself. Not until the very end of the war, two days before Lincoln's assassination, did Federal troops march through its streets.

For Welles and his colleagues, the news of victory at Mobile could not have come at a better time. Union morale had slumped;

there was even serious talk that Lincoln might not be renominated for the presidency. At this gloomy time the joyous news from Farragut buoyed spirits. Within a month the fall of Atlanta and Sherman's subsequent march through Georgia were to renew the energy of a war-weary North and give it the strength to carry through to the end.

Mallory showed no shock at the news from Mobile Bay. It was hardly unexpected. By now accustomed to bad news, the Confederate naval secretary, in a somewhat astonishing turnabout, went on a rhetorical attack. He reported that the Confederate navy had "snatched credit . . . from defeat." In the face of the "inevitable" the southern seamen had displayed unparalleled "heroism." Mallory then went on to extol the virtues of *Tennessee* as if to demonstrate how prescient he had been in building such iron monsters. Yet *Tennessee,* now in Federal hands, had become useless to the South. Mallory's strategy—the use of a few "mighty ironclads" to defend his rebellious nation—had failed.

I I I

Once more Farragut was the hero of the Union. So it was natural that the administration would seek to use his talents where they were most sorely needed: in the North Atlantic Blockading Squadron. On 5 September the admiral was ordered to come north to assume command of the navy's most difficult station. But Farragut was tired, perhaps even exhausted. He wrote to Welles on 27 August: "I am willing to do the bidding of the Department to the best of my abilities. I fear, however, my health is giving way. I have now been down in this Gulf and the Caribbean Sea nearly five years out of six, with the exception of the short time at home last fall, and the last six months have been a severe drag upon me, and I want to rest, if it is to be had."[34]

Clearly Farragut was in no mood for another arduous campaign.

Welles handled Farragut badly. The secretary was in such need of a capable commander on the North Atlantic blockade that he dismissed the admiral's request for rest and instead ordered him to the service. Farragut was angry. In a testy letter of 22 September he told the secretary that he was "surprised" and could only conclude that Welles had not received his letter of 27 August.[35] Welles backed down and ordered Admiral David Dixon Porter to command the North Atlantic blockade. Porter accepted the command with eagerness. It was a dangerous undertaking, perfectly tailored for a leader with Porter's overweening self-confidence.

As for Farragut, he came home to parades, celebrations, and a promotion to vice admiral. He remained on duty for the remainder of the war, but in posts far less demanding and dangerous. In 1866 he was further elevated to the rank of full admiral. The following year he hoisted his flag on America's newest and most powerful warship, the screw frigate *Franklin*. With her as his flagship Farragut took command of the European squadron. Feted by a European public that admired him nearly as much as did the American, the admiral came home in November 1868. He visited California early in 1869, and on the return east he took ill in Chicago. He never fully recovered, and on 14 August he died at Portsmouth Navy Yard. His funeral in New York City was thronged with solemn mourners, among them President Grant.

12

Atlantic Ports

I

War on the western rivers and in the Gulf had produced victories and heroes. It was hardly surprising, then, that Lincoln and Welles should look toward the West for commanders who might bring them victories in the East, a theater where much effort had been expended but very little had been accomplished.[1]

Concern over the eastern blockade's ineffectiveness turned to acute embarrassment on St. Patrick's Day (17 March) 1862. The powerful Confederate navy side-wheeler *Nashville* made a dash to sea from Beaufort, North Carolina, successfully steaming past the somnolent Federals. It was a moonless night, and it took only twenty-five minutes for the Confederate vessel to rush by the blockaders. The two Federal ships on station were taken completely by surprise. One, the sailing bark *Gemsbok*, saw *Nashville* but could not pursue her because of light winds. The second, the steamer *Cambridge*, never saw the escape at all. *Gemsbok* fired shots, but to no effect.[2]

Nashville's escape was all the more humiliating because it was an encore performance. In October 1861 she had run to sea past the Federals at Charleston to become the first Confederate warship to fly the Stars and Bars in English waters. She had only recently returned, again past the blockaders, into Beaufort, and was now once more at sea. Fox wrote to Flag Officer Goldsborough that this turn of events was having disastrous effects in Washington. "This is not blockade," he told Goldsborough. "It is a Bull Run to the Navy."[3]

While it was probably the best known, *Nashville*'s run through the blockade was by no means unique. Statistics on the number of blockade-runners that made it past the Union cordon undermine the oft-made assertion that the blockade starved the Confederacy. In 1861, for example, the odds of a blockade-runner's being caught were approximately one in nine. That was reduced somewhat in 1862, when the odds fell to one in seven. By 1863 they had fallen again, this time to one in four. But even toward the end of the war, as the blockade tightened, the odds fell only to one in three. In the final months of the struggle the most daring of the runners enjoyed a fifty-fifty chance of getting to the wharf.[4]

Considering all their difficulties keeping station off a hostile coast—wind, currents, logistics, too few ships—the wonder is that the Union blockading squadrons did so well. But the worst handicap was the Union's inept strategy. The Federals needed not simply to place ships offshore in some loosely woven and ineffective net but to seize and hold southern ports. Otherwise any captain worth his salt—and the blockade-runners were among the best on any quarterdeck—would risk running by as long as the odds favored them and the cash reward was high.

Taking ports, of course, required joint operations between the army and the navy, a tough proposition. With virtually no experience in such tactics, Federal forces tended to neglect strategic planning. One man, though, early in the war did see an opportunity along the Atlantic coast to launch a strategic initiative that might have had dramatic effects. This was George B. McClellan.

McClellan recognized that the southern Confederacy was a vast geographical expanse held together by a fragile transportation system. If that system, primarily railroads, could be broken, the Confederate armies would be divided from their sources of supply. Nowhere was this vulnerability more apparent than along the East Coast, where rail lines sped supplies from the coastal ports to the Confederate armies. If those lines could be fractured, the armies of the South would be crippled.[5]

Early in 1862, McClellan ordered his old friend General Ambrose Burnside to launch an inland attack from the base at Hatteras Inlet. The attack was designed to seize Beaufort and Goldsborough, North Carolina, from which he could then aim a strike at the Wilmington and Weldon Railroad. Cooperation between the land forces under Burnside and the naval element commanded by Flag Officer Louis Goldsborough was key to the whole operation. The joint thrust was first aimed at Roanoke Island. This was a site which the Confederates had been busily fortifying since the summer of 1861, when the Federals had seized the nearby Hatteras forts.[6]

Burnside was ordered to gather fifteen regiments for an amphibious assault on Roanoke Island. While the troops were assembling at Annapolis, the general went to New York in order to arrange for transport. Then Burnside's first problems arose. Unacquainted with naval requirements, he put together an odd assortment of vessels. Their main defect was that they possessed a variety of drafts, a problem of some consequence since all were bound for the shallow North Carolina sounds. When Goldsborough's fleet finally assembled for review, it was a motley assortment of sail and steam, deep- and shallow-draft boats. Their infinite variety sabotaged any attempts at coherent planning.

On the morning of 13 January 1862 the fleet finally arrived

at Hatteras Inlet. Then, for a variety of reasons (not the least of which was a severe northeast gale), it took until February for the transports and naval vessels to reach Roanoke Sound. By this time the soldiers, having been caged for weeks on board swaying ships, were anxious, seasick, and plagued by lice.[7]

Friday, 7 February, was a near-perfect day for a battle, with smooth water and clear skies. The Union fleet brought such overwhelming firepower that the Confederate defenders had all they could do to keep their heads down and occasionally return fire. Some small enemy vessels made a vain attempt to harass the Federals. But the northerners' most serious problem was the rapidity with which they used up their ammunition.[8]

During the bombardment Union troops crowded to the bulwarks of their transports and clustered in the rigging, straining to get a view of the shelling.[9] About three in the afternoon Burnside ordered the troops ashore at a place called Ashby's Harbor on the west side of the island. Confederates made no attempts to prevent them, and Burnside described the landing in almost lyrical terms. "I never witnessed a more beautiful sight . . . as the steamers approached the shore at a rapid speed each surfboat was let go and with their acquired velocity and by direction of the steersman [they] reached the shore in line."[10] The battle was by no means over. It took another day for the firepower of the fleet and the slogging of the infantry to ensure the surrender of the island. But by the end of the second day, Roanoke Island and with it the sounds of North Carolina were under Union control.

More prescient commanders would have seized the opportunity to move inland as quickly as possible. But at this point fatigue infected the Federal forces. Having used up too much of their ammunition and other supplies, they elected to rest before pushing their advantage. That provided the Confederates with an opportunity to consolidate.

The Federals might still have been able to conquer more inland territory if Washington had not intervened. For political reasons, McClellan's command was reduced to include only that army whose task it was to march on Richmond. Without McClellan's strategic initiative, the Union forces remained stalled on the North Carolina shore. Indeed, McClellan's demotion from general in chief (a position granted to him on 1 November 1861 after General Scott's retirement) to commander of the smaller Army of the Potomac denied the North the kind of strategic coordination that might have shortened the war. As Rowena Reed has noted, "From the moment McClellan was deprived of the chief command the Union had no strategic plan for defeating the Confederacy. Each department commander was permitted to define his own objectives and all competed for the necessary resources."[11]

The Federal navy continued to operate in the North Carolina sounds and in support of the army along the James River and the Chesapeake. But its real focus on the Atlantic coast centered on the three principal ports along the southern shore: Savannah, Charleston, and Wilmington. In defiance of McClellan's grand strategic plan, each of these ports was separately targeted. Furthermore, for all intents and purposes they were seen as navy targets. Most of the navy's efforts were concentrated on Charleston. If the Union army was obsessed with "On to Richmond," the navy was no less preoccupied with "Back to Charleston."

II

When viewed from the water, Charleston· was indeed an impressive fortress. As one approached from the sea, Sullivans Island lay on the starboard side and Morris Island to the port side. Between the two ran the main channel into the inner harbor of Charleston. Both islands boasted well-dug-in fortifications; the passage between them was a mile and a half wide. Towering over the middle of that passage was Fort Sumter, now the ultimate symbol of southern defiance and northern shame. General Pierre Gustave Toutant Beauregard was the commander of this imposing bulwark.

Beauregard was the proud Louisiana Creole who had commanded the forces that first fired on Sumter in April 1861. After Sumter's fall, he had gone west. Disappointed by his performance at Shiloh and his later evacuation of Corinth, President Davis took advantage of Beauregard's announcement that he was in poor health to replace him with Braxton Bragg. When Beauregard recovered, Davis posted him to command the defenses of the Florida, Georgia, and Carolina coasts. Early in the fall of 1862 Beauregard arrived at Charleston to take back his old command. He may well have been overqualified for the job. As was later shown, Beauregard was a fine engineer. He helped design a defensive network (including skillfully used torpedoes) that were to frustrate the Union navy completely. However, the use of this talented, albeit personally obnoxious, general in such a static situation denied the Confederacy an able field commander at a time when it needed such a leader.[12]

In January 1863 Beauregard went on the offensive. From his intelligence sources the general knew that two of the largest Union blockaders, *Powhatan* and *Canandaigua,* had sailed down to Port Royal for coaling. In the early morning haze of 31 January he ordered two ironclads, *Palmetto State* and *Chicora,* to attack the remaining blockaders. Both Confederate vessels were designed as rams; they were also well armed. Their low silhouettes, a hazy morning, and inattentive lookouts permitted them to come well within range before being spotted.

Mercedita took the brunt of the attack from *Palmetto State.* The Confederate fired off a shot, then drove her ram straight through the steam drum of *Mercedita*'s port boiler. Unable to move, *Mercedita* next found that she could not depress her guns low enough to shoot at *Palmetto State.* She surrendered. *Palmetto State* then fired on *Keystone State,* with equally devastating results. *Keystone State* was forced to withdraw from action. In the meantime, *Chicora* was busily engaging some of the other Federal vessels in a long-range gun duel. After approximately three hours the two Confederates withdrew to the shelter of Charleston Harbor and the loud huzzahs of the town's citizens. The Rebel sortie had been so successful that for the time being, the Federals were forced to withdraw offshore. Beauregard declared that the blockade was broken.[13]

Already under tremendous pressure from Washington to assault Charleston and having begun to plan just such an attack, Flag Officer du Pont received the bad news from Charleston with surprise. He was at Port Royal aboard his flagship, *Wabash,* awaiting word from another part of his command, the area near Savannah.

After *Monitor* showed her power in Hampton Roads, the entire Union Navy Department was infected with what some have called "iron fever," the belief that nothing could stand in the way of ironclad monitors with huge guns. It was this faith that convinced du Pont's superiors that he could take Charleston if given these vessels. Du Pont himself was more skeptical. In the early summer of 1862 he confided to his wife that he had serious misgivings about the usefulness of monitors in attacking land fortifications. Du Pont believed that the best way to capture Charleston was to "squeeze" it between land and sea, but the department wanted none of it. Clearly its course was fixed, and in January 1863 the orders arrived for the attack. Welles told du Pont he was sending him enough monitors to "enter the harbor of Charleston and demand the surrender of all its defenses." It would, the secretary added, be an operation resting "solely upon the success of the naval force."[14]

As he gathered his forces at Port Royal for the attack, du Pont decided to do a bit of field testing with the new monitors. On 20 January he ordered John Worden, captain of the monitor *Montauk,* to attempt to take Fort McAllister, which guarded the Ogeechee River just south of Savannah. As a collateral mission, du Pont also suggested moving past the fort to destroy a railroad bridge and a blockade runner he suspected of preparing for sea. The real intent of the mission, however, was to try *Montauk* against a land fortification.[15]

Worden accompanied by four conventional gunboats carried out his mission, but without the desired results. He bombarded the fort, failed to capture it, and returned to Port Royal, where an anxious du Pont awaited news of the results. Worden's experience was worrisome. After four hours of firing his eleven- and fifteen-inch guns and expending all his ammunition, he had virtually nothing to show. His own vessel had been hit thirteen times, with no damage reported. Du Pont's conclusions were not what Welles and Fox wanted to hear. The monitors, whatever their own invulnerability, were simply not good offensive weapons to use against land fortifications. Their very slow rate of fire, from only two guns, meant a limited number of shots on target. Furthermore, the practice of turning the turret away from the enemy after firing and then turning it back signaled the enemy when to go to its bombproofs and safety.

Du Pont expressed serious reservations about the usefulness of the monitors; he also informed Welles that this experience and his previous operations along the coast had convinced him more firmly than ever that success against the forts required troops. His message was not well received in Washington, where so much had been gambled on these ugly water beetles and their power to control the coast. Rather than face facts, Welles and Fox began to suspect that du Pont was a defeatist, a fatal weakness for a commander about to go into battle.[16]

Notwithstanding his reservations, by early April du Pont was off Charleston, under orders to bludgeon his way into the Confederate citadel. Some days before the attack he moved his command to *New Ironsides*. She was an ironclad built along the lines of a conventional steamer, with heavy iron plating and guns mounted in broadside, the only nonmonitor in the attack force. Altogether, nine vessels (*New Ironsides, Weehawken, Montauk, Patapsco, Catskill, Nantucket, Nahant, Passaic,* and *Keokuk*) were expected to pass in line up the main channel, close on Fort Sumter within six to eight hundred yards, and open fire. When Sumter was reduced, they would move back toward Morris Island and demolish its batteries.[17]

Knowing that Beauregard had placed torpedoes in the channel, du Pont ordered *Weehawken* to take the lead. Fitted with a clumsy raft device on her bow, she was expected to sweep the infernal machines aside.[18] At twelve-thirty on the afternoon of 7 April du Pont's line began to move, but trouble hit almost immediately. *Weehawken*'s raft fouled her anchor, and it took some minutes before she could get under way. After freeing the anchor, she made speed again. Then the trouble began in earnest.

As *Weehawken* steamed ahead, her lookouts called the pilot's attention to a number of buoys lying in their path. Their presence could mean only one of two things, neither of them pleasant. They might be range markers upon which the Confederates had zeroed their guns, or they might mark underwater torpedoes. The order was given to move forward, and it was then that the Federals discovered the meaning of the buoys. Just off *Weehawken*'s bow a geyser of water shot up. The torpedo's explosion shook the monitor but did no real harm. *Weehawken* and her sisters started to come about. In the midst of this tricky maneuver, the Confederate batteries opened a hail of fire. *New Ironsides*, with her deep draft, was faced with a particular problem, since the narrow channel in which she was moving could barely accommodate any move to port or starboard. As she began to swing, she drifted toward shallow water. Twice she dropped anchor to prevent being stranded, and twice she collided with neighboring monitors. At this point, in the words of her surgeon, the flagship "was of no more use than if she had been at the Philadelphia navy yard."[19]

The monitors did little better. *Weehawken* counted fifty three hits against her armor; they dislodged some plates and caused her to take water through a hole on the deck. *Passaic*, too, took hits. Farther down the line the story was much the same: hits by the enemy, few shots returned, and trouble with armor and the turret mechanisms. In the face of heavy and effective fire, du Pont ordered a withdrawal at about 4:25 P.M.[20]

That evening du Pont summoned his commanders to the

flagship. They sat in his cabin, and one by one, they reported on the condition of their vessels and their men. As each intoned his gloomy report, du Pont made no response.

Commander A. C. Rhind of *Keokuk* drew a grave picture of his vessel's plight. She had had seventeen shots pass through her armor, and five rounds had hit below the waterline. She was taking water, and Rhind could give no assurance that she would still be afloat by morning. No other vessel was so badly wounded, but all were injured. Some captains spoke out openly and recommended against renewing the attack; others, through their silence, implied assent. After hearing them all, du Pont adjourned the meeting to take his own counsel.

At eight in the morning du Pont watched from the deck of *New Ironsides* as *Keokuk* sank to the bottom. That sealed his decision: There would be no attack.[21]

Du Pont's decision brought a barrage of venomous attacks in the northern press and in the corridors of the Navy Department. The *Chicago Times* reported that Welles and Fox believed up Pont to be an "Incompetent and a coward." The Senate and the House demanded that the secretary forward to them dispatches relating to the failure at Charleston. Du Pont provided evidence, supported by his captains, that to attack again with the monitors was "madness" and "sheer folly." Fox and Welles refused to give in, and in both public and private they continued to aim their barbs at du Pont.

On 25 May five of du Pont's commanders, at the request of the department, forwarded to the secretary a report concerning the "qualities of the vessels."[22] Read by more discerning and less biased eyes, their report might have provided a cure for Washington's "iron fever." However, pride and politics held sway, and the commanders found their observations not so much dismissed as simply ignored. Nevertheless, they had provided a cogent analysis of the flaws of the new technology.

From an engineering point of view, one of the monitors' principal defects was ventilation. Sealed as they were, the vessels depended upon steam-powered blowers to move air through the vessel. These blowers were not always reliable, particularly since the belts driving them were wet from the chronic leaks that bedeviled the ironclads. The result, of course, was a scene straight from the *Inferno*.

Ship handling was also a problem. As had been demonstrated by *Monitor* off Hatteras, low freeboard gave the slightest sea every opportunity to wash over decks and turrets, invading every opening and filling the bilges beyond the pumps' capacity. But even in smooth water problems arose, mainly in the pilothouse. To protect the men inside from enemy fire, the builders had left only minimal eye slits through which lookouts could peer. Therefore, pilots' range of vision was highly constricted. The pilots' complaints were echoed by the gunnery officers, whose line of sight from the turret was equally compromised. Furthermore, the mass of the bulky iron hull virtually paralyzed the ship's compass. It was so slow in coming around when the ship changed course that it was nearly useless for telling direction. In many ways the monitors were navigated blind.

From a tactical standpoint, the most debilitating defect was the monitors' slow rate of fire. While they could withstand a fairly heavy bombardment, they could not return the favor. Under ideal circumstances, the time required to load, point, and fire their heavy guns was never less than seven minutes and often more. Within its turret each monitor generally carried two large guns. Considering the confined space, unreliable mechanisms, and damage from enemy fire, firing both pieces alternatively gave a rate of fire that never went much beyond a pitiful eight rounds per hour.

Welles and Fox stood firm: Not the monitors but du Pont had failed at Charleston. The navy's chief engineer, Alban Stimers, agreed. He concluded from an examination of the vessels after the repulse that the force was fully able to take Charleston and that the only thing wanting was determination. For that report and certain "falsehoods" uttered to newspaper reporters as well as "Conduct unbecoming an officer" du Pont brought charges against Stimers. The whole business became a public scandal.[23]

On 3 June Welles wrote to du Pont how disappointed he was that none of the admiral's dispatches indicated a commitment to renew the attack on Charleston. According to the secretary, this was unacceptable. "From the tone of your letters it appears that your judgment is in opposition to a renewed attack on Charleston, and in view of this fact . . . the Department had concluded to relieve you of the command of the South Atlantic Squadron. . . ."[24]

Du Pont's replacement was to be Andrew Foote. Foote's untimely death forced Welles to turn to an officer for whom he had little personal liking but whose professional credentials and political connections made him the inevitable choice. At last John Dahlgren was to hold a crucial command.

Not unexpectedly Beauregard and Mallory took delight both in the January attack that had driven off the blockading Federals and now in du Pont's political defeat. Yet not all was well between these two men.

Beauregard was highly critical of the Confederate navy's plans for defending Charleston. Although *Chickasaw* and *Palmetto State* had triumphed, their victory was against a temporarily weak enemy and their attack had been by ramming, not by gunfire. At Charleston, as everywhere else, Mallory had emphasized the construction of heavy ironclads. And as before, he encountered the same obstacles, with the same results: too few vessels with too many defects.

Beauregard was quick to point out to Richmond that in the defense against du Pont's attack in April the Confederate navy had not fired a single shot. Army guns and torpedoes had defeated the enemy. In his estimation, Mallory was wrong to emphasize the importance of large ironclads. The general believed in torpedoes and small, fast shallow-draft gunboats that could be fitted with spar torpedoes, an explosive device attached to a long pole at the bow. Such vessels, according to Beauregard, would wreak havoc with the clumsy Union ironclads. In

November 1863 the general detailed his criticisms of Mallory's plan in a letter to a South Carolina congressman, William P. Miles. Among the defects he cited to Miles were the facts that Mallory's boats were slow, drew too much water to be useful in shoal areas, and were "costly, warm, uncomfortable and badly ventilated, consequently sickly. . . ."[25]

Mallory, of course, thought otherwise and defended his plan for strong ironclads as the only sound course to follow. Beauregard was unpersuaded. It seemed to him that Mallory's strategy had become a personal, not a pragmatic, choice, that he felt his career to be inextricably linked to the fate of these iron monsters. He wrote to Miles: "Of course, I do not suppose that Mr. Mallory can possibly admit they [large ironclads] are worse than useless, since . . . they are to a certain extent the children of his own creation, and if he be a good father he cannot disown them or admit that they are defective, any more than the owl can admit that its young ones are ugly."[26]

III

Dahlgren wasted no time in getting to work. He took command on Monday, 6 July 1863, and that Friday launched his first attack. It was a combined effort against Morris Island and Battery Wagner. The army sent five thousand troops under the command of Brigadier General Quincy A. Gillmore. At a range of approximately twelve hundred yards distant from Wagner, Dahlgren's ironclads hurled their shot at the Confederates. By the end of the day, they had sent 534 shot and shells into the fortification, with little discernible result. When the army made its assault after the bombardment, it was repulsed with heavy losses.

Undaunted, Dahlgren determined to try again. He was convinced that a Federal "foothold on Morris Island must lead to the fall of Sumter, and the possession of the main Ship Channel." That meant more attacks by land and by sea. On 18 July a tremendous bombardment lasting eleven and a half hours was laid down on Battery Wagner. The Confederates retreated to their bombproofs. When the naval fire lifted and the Federal troops charged forward, they found an enemy still strong enough to repulse them with heavy losses.

Among those killed in the assault was Colonel Robert Gould Shaw, who led the all-black Fifty-fourth Massachusetts against a withering enemy fire. In September the penultimate attack was undertaken. For forty-two hours both the army and the navy fired on Battery Wagner. The Federals kept up the barrage of shells day and night. In the evening calcium lights cast an eerie glow over the area. Wagner put up a gallant defense, but it was hopeless. Toward midnight Colonel L. M. Keith, commander of the battery, sent an urgent message to Beauregard informing him that to defend his post further would mean sacrificing the entire garrison. After fifty-eight days of attack, on the night of 6 September, the Confederates managed to slip away, leaving the Federals to occupy an empty fort by the light of the morning.[27]

Despite Dahlgren's great hopes, the capture of Morris Island and Battery Wagner brought the Federals no closer to capturing Charleston. From their new position they could lob an occasional shell into the city, but that sort of sporadic attack only stiffened Confederate resolve.[28] Union monitors and *New Ironsides* were eventually able to reduce Sumter to rubble, but the Stars and Bars still blew over the debris. Nor was even this accomplished without paying a price. In addition to *Keokuk*, the Federal squadron counted three more vessels lost.

In December 1863 the monitor *Weehawken* foundered, taking thirty-one men to their deaths.[29] *Housatonic*, a new steam sloop, met her fate at the hand of the enemy. She was sunk by the Confederate submarine *H. L. Hunley*, thus earning the unhappy distinction of being the first vessel ever sunk by such a machine. *Hunley* was built at Mobile and brought to Charleston by Beauregard's order in the summer of 1863. During two dives in Charleston Harbor she sank, taking thirteen men to their deaths. Determined to use *Hunley* nonetheless, Beauregard ordered her into action against the Federals but insisted that she attack on the surface. On the night of 17 February 1864, armed with a spar torpedo carrying ninety pounds of explosive, she made her way surreptitiously toward *Housatonic*. The night was clear and bathed in moonlight. Seas were calm, and *Housatonic* was lying east southeast about five and a half miles away from Fort Sumter. Gazing landward, the lookout spotted a curious object floating nearer; it looked like a log. But it was moving at a speed of three to four knots, far too quickly for a piece of flotsam. Within three minutes of the sighting the submarine was alongside and making contact on the starboard quarter. Almost as soon as she touched, *Hunley* and her torpedo went up in a roar, tearing off the starboard quarter of *Housatonic* and sending her to the bottom. Miraculously, only five of *Housatonic*'s crew were lost. *Hunley*, however, went down with all hands.[30] She was the first submarine to sink an enemy in combat.

Last of the Federal squadron to be lost off Charleston was the monitor *Patapsco*. While screening vessels sweeping for torpedoes, she struck one herself on the evening of 15 January 1865. Going down in less than a minute, she took sixty-two men with her.[31]

Patapsco's loss came at the very moment when the Confederates were preparing to evacuate Charleston. Beauregard's decision to abandon the city had little to do with Dahlgren's shelling. He was far more concerned with General William Tecumseh Sherman, who was marching north after having driven across Georgia to the sea. On the night of 17 February 1865, the Confederate forces retreated from Charleston. The city had resisted the Federal siege for 567 days.

While Dahlgren and the nation focused their attention on Charleston, there was still the question of Savannah. In February 1862 the Union army had taken Fort Pulaski, at the mouth of the Savannah, but the city was still firmly in Confederate hands. Although the Federals made no major assault against Savannah, they kept a blockading force in the area. On occasion, as when du Pont ordered the attack on Fort McAllister, special attention was paid to the Confederates in that area. On 17 June 1863 a notable engagement took place in those waters when two monitors under the command of the indefatigable John Rodgers—*Weehawken* and *Nahant*—engaged the Confederate ram *Atlanta*.

Atlanta was originally the British blockade-runner *Fingal*, built in Glasgow. She was obtained by the Confederates in 1862, cut down, and converted into an ironclad ram fitted with a spar torpedo designed to explode on contact. Thanks to the information they'd extracted from Rebel deserters, the Federals knew that *Atlanta* was preparing to attack. It was that news that brought the monitors to the waters of Warsaw Sound at the mouth of the Wilmington River.

Early on the morning of 17 June *Atlanta* got under way. She had come only a short distance when her deep draft caused her to run aground. It took fifteen minutes to back her off, but by that time the element of surprise was gone, and *Weehawken* was making straight for her. In trying to maneuver, *Atlanta* hit bottom again. *Weehawken* opened fire with telling effect and was soon joined by *Nahant*. Immobile and under fire, *Atlanta* surrendered.[32]

With *Atlanta*'s demise the Confederates at Savannah lost their only offensive capacity, but that still left them in possession of the land fortifications protecting the port. The blockade continued, but without troops to take the forts, all the Federals could do was try to keep the port closed. Savannah finally fell from the land side when, on 20 December, the Confederates abandoned the city in the face of certain capture by Sherman's army.

I V

The frustrating experience of the South Atlantic Blockading Squadron at Charleston and Savannah was mirrored by that of the North Atlantic Squadron. Once Norfolk was back in Union hands (10 May 1862), and the waters of the North Carolina sounds were secure, the only significant port that remained in Confederate hands was Wilmington, North Carolina. Wilmington was every bit as tough as Charleston, and even more problematical. Geography gave it advantages that Charleston did not possess and made it one of the chief destinations of the blockade-runners.

Tucked twenty-eight miles up the Cape Fear River from the Atlantic, Wilmington itself was quite safe from any attack by the Federal navy. Only 570 miles from Nassau and 674 from Bermuda, it was close enough for a quick dash by blockade-runners operating from those ports. The runners could sail into the river through the New Inlet passage, guarded by Fort Fisher, or from the south, near Cape Fear and Smith's Island. Both passages were well defended by the Confederates. Since the Federals had to watch both entrances and at the same time stay far enough offshore to be out of range of the shore batteries, they found themselves patrolling along an arc of nearly fifty miles.

Wilmington also had the marked advantages of good rail connections and proximity to the Army of Northern Virginia's operational area. As the fortunes of the Confederacy declined, and as other ports were either captured or more securely blockaded, Wilmington grew more and more important to the South. By late 1864 it was virtually the last source of critical supplies for the army.

Although Welles had seen, as best he could, to the blockade of Wilmington, he had not been able to do much more than send ships and hope for the best. The officer in command of the North Atlantic Blockading Squadron, Samuel Phillips Lee, was competent and conscientious. Indeed, through his efforts Wilmington had become a more difficult port to enter and leave. Nevertheless, Lee knew that the only sure means of closing Wilmington was to capture it. Neither he nor Welles, however, had ever been able to persuade the army to send troops in sufficient numbers to take the town and its defenses.

In September, to his surprise, Lee was told that he would exchange commands with Farragut. When the latter declined the new post, Welles still insisted on transferring Lee, and in Farragut's stead he appointed Porter. Events were taking a turn for the better. Lieutenant General Grant, since March 1864 general in chief, informed Welles that he might be able to spare sufficient men to assault Fort Fisher. The offensive was planned for October. Porter conferred with both Fox and Grant to lay plans for the grand assault.

As the commanders laid their plans, it became obvious that the navy had misread Grant. The army did not share the navy's enthusiasm for a full-scale attack culminating in the capture of Wilmington. It had in mind a more modest operation, which might well be termed successful if it simply closed off the port. Porter was miffed but proceeded to plan with his usual gusto, muttering about the army's fixation on Richmond and the delays caused by its lassitude. In private correspondence he told Fox, "I hope never to see the army again as long as I live."[33]

However, not all the news for Porter was bad. In the midst of his trials with the army, he received news of one of the most courageous naval exploits of the war.

After securing the waters of North Carolina's Albemarle Sound, the Federal blockaders had become complacent. In April 1864 the Confederates seized an opportunity to strike at them. Up the Roanoke at the town of Edwards Ferry, Commander James W. Cooke, of the Confederate navy had been supervising the construction of the ironclad ram *Albemarle*. She was commissioned on 17 April, and that day she headed down the river toward the Federal position at Plymouth. After some delay caused by low water and faulty machinery, she finally attacked early on the morning of the nineteenth. Two Union gunboats, *Miami* and *Southfield,* fought back. *Southfield* went to the bottom after being rammed by *Albemarle,* leaving the rest of the Union boats to retreat with all due haste. The next day Plymouth fell to Confederate troops. It was a complete rout for the Federal forces and a turnabout in the war. For one of the few times during the fighting, the Confederates held supremacy on the water.

Plymouth's fall was bad news to the North. Strategically it was unimportant as long as the entrances to the sound were still in Union control. Psychologically, however, it was over-whelming. Furthermore, as long as she was afloat, *Albemarle* remained a potential threat. This threat was brought home in May 1864, when *Albemarle* sortied and attacked Union vessels in the sound.[34] Although she was repulsed, it was clear that the ram was a formidable weapon. As long as she stayed afloat, Federal control of the sound was in peril. *Albemarle* must be destroyed.

It was not clear, however, how this could be accomplished. The entrances to the sound were too shallow for Union iron-clads. Then a brash young naval lieutenant, a Naval Academy dropout named William Barker Cushing, proposed a daring scheme. On at least two prior occasions, Cushing had led night raiding parties behind enemy lines, securing intelligence and prisoners. Always eager for adventures, Cushing devised another to destroy *Albemarle.*[35]

Under Cushing's supervision, a fast steam launch, about forty-five feet in length, was fitted out for attack. A spar tor-pedo was placed forward of the bow and fixed to a contraption with a lanyard leading back to the launch. When pulled, the lanyard would release the torpedo, allowing the launch to back down; another pull on a second lanyard would explode the tor-pedo and sink the ram. Though his plan was risky, Cushing found volunteers to accompany him, including at least one sea-man who had been with the lieutenant on his previous adven-tures.

On the night of 27 October Cushing's launch stole silently up the Roanoke River toward *Albemarle*. Miraculously, Confederate pickets never heard or saw the low silhouette gliding past them. Cushing made it almost all the way, but within hailing distance of the ram, a sailor aboard the iron mountain called out and sounded the alarm. It was too late. Through a hail of fire, Cushing ran forward, hit the ram, pulled the first lanyard, and then almost simultaneously jerked the other. A loud explosion and a geyser of water flew up over them. *Albemarle*'s crew pumped furiously, but to no use; the ram settled to the bottom of the river. So did Cushing's launch, and it was every man for himself. Union and Confederate sailors splashed about together in the debris-strewn water.

Some volunteers who were unable to swim drowned; others were scooped up by Confederate picketboats. A few, including Cushing, struggled to shore. Somehow Cushing managed to creep twelve miles through enemy lines alone until he reached the sound, found a small boat, and set out on the water. After ten hours of paddling he was finally picked up by the Union gunboat *Valley City*. Needless to say, as soon as the story reached the press, William Cushing became a national hero. Porter forwarded a report of the action to Welles and urged him to promote Cushing for his daring. In later years, as he reflected on the exploit, Porter wrote that Cushing's tale "should be written in letters of gold on a tablet for the benefit of future ages."[36]

Cushing's derring-do paved the way for the recapture of Plymouth, and within two weeks the Stars and Stripes were once more flying over the town.

V

Though the recapture of Plymouth was encouraging, Porter thought of little else but Wilmington. Unfortunately the army continued to hang back. Porter fumed at the delays, and Welles even wrote directly to Lincoln, urging him to order troops forward.

Although sixty-five hundred troops were finally assigned to the expedition, Grant appointed one of his least capable generals, Benjamin Butler, to command. Butler had most recently embarrassed himself in a bungled attempt on Richmond, and Grant was probably anxious to have him out of the way. Wilmington was a minor venture as far as the army was concerned and thus a perfect task for this weak general, whose incompetence was exceeded only by his political clout.

The fleet set sail from Hampton Roads and assembled off Fort Fisher on 20 December. Confronting the Confederates was the largest and most powerful assemblage of Union naval might of the entire war. Indeed, it is quite likely that the force that stood offshore was the most powerful naval fleet ever assembled up to that time. The Union fleet totaled sixty warships, mounting more than six hundred guns, whose weight of fire exceeded twenty-two tons.

At first, Porter and Butler neglected to use the force that they had mustered. Instead of assault, they planned what they thought was a clever stratagem. On the evening of the twenty-third *Louisiana,* a decrepit gunboat, was towed to a place about 450 yards off Fort Fisher. She was loaded with 350 tons of powder. The plan was to blow her up. The concussion of the blast would then sweep across the fort, disabling both the structure and the men inside. General Richard Delafield, chief engineer of the army, thought the idea ridiculous and told the War Department so.[37] But Butler and Porter opposed him, and at their orders, *Louisiana* took her place. At 1:40 A.M. the explosion went off; it was a colossal failure. The Confederate garrison was undisturbed, and in the morning the fort loomed over the beach as dark and grim as ever.

Fort Fisher was constructed on a peninsula lying roughly on a north-south axis, with the Cape Fear River on the west and the Atlantic on the east. The entire peninsula was not much more than a large spit of sand into which had been burrowed a fortress, whose strength came from powerful batteries protected by thick mounds of sand. It was shaped in a ⌐, with the longer portion, three-quarters of a mile, fronting the Atlantic and the short leg, one-quarter of a mile, running across from east to west.

Fisher presented an imposing sight.[38] For nearly four years the Confederates had been at work improving their position. Everything had been done in accordance with the best military engineering. Fields of fire were well covered, and numerous bombproofs were provided for troops to take shelter in during bombardments. Forty-four heavy guns were in place, as were several smaller pieces. The north side mounted most of the guns and was protected by a nine-foot-high palisade of logs as well by as electrically detonated mines.

The fort did have its weaknesses: Ammunition, for instance, was in short supply. And once infantry moved close in, the only way the defenders could return effective fire was to move out of their covered positions and expose themselves on the top of the sand fortifications. The force manning the fort was much smaller than the Federal army, just shy of two thousand troops. Still, the Confederates were well prepared to repel any Union attack.

V I

It was not until midday on the twenty-fourth, many hours after *Louisiana's* explosion, that Porter put his fleet in position to begin the bombardment. The delay now seems a bit strange. It would have made better sense for Porter to keep his force closer in, ready to move against the enemy while it was still in shock. Perhaps Porter, always a navy partisan, believed that he could preempt an army victory. All he needed to do was rain fire on the fort and force its surrender before Butler could even get ashore. If that was his belief, he was very much in error.

On the day before Christmas for five and a half hours Porter's ships laid down an extraordinary barrage. At times the rate of fire reached 115 rounds per minute. There was incessant noise, black smoke, and something that resembled a desert sandstorm on the shore. Most shipboard spectators could hardly believe that anyone could survive such an ordeal, let alone come through it ready to fight. They were soon proved wrong.

During the bombardment the troop transports arrived, under the command of Butler and his immediate subordinate, Godfrey Weitzel. While the navy continued its barrage, Butler's troops began to move ashore. They landed to the north of the fort, organized, and then edged their way toward the Confederate position. As they got closer, Butler and Weitzel were taken aback by what they found. Aside from minor damage, the fort was virtually untouched. Two days of sound and fury had accomplished almost nothing. The mounds of sand had swallowed up Federal shot, muffling their effect, while the Confederates kept their heads down in their bombproofs. In fact, the losses from exploding ordinance on the naval vessels (twenty men killed) exceeded the number of casualties in the fort (one man killed). As soon as the naval fire lifted, Colonel William Lamb, commander of the garrison, had his men at their guns. He was even able to man the palisade.

Butler was in a tough spot. Thus far the gunfire assault had been a bust. It had, however, consumed enormous quantities of shot and powder. Now Porter told him they were running short on ammunition and could not promise anything like an encore performance. At the same time the barometer was dropping. If the weather turned dirty, as seemed likely, the three thousand men thus far put ashore might be the only ones on that beach for some time. Assaulting the Confederates with the small force at hand would be suicidal. Some suggested laying siege to the fort; but that had never been Butler's idea, and his mind had not changed. Instead, he told Porter: "I caused the troops . . . to reembark, and see nothing further that can be done by the land forces. I shall therefore sail for Hampton Roads as soon as the transport fleet can be got in order."[39]

Butler's decision caused Porter to let loose a torrent of verbal abuse that continued long after the war was over. In all fairness it should be noted that Butler's decision was probably correct. It had taken the Federals so long to marshal their forces against Fisher that the enemy had had plenty of time to prepare a warm reception. By the time Butler got ashore, it was clear he did not have a force sufficient to take the fort. Perhaps it might be argued that he did not come well prepared, but if that was the case, then the navy might be faulted for overselling its services, causing Butler to underestimate the land force required for the action.[40]

There had to be another attempt at Fort Fisher. Fox wrote to both Grant and Porter: "The country will not forgive us another failure at Wilmington."[41] In his usual manner Porter told Fox that he was eager to have another go at it. He had no faith in the army, including his old friend Grant. He was, he told Fox, willing to go it alone, promising to silent Fort Fisher's guns in twenty-five minutes. "I don't believe in anybody but my own good officers and men. I can do anything with them, and you need not be surprised to hear that the webfooters have gone into the forts."[42]

Fortunately the navy was not forced to go it alone. Grant sent General Alfred Terry with twelve thousand men and a siege train that was to be held in reserve. General Terry was ordered to "consult with Admiral Porter freely" about strategy and deployment. Porter, too, was cooperative, assuring Grant, "There is no use in fretting over the past."[43]

On Thursday, 12 January, the fleet was once more off Fort Fisher. Early on the morning of the thirteenth the second bombardment began. Porter had learned from his mistakes. This time he moved his vessels closer to the target and concentrated his fire on the land face of the fort, where the main attack was to take place. In addition, he told his gunners not to engage in fancy firing at flagstaffs. It had become a custom among naval gun crews to aim for the enemy colors, a romantic but not necessarily important target. This time, Porter told them, they should "pick out the guns."[44]

Porter, however, was not above making his own beau geste. He decided that the navy ought to have a more direct role in taking the fort. In his General Order 81, he instructed his commanders:

> That we may have a share in the assault when it takes place, the boats will be kept ready, lowered near the water on the off side of the vessels. The sailors will be armed with cutlasses, well sharpened, and with revolvers. When the signal is made to man the boats, the men will get in, but not show themselves. When signal is made to assault, the boats will pull around the stern of the monitors and land right abreast of them, and board the fort on the run in a seaman-like way.
>
> The marines will form in the rear and cover the sailors. While the soldiers are going over the parapets in front, the sailors will take the sea face of Fort Fisher.[45]

Though careful planning and cooperation, Porter and Terry accomplished their mission. Porter's vessels hurled their fire at the north face, dismounting guns and blowing wide gaps in the palisades. They kept up the fire during the night, preventing the enemy from repairing the damage. For his part, Terry got his men ashore with adequate provisions and ammunition. Porter's naval battalion proved the key to the assault, although at a high cost. Sixteen hundred sailors and four hundred marines went ashore against the sea face, while the army moved against the north side. The seamen's attack was brave but uncoordinated. The two thousand men had never before fought together, and their command structure was inexperienced and wobbly. Confederate fire blasted through their ranks and took a fearful toll: eighty dead and nearly four times that number wounded. Caught in the open, the sailors and marines were repulsed, but not before accomplishing an important objective. Their attack forced Lamb to divert men to the sea face, thus weakening his north front, where the main attack was taking place. Terry's troops, after fierce hand-to-hand combat, broke through and invaded the fort. At a critical moment in the seesawing battle, naval gunfire was fired at right angles into the Confederate defenders. With friendly troops hotly engaged in the same sector, the fire had to be delivered with "deadly precision," and it was. From 3:00 in the afternoon—when the first wave of troops moved up the beach—until well into the night, the battle continued. Finally the defenders were driven back into the recesses of the fort. Their ammunition was running low, and there was no hope of reinforcement. Their commander, wounded, offered to surrender. According to Porter, at 10:00 P.M., when the "joyful tidings were signaled to the fleet we stopped our fire and gave . . . three of the heartiest cheers I have ever heard."[46]

Fort Fisher's fall marked the end of Wilmington as a port. Grant dispatched additional troops to move on the city itself, and with naval support, the forces closed in. The pressure was relentless as the Union forces drew nearer the city. On 17 February Charleston fell. Five days later, on Washington's Birthday, the last useful seaport in Confederate hands surrendered. Raphael Semmes late wrote of Wilmington's demise: "[W]e had lost our last blockade-running port. Our ports were now hermetically sealed. The anaconda had, at last, wound his fatal folds around us."[47]

13

Raiders

I

Few images are more romantic in American history than that of the lone American sea captain bravely striking at the commerce of our enemy. The fabled Yankee privateer boldly sailed into the midst of an enemy, cut out a richly laden merchantman, and then returned home to the huzzahs of neighbors and the clink of gold coins. It was a tale told and retold through all America. Patriots sang about these brave seamen, wrote stories about them, and grandly exaggerated their accomplishments. These men were the folk heroes of a new nation struggling to survive in a hostile world.

But America's fondness for raiding an enemy's commerce was based as much on hard reality as on fanciful notions of adventure at sea. Neither willing nor able to support a strong navy, the new nation found that its best defense was a twofold threat: its navy and its privateers.

Privateering—the arming and equipping of private vessels

to raid the enemy in time of war—was an accepted activity well into the nineteenth century. But while every maritime nation dabbled in privateering, Americans seemed to take to it with particular gusto. They had begun the practice during the time of the colonies, continued it in the Revolution, and brought it to new heights in the early days of the Republic. The nation's fascination with privateering stemmed from the twin motives of patriotism and greed. Privateering was a chance to strike at the nation's enemies and get rich in the process, since owners and crews of privateers were entitled to keep what they captured. But though stories of great rewards enticed young men to sign on, the truth was usually some distance from the tales told in taverns. Privateering was a risky business, and large numbers of young sailors came home with little or nothing. Some adventurers lost everything, including their lives.

Professional naval officers generally disdained privateersmen. They viewed them as seagoing rascals, closely related to pirates. Privateers were loners, greedy and undisciplined, men who cared more for lining their pockets than for striking a blow at the nation's enemy. Naval officers, on the other hand, claimed to value discipline, patriotism, and coordinated efforts.

The American navy did not always achieve this ideal in the antebellum period. Lack of professionalism and a shortage of ships dictated a policy that often listed more toward privateering than toward disciplined and coordinated naval action. During the Revolution, Naval War with France, and War of 1812, virtually all the blue water naval victories involved raids by one gallant American ship on the enemy. Out of necessity and weakness, raids, harassments, and disruptions were the chief pillars of American naval strategy from the time of the Revolution to the opening of the Civil War. It was not necessarily a policy popular with most naval officers, who would have liked to think in the grander terms of fleet action. Alfred Thayer Mahan, a young American naval officer in the Civil War and the future naval theorist, abhorred the policy of commerce raiding, as did many of his brother officers. Nevertheless, because of limited resources, the navy was often forced to turn to this less orthodox means of resistance.[1]

Love of privateering and a naval strategy based on raiding thrust the United States into taking a position in 1856 that it lived to regret in 1861.

On 16 April 1856 representatives of Austria, France, Great Britain, Prussia, Russia, and Turkey agreed at Paris that henceforth privateering would be abolished.[2] Invited to become a signatory to he agreement, the United States declined. In a statement that the government came to rue, William L. Marcy, secretary of state, lectured the Europeans:

> It certainly ought not to excite the least surprise that strong naval powers should be willing to forego [sic] the practice, comparatively useless to them, of employing privateers upon condition that weaker powers agree to part with their most effective means of defending their maritime rights. It is, in the opinion of this government, to be seriously apprehended that if the use of privateers be abandoned, the dominion over the seas will be surrendered to those powers which have the means of keeping up large navies.[3]

In 1856 Marcy's answer made sense to Americans. But five years later, in 1861, the world had turned upside down. The North was in the position of the European nations, a dominant naval power trying to cope with a weaker foe whose only recourse was to raiding and privateering. On 24 April 1861, fewer than two weeks after Sumter's fall, Secretary of State William Seward instructed the American minister in London, Charles Francis Adams, to inquire of Her Majesty's government "whether it is disposed to enter into negotiations for the accession of the government of the United States to the declaration of the Paris congress."[4] But it was too late. The British and French governments responded that they were willing to talk but that any agreement they might reach could not apply to the current "internal difficulties" in the United States.[5] Naturally negotiations broke down, and Seward had to instruct his ministers in England and France to withdraw the offer.

While Lincoln and Seward lamented their predecessors' shortsightedness, the Confederates took every advantage of their freedom. In the grand American tradition, they made ready to torment their powerful adversary with privateers and naval raiders.

Apart from the blockades and the lack of domestic ship-building (which severely limited the number of ships available) the Confederates had also to cope with the rules and procedures of international law. Some cynics might have agreed with Cicero that "The laws are silent in the midst of arms," but in fact, war in the nineteenth century, especially at sea, did conform to agreed-upon conventions. To be sure, these conventions most often favored the strong.

In the case of the Civil War the Union navy, weak at the outset, rapidly grew to strength. It was clearly in the interest of the increasingly aggressive North that the most stringent interpretation be placed upon the rights of belligerents. As the North emerged as a power on the seas, other nations realized that it was in their interest to placate the now-formidable Union. At times it seemed that the laws existed only to ensure the Federals' right to victory.

The Confederacy's ability to strike at sea was enhanced when, on 13 May 1861, the government of Great Britain issued a proclamation of neutrality, a measure promptly imitated by other European powers. In effect, this allowed Confederate naval vessels and privateers to be treated as legitimate ships of war. This proclamation received additional elaboration on 31 January 1862, when the ministry laid down particular rules.

1. Ships of war were not to enter Nassau or to use the Bahamas anchorages.
2. Time in other ports was not to exceed twenty-four hours. If two enemies should enter the same port,

their time of departure was to be separated by twenty-four hours.

3. The quantity of fuel which might be supplied was to be limited to sufficient to reach the nearest harbour in the applicant's own country. This privilege was not to be extended to any particular ship more often than once in three months.

4. "Prizes" were not to be taken into British ports.[6]

Not surprisingly, these rules were frequently ignored by local crown officers. The laws of other European nations, especially those of France, were even more fluid.

Great Britain was the nation whose yards were most likely to build ships for the South, and here the Confederates had to deal with the provisions of the Foreign Enlistment Act of 1819. Under this law, it was illegal to equip, furnish, fit out, or arm within British jurisdiction a vessel whose purpose was to attack the commerce of a friendly power. Curiously, the construction of such vessels was not prohibited. Nothing in the law prevented a belligerent from building a ship in Great Britain and then taking it elsewhere to be equipped, fitted out, and armed. This was a loophole large enough for many a Confederate ship to sail through.

With both law and tradition now on his side, President Jefferson Davis issued a call on 17 April 1861 to "all those who may desire, by service in private-armed vessels on the high seas, to aid this Government in resisting so wanton and wicked an aggression, to make applications for commissions or letters of marque and reprisal to be issued under the seal of these confederate states."[7] Within twenty-four hours applications had begun to arrive. Captains and shipowners, with visions of loot dancing in their heads, laid plans to waylay Union commerce. During the course of the war, though, only fifty or so commissions were actually granted. This seems an especially small number compared with the hundreds of commissions that American authorities issued in the Revolution and War of 1812.

One limiting factor was legal. The Confederate States adhered to law and would issue commissions only to vessels actually present within southern jurisdiction, not to individuals. This was a prudent policy and prevented a trade in commissions from developing. Unprincipled men might have taken blank commissions, found themselves ships beyond the bounds of the Confederacy, and launched themselves into piracy under the guise of Confederate privateering. That sort of nefarious conduct, known in previous wars, was not something the Confederate leaders would countenance. In the long run, it would not have served the interests of their cause. The Confederates needed respectability. Playing loose with privateering, particularly in light of its questionable standing since the Declaration of 1856, would have served them ill in their quest for international standing.[8]

Adherence to law undoubtedly reduced the number of Confederate privateers, but what really harmed southern privateering was something far more simple and mundane: the lack of profit. In accordance with long tradition and law, owners of privateers were permitted to keep all the proceeds, minus a small percentage for the government, from the sale of their captures.[9] After paying expenses, shares from the sales of the captured goods were divided between the owner and crew of the vessel. But before any sale could take place, a very important condition had to be fulfilled.

By law and tradition, the captured prize had to be condemned by a properly constituted court. These courts could be held only within the jurisdiction of the government issuing the original commission. The hard fact was that Confederate privateers, in order to realize any gain from their hazardous enterprise, had to bring their prizes home. Getting out to sea past the Federals was dangerous enough, but getting back with prizes was harder still. Legal Confederate privateering was not an attractive proposition, and while fifty commissions were issued, probably considerably fewer than that number ever got to sea.

Confederate privateers never amounted to much more than
paper sharks.

I I

Navy raiders, however, were another matter. Astute as usual,
Stephen Mallory understood what the Confederate navy needed
in order to raid on the high seas: "vessels built exclusively for
ocean speed, at a low cost, with a battery of one or two accurate
guns of long range, with an ability to keep the sea upon a long
cruise and to engage or to avoid an enemy at will."[10] Virtually
no vessels then under Confederate control fitted this description, and the possibilities of southern yards' being able to construct such cruisers were remote. Mallory's only alternative was
to scoop up what was available within the South. At the same
time he began to look abroad for new vessels.

Among the first homegrown cruisers that put to sea was
Sumter, the ship that evaded and embarrassed the Federals off
Pass à l'Outre in late June 1861.[11] Once he had sailed beyond
the Federals' grasp, *Sumter*'s captain, Raphael Semmes, laid a
course into the West Indies and down toward Brazil. Three
days into the cruise *Sumter* took and burned her first victim—
the ship *Golden Rocket* out of Bangor, Maine. Thus began the
career of the South's most famous captain.[12]

Born in Maryland, Semmes entered the American navy in
1826. He served in the Mexican War and shortly afterward wrote
of his experiences in *Service Afloat and Ashore During the Mexican
War*. David Dixon Porter, another officer with literary preten-
sions, noted: "Semmes had little reputation as an officer. He
had no particular taste for his profession, but had a fondness
for literature and was a good talker and writer."[13] Semmes must
have enjoyed serving the Confederacy more than he had the

Republic, for his record during the Civil War is nothing less than remarkable.

After pausing to burn *Golden Rocket,* Semmes returned to the prowl, and within three days he had taken seven more vessels. Concerned lest the Federals pick up his trail, Semmes now bore down toward Curaçao. In late July he took two prizes off the Venezuelan coast. From there Semmes sailed and steamed north, and for the next twenty-three days he lingered in and around the French and Dutch West Indies. Although he was treated with politeness, Semmes did not receive the cordial reception which he had hoped for. The island officials had no intention of violating international law, and Semmes decided to look for a friendlier atmosphere in Brazil. There he might also encounter Union ships homeward bound from California.

But the pickings near Brazil were thin: only two vessels in September and October. By early November Semmes was back in the West Indies at Martinique. There he barely managed to escape the clutches of the USS *Iroquois,* whose captain (James Palmer) had afterward to explain to Secretary Welles how this Confederate raider had managed to elude him.[14] Altogether in his cruise Semmes and his crew had taken eighteen enemy vessels. It was an impressive feat.

Semmes now fled for Europe. With a leaky ship in need of repair and refitting, and crowded with prisoners, Semmes crossed the Atlantic amid winter storms and arrived at Cádiz on 3 January.[15] By now Federal warships (*Iroquois, Powhatan, Niagara, San Jacinto, Richmond,* and *Keystone State*) were close on his trail. Spanish authorities allowed Semmes time for a few repairs, not to remain. On 17 January *Sumter* left Cádiz, and the next day she put in at Gibraltar. "Poor old Sumter" was Semmes's sad comment as he lamented the condition of his ship.[16] Her boilers were condemned, and she was in no fit condition to sail. On 12 February the Federal screw sloop *Tuscarora* entered the harbor; within a short time she was joined by *Kearsarge* and *Ino.* They retired across the strait to Alcegiras to await *Sumter.*

Semmes knew it would be hopeless to defy them. On 9 April he discharged the crew and a few days later left for Nassau himself. In Nassau Semmes found orders from Mallory directing him to proceed to Liverpool. Eight months later *Sumter,* still riding at anchor in Gibraltar, was sold to a British firm, Fraser Trenholm, which renamed her *Gibraltar* and sent her into the business of blockade-running.

Another successful Confederate cruiser that had her origins as a domestic conversion was *Nashville.* Her career was shorter and far less spectacular than *Sumter*'s, but important nonetheless. A converted passenger steamer, she became the first Confederate warship to show the flag in Europe. She first ran past the blockade at Charleston on 21 October 1861. After coaling at Bermuda, she departed on 5 November and set her course for England. On the eighteenth *Nashville*'s captain, R. B. Pelgram, reported sighting and overtaking the clipper ship *Harvey Birch.* Pelgram took her crew aboard *Nashville* and then burned her. Two days later he dropped anchor in Southampton.[17]

Pelgram's arrival at Southampton followed close on the heels of the notorious *Trent* affair. Captain Charles Wilkes, commander of the Yankee steam frigate *San Jacinto,* had stopped the British mail steamer *Trent* in international waters and forcibly removed two Confederate diplomats, James Mason and John Slidell. Such high-handedness inflamed the British. Confederates on both sides of the Atlantic had high hopes that this incident would rupture relations between the governments of Great Britain and the United States. *Nashville* could not have arrived at a more promising time.[18] Captain Pelgram was treated with "courtesy and kindness . . . by all."[19]

While Pelgram was preparing to depart, *Tuscarora* arrived at Southampton and took up an anchorage not far from *Nashville.* When it came time for *Nashville* to leave for home, HMS *Shannon* positioned herself alongside *Tuscarora* with her "steam up and guns shotted," so that the Federal might be encouraged to obey the law and not leave port within twenty-four hours of

Nashville's departure. On 3 February *Nashville* left for home. *Tuscarora's* captain, Tunis Augustus MacDonaugh Craven, muttered "collusion," but there was nothing he could do.[20]

On 20 February Pelgram arrived in Bermuda; there he recoaled for the sprint into Beaufort. Having left Bermuda on the twenty-fourth, *Nashville* captured and burned a small schooner on the twenty-sixth. Two more days brought her off Beaufort during the early-morning hours. When challenged by a Yankee blockader, Pelgram hoisted American colors. The deception worked. By the time the Federals figured out that they had been snookered, *Nashville* was safely out of range and on her way to the safety of Morehead City.[21]

Nashville's triumph was short-lived. For reasons that are unclear, she was sold to a private owner at Morehead City. She became first a blockade-runner, then a privateer; in neither career did she earn much distinction. Fate and the enemy caught up with her in February 1863, when the Union army captured her in the Ogeechee River near Savannah and put her to the torch.[22]

I I I

Sumter and *Nashville* had thwarted Union commerce, panicked the North, and forced Federal warships to chase them all the way to Europe. Their early sorties showed what might be done with a good ship, a bold captain, and a modicum of luck. This good beginning gave the government in Richmond high hopes for a new set of cruisers it was planning to build in Europe. Central to this effort was Commander James D. Bulloch, the Confederate naval agent in Great Britain, who was charged with obtaining warships for the Confederacy. Born near Savannah, Georgia, in 1823, Bulloch came from a distinguished family. His nephew was the future president Theodore Roosevelt. He had served in the United States Navy and then the merchant service for more than twenty years. When war broke out, Bulloch immediately offered his services to the Confederacy.[23]

Bulloch arrived in England early in June 1861. Over the next four years he played a central role in the network of intrigue which surrounded the Confederacy's attempts to build and buy warships in Britain and on the Continent. Though Federal agents and diplomats did their best to frustrate him, Bulloch often managed to get the best of his adversaries, in particular the Union minister to England, Charles Francis Adams. Bulloch's story is worthy of a spy novel: furtive detectives following suspects, allegations of bribery, and secret correspondence written in code. Bulloch, a suave and resourceful manipulator, moved easily in this shadowy world.

Bulloch's machinations often involved England's most famous shipbuilding firm, John Laird and Sons of Birkenhead. It was with it that he enjoyed his greatest success and his most appalling failure. The latter centered on the construction of the so-called Laird rams. In June 1862 Bulloch contracted with Laird to build two seagoing armored rams, intended to help the Confederacy break the blockade. Simply labeled Hulls Number 294 and 295, these vessels were built, ostensibly under private contract, for James Bulloch, with no mention of the Confederate States. The ploy was clever, but not clever enough. His attorneys tried to bring the narrowest possible interpretations to the law (the five-inch armor sheathing on a ship did not necessarily make it a warship!). But even Bulloch could not delude the Britons. With Charles Francis Adams hot on the scent, the British officials were hard pressed to continue this charade.

Ever inventive, Bulloch then tried to sell his ships via a French banker to the khedive of Egypt. His stratagem failed, and finally, on 9 October 1863, the rams were seized by Her Majesty's government. The government paid Bulloch thirty thousand pounds beyond his initial outlay for the ships. The naval agent had made a tidy profit, which he quickly turned over to other Confederate activities.[24]

Though Bulloch and his cronies might lament Laird's rams,

they could take credit and comfort from other triumphs. Through their efforts, a trio of infamous raiders was let loose on Yankee commerce.

The first of Bulloch's British-built raiders was *Florida.* Built in the yard of William C. Miller and Sons at Liverpool, she put to sea in March 1862. *Florida* obtained port clearance by posing as a peaceful merchantman, *Oreto,* traveling without guns, ammunition or other accoutrements of war. At nearly the same time, however, *Bahama,* another vessel of British registry, sailed toward the Bahamas, laden with all the stores that would transform *Oreto* into the Confederate raider *Florida.* In Nassau the newly baptized *Florida* took on her weapons, sailed into the Gulf, and made straight for Mobile. Defiantly she sailed past the blockaders and up to the town, where she enlisted a full crew eager to sortie out and destroy Federal shipping. On the night of 15 January 1863 *Florida,* under the command of John Newland Maffit, once more passed the Union blockaders and headed to sea to begin her adventures.[25]

For the next twenty months—apart from six months spent recuperating in a French dockyard—*Florida* cruised the eastern Atlantic. Altogether she took thirty-seven prizes, among them the ship *Jacob Bell* outward bound from Foochow, China, en route to New York. With a rich cargo of tea and silks, *Jacob Bell* was worth at least $1.5 million, the richest capture of any Confederate vessel in the war. Alas, her capture did little to enrich the South. Like most other high-seas captures, she could not be safely brought to port. Instead, she was put to the torch and sunk.[26]

The USS *Wachusetts* finally ended *Florida*'s career as a raider in one of the most daring and outrageous acts of the war. *Wachusetts,* a screw sloop launched in Boston on 19 October 1861, had spent a good deal of her time tracking down raiders. In 1862 she had been flagship for a seven-ship squadron under the command of Charles Wilkes. These ships were unsuccessfully deployed in the West Indies to destroy Confederate raiders. After her long warm-water cruise *Wachusetts* came north for a much-needed overhaul and was not put back into commission until January 1864. Under her new captain, Napoleon Collins, she was dispatched to the coast of Brazil for "the protection of the rights and property of American citizens on the coast, and especially the guarding of American commerce against the depredations of piratical cruisers."[27] For the next nine months Collins chased down rumors and ghosts along the coast of Brazil. He and his crew put in a good deal of sea time, stopping "suspicious" vessels and comforting American captains, who saw raiders everywhere.

Having gone north from Rio early in October, *Wachusetts* dropped anchor in the Brazilian port of Bahia. *Florida* was reported to be in the area, and Collins was on the prowl. He need not have worried. On 4 October the fox came to the hound. At seven-fifteen in the evening, during the second dog watch, a lookout reported a sail coming into the harbor, and Collins dispatched a small boat to identify the stranger. When the boat returned with the news, he could scarcely believe the report: The strange sail was none other than *Florida*. Collins got up steam, heaved short on the anchor cable, and sent his crew to general quarters. But *Florida* merely rode calmly at anchor. Her captain, Charles Manigault Morris, had no intention of provoking any untoward action. He was there, as he told the Brazilian officials, to procure provisions and make repairs so that he might safely proceed to sea. Since Bahia was a neutral port, Morris had every reason to expect this courtesy, and furthermore, when he did put back to sea, he was entitled to a twenty-four-hour head start on *Wachusetts*. The Brazilian officials acknowledged Morris's rights and so informed him and Captain Collins.[28]

Napoleon Collins was frustrated by months of aimless searching for his quarry. International law notwithstanding, he decided to act. Apparently in consultation with the U.S. consul at Bahia, Thomas F. Wilson, Collins decided to ram and sink *Florida* and then let the diplomats sort out the inevitable legal tangle. A few hours before dawn on 7 October Collins slipped his cable and made for *Florida*, then riding at her anchor about five-eighths of a mile distant. The noise of *Wachusetts*'s anchor chain alerted *Florida*. In the few minutes available, she managed to move just enough so that instead of smacking her dead amidships, *Wachusetts* gave her a more glancing blow on the starboard quarter. The force of the blow took down her mizzenmast and her main boom and carried away a portion of the bulwarks. A brief scuffle followed as *Wachusetts* backed off, but in a few minutes *Florida* surrendered. As quickly as he was able, Collins passed a line over and took *Florida* under tow out to sea. On 11 November *Florida* arrived at Hampton Roads.

While the Brazilian and Confederate governments protested loudly, *Florida* swung at her anchor in Hampton Roads. Then, on 19 November, in an incident which could hardly be characterized as accidental, an army steamer crashed into the raider, holing her. *Florida* took water and finally went to the bottom in nine fathoms. Although regrets were expressed by Federal officials, one suspects that what they really felt was relief.

I V

James Bulloch was nothing if not assiduous. Even as he finished the contracts for *Florida*'s construction in June 1861, he began to discuss another project with Laird and Sons. On 1 August Bulloch, ostensibly acting as a private individual, signed a new contract for the construction of a steamer of the most modern design. To the Lairds, she was Hull Number 290; she became the Confederacy's most famous raider, *Alabama*.

Bulloch had learned a good deal from his experiences with *Florida* and from observing the Royal Navy. He realized that he needed a vessel that was fast, well armed, and, perhaps most important of all, able to keep to sea for long periods of time without having to come into port. The result of his considerable thought was a remarkable vessel.[29]

Alabama was bark-rigged, with very tall lower masts which

allowed her to carry large fore and aft rigged sails. In addition, she had two engines driving a single screw which, when not in use, could be lifted to enhance her sailing qualities. Her bunkers carried a very heft 350 tons of coal, and she had fresh water condensers on board, thus reducing her need to dock for fuel and water. Bulloch and others agreed that "she was as fine a vessel . . . as could have been turned out of any dockyard in the kingdom, equal to any of her Majesty's ships of corresponding class in structure and finish, and superior to any vessel of her date in fitness for the purposes of a sea rover, with no home but the sea, and no reliable source of supply but the prizes she might make."[30]

Bulloch made sure that no armament was put aboard and that 290's ownership was kept private. While the American consul at Liverpool, Thomas Dudley, and his London superior did everything they could to thwart the venture, Bulloch stayed well within British law. On 15 May 1862 Hull Number 290 went into the water at Birkenhead.[31]

Conforming to the law, Bulloch knew, might not be enough to ensure *Alabama*'s safety. In international diplomacy, nothing was certain except that nations would always follow self-interest. Amid rumors that the British ministry was becoming nervous about *Alabama,* Bulloch "received information from a private but most reliable source, that it would not be safe to leave the ship in Liverpool another forty-eight hours."[32] On the morning of 29 July *Alabama* left the dock at Liverpool. According to her owner, she was going out on a festive trial run, decked in flags and carrying guests. She made a few runs past the lightship, and then, after putting her guests aboard a tug, *Alabama* headed to sea.

Every move had been carefully planned. The day before *Alabama* disappeared from Liverpool, the owners of a small British bark in London had ordered her to proceed with her cargo to "the bay of Praya, in the island of Terceira, one of the Azores." There the bark—*Agrippina*—should await the arrival of a "steamer" whose captain would present "a letter . . . with authority to take whatever quantity of coal and other articles of your cargo he may require." This "cargo" included "a 7-inch 100 pounder rifled gun, Blakely pattern, 84 cwt.; one 8-inch solid shot 68 pounder, smooth bore, 108 cwt.; and six 6-inch 32 pounder guns, 55 cwt. each."[33]

As *Alabama* and *Agrippina* moved toward their rendezvous, Bulloch, who had remained behind in England, awaited another arrival. On 8 August Raphael Semmes and Lieutenant John McIntosh Kell, both late of *Sumter,* arrived with other Confederate naval officers. They had been assigned to *Alabama,* and within a few days Semmes, Kell, their brother officers, and Bulloch were en route to Terceira. The transfer of guns and supplies went quickly. On Sunday, 24 August, *Alabama* steamed out of the bay. As soon as she was in international waters, she hoisted her true colors, the Stars and Bars. At midnight Bulloch bade good-bye to Semmes and wished the captain "a glorious cruise."[34]

Bulloch's wish came true. On 5 September, barely a hundred miles from Terceira, *Alabama* took her first prize, the whaler *Ocmulgee.* Her oil-soaked decks and the barrels of sperm oil below made for a brilliant fire. For nearly two more years this good ship, superb captain, and able crew (many of whom were, in fact, British) cruised the oceans of the world. She headed toward Newfoundland, where she captured Union merchantmen carrying grain, then south toward the West Indies and into the Gulf of Mexico. There she encountered the USS *Hatteras*; it was the only time in the entire war that a Federal warship was defeated on the high seas. A triumphant Semmes then laid a course for the coast of Brazil, by now a favorite hunting ground for Confederate raiders. He had hoped to find prey homeward bound from the Far East, and sure enough, eight hapless merchantmen sailed into Semmes's trap.

On 10 April *Alabama* came within sight of the towering mountains of Fernando de Noronha.[35] To his satisfaction, Semmes was able to report that the lonely Brazilian authorities on this remote island (which served mainly as a penal colony) welcomed him and extended every courtesy. After a two-week stay "Alabama with full coal-bunkers and a refreshed crew was again in pursuit of the enemy's commerce." By now, however, success was taking its own toll. Semmes had more than a hundred prisoners belowdecks: just feeding and caring for them were becoming a serious drain. On 11 May he put into Bahia, and the next day, with permission of the local authorities, he put his human cargo ashore. With his burden lightened, Semmes continued to sail the coast. But time was running out. If Semmes stayed in these waters, the Federals would soon catch up with him. Semmes decided it was time to leave, and by late July he was off the Cape of Good Hope.

Semmes sailed into the Indian Ocean. For nearly six months *Alabama* traveled in a roughly counterclockwise direction around the ocean, capturing and destroying enemy shipping. She stopped for two weeks at Poulo Condore (a small group of islands off Vietnam) and then made her way to Singapore. The New Year saw her coasting Sumatra and then sailing across the Bay of Bengal to Ceylon. On 30 January *Alabama* crossed the equator, bound back toward Cape Hope. At Cape Town Semmes took on coal and made a fateful decision. After so long a cruise his ship was in dire need of repair above and below the waterline. He decided to head for France. Before leaving Cape Town, he picked up a bundle of newspaper from America and read with unconcealed joy that his trip through the Indian Ocean had almost halved American commerce in that region.

But there was worse news, too. In the spring of 1864 the Confederate army was in retreat. Lee could barely hold northern Virginia, and Sherman was closing in on Atlanta. Somehow, Semmes hoped that he could refit his vessel and quickly rejoin the fray. On 11 June 1864 *Alabama* entered the harbor at Cherbourg, France. He asked the authorities for permission to land his prisoners and repair his ship. The former was granted, but the latter was in doubt.

As soon as *Alabama* was recognized, the United States minister in Paris, William L. Dayton, telegraphed an urgent message to Captain John A. Winslow at Flushing in the Netherlands. Winslow was commander of USS *Kearsarge*. Commissioned in January 1862, *Kearsarge* had thus far spent her entire career searching for Confederate raiders, first *Sumter* and *Rappahannock* and now *Alabama*.[36] With all the dispatch he could muster, Winslow summoned his crew back to their ship and headed for Cherbourg. The events that followed were both glorious and tragic.

In earlier years Emperor Napoleon III had beguiled the Confederacy with talk of recognition and assistance. But with the Union juggernaut so clearly grinding down a faltering Confederacy, there was little chance that he would aid *Alabama*. The French authorities informed Semmes that he could remain in port only so long as it took him to prepare his ship to go safely back to sea.

Semmes had three choices: He might fight, run, or, as he had done with *Sumter*, simply leave his ship. He choose the first. The decision was both rational and romantic. If he did manage to run past *Kearsarge*, where could he go? After so long a voyage *Alabama*'s bottom was foul. Her powder and shot were running low, and even the powder left in the magazine was showing signs of decay. In the last target practice, fully one-third of the rounds fired had proved defective.

Despite his problems, Semmes was still hopeful. *Kearsarge* had no overwhelming advantage, at least none that was apparent. She was about the same age as *Alabama* and of roughly equal tonnage. She did have an armament advantage, with her eleven-inch guns, but in total weight of broadside she outthrew *Alabama* by only seventy pounds. As for crew, *Alabama* had only 149 men, compared with 162 on *Kearsarge*. But those 149 had been through a great deal together, and their morale and spirits were high.[37]

There was one factor of which Semmes may have been ignorant. Winslow had made certain alterations to *Kearsarge*'s hull. He had constructed field-expedient armor by draping anchor chain down the side of the hull to protect the engine compartments. The idea was not new (Farragut had used it in the Mississippi), and the "armor" was hardly shotproof. Nevertheless, in a closely fought battle, it might well provide an extra margin of safety.

On 14 June *Kearsarge* arrived off Cherbourg and hovered just beyond the entrance. Semmes wasted no time. If he must fight, he would at least do it when he chose, and with characteristic southern flair he dispatched a challenge to Winslow. He begged the Union captain not to leave the area. *Alabama* needed only a day or so to make "necessary arrangements," following which she would steam forth to engage.[38]

True to his promise, Semmes left port shortly after nine o'clock on the morning of 21 June. From the deck of the nearby French warship *Napoleon,* a cheer went up, and the ship's band began to play "Dixie." As they cleared the breakwater, Semmes summoned his crew aft. With his usual flair for drama, he charged them: "Remember that you are in the English Channel, the theatre of so much of the naval glory of our race, and that the eyes of all Europe are at this moment, upon you. The flag that floats over you is that of a young Republic, who bids defiance to her enemies, whenever and wherever found. Show the world that you know how to uphold it!"[39]

Kearsarge held her position about nine miles off the coast, far enough to sea so that there could be no risk of violating French law. *Alabama* steamed toward the Federal vessel, and the two began to stalk each other. Less than a century before, not far from here, another American naval officer had fought a similar battle. In 1778, when John Paul Jones had engaged HMS *Serapis* off Flamborough Head, he understood that his ancient vessel could not long endure a gun duel. It was his tactic, then, to grapple and board so that the enemy's firepower and mobility might be annulled. It seems likely that Semmes had the same notion. He knew that *Alabama* was weary and could not last in a protracted fight with *Kearsarge.* Before leaving Cherbourg, Semmes had drilled his men in boarding techniques. If he could close with Winslow and board, he would trust to the élan and experience of his crew. But Winslow would not permit this, and since *Kearsarge* had greater speed, he was able to set the rules of engagement. There would be no heroic boarding.

Semmes fired first. His opening shots missed their mark, as so many of them would. Those that did hit sometimes failed to explode, including one that actually dug itself into *Kearsarge's* stern post and then failed to detonate. Had that shot done its job, the battle might well have ended differently.

The two vessels circled, with barely a half to three-quarters of a mile standing between them. From the beginning the outcome was clear. *Kearsarge's* greater and more accurate firepower, her mobility, and her hasty armor all worked to her great advantage. *Alabama* was hit several times. Finally a fatal shot tore into her engine room, leaving a gaping hole through which torrents of water poured.

Concerned for his men, Semmes ordered the flag lowered. But Winslow, suspecting a ruse, continued firing. Meantime, Semmes ordered the one remaining small boat hoisted out to carry the wounded over to *Kearsarge* as *Alabama* began to settle by the stern. When the guns fell silent, spectator craft, including an English yacht named *Deerhound,* moved closer to lend a hand. Crewmen aboard *Alabama* dived into the water, hoping to avoid being sucked down when the ship made its final plunge. Clinging to debris, spars, boxes, and anything else that could float, the Confederate sailors struggled to stay alive. In a gesture befitting tradition and his own character, Semmes stayed aboard until the last minute. At last, *Alabama* sank beneath the gray-blue waters.

Semmes and forty-one others from *Alabama* were rescued by *Deerhound* and deposited on the dock at Southampton, safe and beyond Federal control. Many survivors were picked up by two small French craft; some of them were taken over to *Kearsarge,* while others were delivered to the quay at Cherbourg. Twenty-six men from *Alabama* were either killed in battle or lost by drowning; another twenty-one were listed as wounded.

In comparison, *Kearsarge*'s casualties were rather light. There were only three wounded and one killed. Despite the 370 shot hurled at her, the vessel itself was relatively unscathed.

During her brief career, only twenty-three months at sea, *Alabama* had taken more than sixty prizes worth millions of dollars. She had done several times that damage by diverting Union trade from its normal course, increasing marine insurance rates, and encouraging northern shipowners to seek other flags for their vessels. *Alabama* was a proud ship, and she sank in glory.

V

Confederate energies on the high seas had been spent in destroying the foreign commerce of the Union. Their efforts had been fairly successful, but now, late in the war, Mallory thought that other targets needed attention. For political reasons he thought it might be wise to inflict special torment on New England, a region that in the antebellum years had been home to the most rabid abolitionists and other enemies of the South and one that was still viewed with special hatred by many in the Confederacy. That could be best accomplished by attacking the fishing industry, in particular the greatest fishery of them all, whaling. In a letter of 21 March 1864 to Bulloch the secretary wrote that such attacks "would have a decided tendency to turn the trading mind of New England to thoughts of peace." That Mallory could even conceive of such a notion is a sign of the desperation and the wild notions then infecting Richmond. Still, the idea appealed to Bulloch, and the faithful agent went to work.[40]

This time building was out of the question. Adams's spies were everywhere. And with Union victory an increasingly likely prospect, the British ministry was beginning to realize that there might be postwar costs for any dalliance with the South. Furthermore, building took too long. The Confederacy could hardly afford to wait more than a year to get a raider to sea. From now on the South would have to buy its ships.

Bulloch first saw *Sea King* in the fall of 1863, when he examined her at her berth in the Clyde. She was then loading for India, and in the haste of the moment the agent did not have enough time to make a full inspection. Ten months later she was back, and Bulloch decided to have a second look. He was pleased with the looks of the vessel, and he bought her.

Oddly enough, long before Bulloch bought *Sea King*, she was already suspected of being a part of the Confederate navy. On 11 April 1864 Napoleon Collins, the nemesis of *Florida*, wrote to Welles from the waters off Brazil: "Captain Babcock, of American whaler *Lydia*, was informed by an English merchant at Hobart Town, [Tasmania,] a man of good standing and reliable, whom he feels sure would not attempt to deceive him . . . that there was a steamer fitting out in England called the *Sea King*. She was to be ready to sail from England by middle of January. She was to proceed to Australia. . . . Her object was to prey on the whalers in that sea."[41]

Collins erred only in reporting that *Sea King* was intended to sail in January; her departure was even earlier than that. What is surprising is that Welles, even after Collins's report was verified in England, failed to act. Very little was done to provide *Sea King* with a proper reception at sea, and no measures were taken to protect her intended quarry in the Pacific. This inattention later proved costly.

The plot was familiar. From his Liverpool office Bulloch bought supplies and recruited seamen, while doing everything he could to hide his connection with the vessel preparing for sea. On the morning of 8 October *Sea King* sailed from London. At almost the same hour *Laurel*, chock-full of guns, munitions, sailors, and supplies, left the dock at Liverpool. Ten days later the two rendezvoused at a remote spot near Madeira, where

Sea King underwent her transformation from merchantman to the Confederate States ship *Shenandoah*.[42]

Among the first to go aboard *Shenandoah* at Madeira was her new captain, James Iredell Waddell. A North Carolinian, Waddell was one of the few Confederate naval commanders to have attended Annapolis. High-spirited and aggressive, Waddell walked with a limp, an unfortunate souvenir from a duel. His last assignment in the United States Navy had been with the East India Squadron. He looked forward to returning to Pacific waters under another flag.[43]

Waddell's orders were simple: He was to sail into the Pacific and destroy the enemy's whaling fleet. As Waddell broke the seal and read his instructions, he experienced both elation and sadness. There is a sense of pathos in the long injunction given him by his superiors. He may have felt his solitude when he read that "Considering the extent of ocean to be sailed over, the necessarily incomplete equipment of your ship . . . and the approaching isolation from the aid and comfort of your countrymen," he was to consider himself and his ship on their own. Even if he triumphed, he was told that there could be no homecoming, for no foreign port would receive him and no Confederate port was open. At the end of *Shenandoah*'s voyage he was to "sell her."[44]

At two in the afternoon of 19 October *Shenandoah* weighed anchor and got under way. Four hours later she parted company with *Laurel*, hoisted the Stars and Bars, and set her course for the south, bound toward Cape of Good Hope. Although shorthanded, Waddell could boast a good crew and experienced officers. Among the latter was Irvine Bulloch, James's younger half brother and a veteran of *Alabama*. Also in the wardroom was an experienced freshwater sailor, Second Lieutenant Dabney Minor Scales, who had seen action on board *Arkansas* during her fiery dash past the Union squadron at the mouth of the Yazoo.

On 30 October Waddell took his first vessel. He took eight more in the Atlantic and then rounded the Cape and made for

Australia. *Shenandoah* entered Port Phillip Bay near Melbourne on the afternoon of 25 January. As soon as the anchor was down, Waddell forwarded a request to the local authorities that he be allowed sufficient time to repair his machinery and recoal. In the weeks to come, the citizens of Melbourne witnessed a clever dance as Waddell negotiated with local authorities, who were frightened by the protests of Union diplomats. This adept political performance took place against a backdrop of public support and sympathy for Waddell and his "Dixie tars." After making repairs and taking aboard 250 tons of Cardiff coal, *Shenandoah* put to sea, bound this time toward the North Pacific in search of Yankee whalers.[45]

On 1 April *Shenandoah* was at Ponape in the Caroline Islands, where she took four whalers. From them Waddell took charts of the North Pacific, including the Okhotsk and Bering seas. The captains had conveniently marked the charts with the whaling grounds. Waddell remarked: "With such charts in my possession I not only held a key to the navigation of all the Pacific Islands, the Okhotsk and Bering Seas, and the Arctic Ocean, but the most probable localities for finding the great Arctic whaling fleet of New England, without a tiresome search."[46]

Waddell was right: No search was necessary. Like a hawk, he flew straight to his prey. The whalers had set out as hunters, and now they were hunted. In two months Waddell took twenty-five whaling vessels, twenty-four of them within the space of one week. As the smoke rose from burning whalers, florid newspaper accounts reported the "Confederate pirate" sighted thousands of miles apart on the same day.

Waddell and his crew found the work disheartening. While he was a good officer and patriot, Waddell had no love for destruction. Though he might burn ships, he was careful to save lives. Furthermore, Waddell was not unaware that his success in the North Pacific might be for naught. When he had left England, Confederate fortunes were ebbing, and while the news had been sparse since then, he heard nothing to raise his hopes.

Fearful that his trail had been picked up by the Federal cruisers, Waddell left the chilly waters of the North Pacific in July. He headed south toward the coast of Lower California and Mexico, hoping to snatch steamers shuttling between San Francisco and Panama. As *Shenandoah* tracked back and forth, finding nothing, her crew became restless. It was an international force; about forty new men had signed on at Melbourne. Their loyalties to the Confederacy were weak at best and under the strain of this prolonged cruise were fading fast. From some accounts, it would appear that discipline aboard the ship was collapsing and that Waddell, under great pressure himself, was devolving into a petty despot.

On 2 August *Shenandoah* stopped and boarded the British bark *Barracouta*. From newspapers aboard her the men of *Shenandoah* learned the sad fate of the South. The officer of the watch, Dabney Minor Scales, recorded the moment in the log: "Having received by the bark *Barracouta* the sad intelligence of the overthrow of the Confederate Government, all attempts to destroy the shipping or property of the United States will cease from this date, in accordance with which the first lieutenant, William C. Whittle, Jr., received the order from the commander to strike below the battery and disarm the ship and crew."[47]

Where to go? Waddell feared that if he surrendered to Federal authorities, he and his men might be tried as pirates. During the war northern officials had often growled threats to hang these Confederate "pirates." Now they would have even more reason, since *Shenandoah* had done much of her work after the war was over. No one wanted to be hanged on a technicality. After some discussion with his officers Waddell decided to disguise *Shenandoah* as a merchantman and hightail it for England. She ran down to Cape Horn around and into the Atlantic. On the morning of 6 November 1865 *Shenandoah* entered the Mersey, masked in the friendly cover of a thick fog. She came up the river and anchored near HBM ship of the line *Donegal*. At 10:00 A.M. Waddell hauled down the Confederate flag and surrendered his ship to Her Majesty's government. It was almost seven months to the day since Lee had surrendered at Appomattox. *Shenandoah* had been at sea for thirteen months, had taken thirty-eight prizes, and in all that time had set her anchor down only twice—Melbourne and Ponape. Remarkably *Shenandoah* had lost only two men.

While *Sumter, Florida, Alabama,* and *Shenandoah* are the best-known Confederate cruisers, they were by no means the only southern ships to wreak havoc against the northern merchant marine. According to J. Thomas Scharf, a former Confederate naval officer and historian of the South's navy, approximately twenty cruisers went to sea against the North and took three hundred Union prizes totaling 120,000 tons and valued at five million pounds (nearly twenty million dollars). Their effectiveness is reflected in the quick increase in marine insurance rates which induced many northern shipowners to reflag their vessels under different colors. Tonnage figures tell the same story. In 1861 the United States registered 2.5 million tons in foreign trade. Four years later the figure was only 1.5 million tons.[48]

Most of the decrease can be accounted for by ships that simply sought service under other flags. Undoubtedly the northern shipowners who placed their vessels under foreign flags had every intention of bringing them back when the war was over. However, that would not be the case. In 1866, under heavy pressure from American shipbuilding interests, Congress enacted absurd legislation prohibiting the readmission to American registry of any vessel that had been transferred to foreign registry during the war. The wartime flight from the flag, combined with an ill-conceived postwar maritime policy, meant troubled times ahead for the American merchant marine.[49]

Besides the economic misery that the raiders inflicted, they were potent psychological weapons. The exploits of *Alabama* and her sisters were followed with rapt attention in the South and elsewhere and often provided an illusion of hope. *Alabama*'s sinking of *Hatteras* was a great moment for the South, as was the time when Lieutenant C. W. Read took his tiny schooner

Archer into the harbor of Portland, Maine. He actually captured the U.S. revenue cutter *Caleb Cushing,* only to be captured himself a few hours later.

There were others whose exploits were sung and written about, but in the end even the valiant efforts of Semmes and Waddell were of little value. The northern commerce they destroyed had no direct effect on the conduct of the war. Mallory's hope that rampaging raiders would force Welles to divert blockaders to chase down the scoundrels proved a chimera. Whatever his faults, Gideon Welles never once lost sight of the fact that maintaining the blockade was paramount. Newspapers might rail, and merchants bombard the Congress with complaints, but he would not be swayed: His blockade always came first.

Curiously, one could argue that the South benefited very little from the raiders. Building and outfitting the ships were expensive, and the raiders did not contribute much to the strategic interests of the Confederacy or take rich prizes home. Still, the men who served on board the raiders were as brave as any who served the southern cause. True, they failed to save their nation, but their courage deserves celebration.

14

Conclusion

I

Everywhere the Confederacy was in free fall, plummeting toward collapse. With all its major ports in Union hands, the South could hope for no help from the outside. Meanwhile, the Union army marched steadily across the Carolinas and toward Virginia.

Lee had drawn his army tight around Richmond, but without reinforcements and with dwindling supplies, each day his army grew weaker. Grant was relentless; assault followed assault. Finally, on Sunday, 2 April, as Davis, Mallory, and other cabinet members sat worshiping in St. Paul's Church, a messenger came quietly toward the president's pew. He whispered to Davis that Lee believed Richmond should be abandoned. Davis left the service and summoned his cabinet.

For Mallory, it was a study in contrasts. That day was one of the grimmest of his life, yet when he left the church, he saw only a beautiful Richmond spring day. "The Temperature wooed the people abroad, a pleasant air swept the foliage and flowers of the Capitol grounds. . . . This old city had never, during the war, worn an aspect more serene and quiet." Inside the Capitol, the cabinet heard Davis describe the wretched condition of Lee's army. Within an hour, boxes of records were being loaded on wagons to make their way toward the depot. At eleven that night one of the last trains to leave Richmond pulled out of the station with Davis and his cabinet aboard.[1]

This flight from the capital took the president's party south to Danville, where they lingered, hoping that a miracle might turn the Federals back. Their hopes were vain. Lee surrendered on 9 April, and on 15 April Generals Beauregard and Johnston informed President Davis that the Confederate cause was lost. On 2 May Mallory tendered his resignation to his president. Shortly afterward he found himself under Federal arrest.

Mallory spent a comfortable ten months playing chess and writing letters at Fort Lafayette. Finally, in March 1866, a sympathetic President Andrew Johnson set him free. Reunited in Pensacola with his beloved Angela and the rest of his family, he resumed his career as a lawyer. It was, both financially and physically, touch and go. His practice was small, and poor health kept him from expanding it. To his son Attila, a student at Georgetown University, he wrote in March 1868, "I am in pain." Indeed for the next few years poor Mallory never seemed far from illness. Hampered by gout, he was also afflicted with a failing heart. On 12 November 1873, after a sudden heart attack, Stephen Mallory died.

In death Stephen Mallory continued to pay the price for having served the Confederacy. He had done his best with the slender resources and forces provided by the Confederacy, but the nation he had served so loyally did not honor him after his death. There were no parades for him, no statues, no monuments to his achievements, for the southern republic Mallory had hoped to help create was only a distant failed memory.

The usually dour Welles joked that the Confederates had fled Richmond with "heavy hearts and light luggage." But only a few days after his flippant remark, Welles himself suffered a severe blow. On the evening of 14 April Welles and his wife were awakened by startling news: President Lincoln had been shot. Welles dressed hurriedly and went to Ford's Theater, but the president had already been carried across the street to the home of a German tailor, Wilhelm Petersen. Welles entered a small bedroom at the rear, where he saw the president lying aslant on a bed that was too short for his lanky frame. There was no hope. Welles sat through the night by Lincoln's side, watching his breathing grow shallow, then finally stop.

For the next three years Welles served President Andrew Johnson as he had served Lincoln. These were difficult years. Unable to agree with the Radical Republicans in the House and Senate that the South ought to be punished and its society reformed, President Johnson found himself at loggerheads with the members of his own party. As Radical power in Congress grew, Johnson, whose political skills were marginal, found himself in a virtual siege.

Welles remained loyal to the president. Although he did not always admire Johnson's tactics, he supported the president's position. Both men had fought to save the Union, but at heart these two were advocates of states' rights. The climactic moment came when the Radicals moved to impeach Johnson. Welles stood with his president and at the trial in the Senate offered testimony on his behalf. Conviction failed by a single vote. Crippled by impeachment, Johnson continued to hold office until 4 March 1868, when Ulysses S. Grant took his oath. Out of a sense of duty, Welles had stayed with the president, but with the Radicals so clearly in control of the party it was apparent that his political career was at an end.

At the change of administration Welles left Washington and returned to Hartford. He had served longer as secretary of the navy than any secretary before or since. He resumed writing and spent the rest of his days publishing essays and editorials and at the same time trying to edit his diaries for publication. He never finished them.

With his flowing white beard Gideon Welles was a common sight along Main Street in Hartford. With the bearing of an Old Testament prophet, he commanded attention, but the years were telling on him. By the fall of 1877 he was noticeably ill, and that winter his condition worsened. For three days he lingered in agonizing pain. Finally, on the evening of 9 February 1878, Gideon Welles, surrounded by his family, died.

Gideon Welles was never meek or accommodating. He was stern, uncompromising, and sometimes brutal toward his political foes, but he was also unquestionably a man of integrity and energy. With admirable aplomb he steered the Union on a steady course to victory.

I I

Out of the chaos of the Civil War the United States Navy emerged as one of the most powerful seaborne forces in the world. It boasted more than six hundred ships, fifty thousand men, and extensive combat experience with new shot, shell, and armored vessels. But its great force was short-lived. Like a sunburst, the navy shone out brilliantly, then just as quickly disappeared. Men went home, ships were sold or scrapped, and the technological lessons America had learned at such great cost were forgotten. The American navy lapsed into a period of decline and neglect.

Much the same might be said of the Union army. But the nation remembered the Federal soldiers, as it did not remember its sailors. In the post-Civil War period Union army veterans wielded enormous political clout. Every president from Grant to Cleveland was an army veteran, and candidates for every office, from selectman on up, did everything in their power to woo the vote of the old Grand Army of the Republic. Regimental reunions held on battlefields, with both blue and gray veterans in attendance, became common. The memories of bloody butchery faded, and out of the carnage of battle arose romantic remembrances of heroism and courage.

Amid the flag-waving, the speeches, and the flood of military memoirs the navy kept a low profile. Farragut, its greatest hero, was not given to public display. Content to be a naval officer, he avoided politics and never published his recollections. His fellow flag officers, with the notable exception of David Dixon Porter, simply became obscure. But the navy deserves to be remembered, for without its notable contribution the North could not have won the war. Four areas deserve particular scrutiny: the blockade, combined operations, riverine operations, and chasing high-seas raiders.

The Blockade

Beginning with the contemporary writings of James R. Soley and continuing well down into modern times, historians have asserted that the blockade "starved" the Confederacy and was one of the leading contributors to its eventual collapse. The first notable challenge to this thesis came in 1931, when Frank Owsley's *King Cotton Diplomacy* described in detail "The Ineffectiveness of the Blockade." Owsley's views gained further credence as other historians began to rely less on anecdotal information and personal reminiscences and more heavily on hard data. It became apparent that when a port was in southern hands, the odds usually favored the success of the blockade-runner. Even during the dying moments of the Confederacy, runners were delivering materials to the doomed cause. Wilmington, North Carolina, for instance, stayed in business until the day Union troops took Fort Fisher, and the same may be said for many other ports.

The Union navy stationed hundreds of vessels along the coasts; this was clearly its major effort in the war. But many of them were sailing vessels and cranky, aged steamers, ill equipped for the business at hand. Even those vessels which were fit for duty had to retire often for repairs and fuel. Thus the total number of vessels actually on station at any one time was far less than the total number carried on the navy list.

The increasing industrialization of the South also hampered the effectiveness of the blockade. While it was unable to build large numbers of ironclads, the South did manage between 1861 and 1865 to make remarkable industrial progress. This was, in fact, its major wartime achievement. An Italian historian remarks that "Never before in history had anything like this been seen. A backward agricultural country, with only small, truly preindustrial plants, had created a gigantic industry, investing millions of dollars, arming and supplying one of the largest armies in the world."

While historians still debate the economic impact of the blockade, they are sure of one of its effects. From a diplomatic and political perspective, the blockade managed to isolate the South. Lincoln's proclamation, backed by Union guns, gave a clear warning to any nation with notions of recognizing the South. Their collusion would raise a serious risk of war with the North, and no European power was ready to run that risk for the questionable benefits of southern friendship.

Combined Operations on the Coasts

Combined operations—that is, the use of army and naval units in a coordinated manner against an enemy—are a bit more difficult to judge. The entire Union command structure was in an evolving and sometimes confused state, so it is not surprising that the kind of careful planning necessary for such operations was lacking. It was an area which held great promise and from which little ever came.

McClellan had thought of striking along the coast and pushing inland to disrupt and confuse the enemy; this was a sound strategy. Had he remained in overall command, Union forces might have conquered the southern coast more quickly. Instead, Union coastal strategists recognized the need to take certain ports but thought little of how to exploit these toeholds.

Union strategy devolved into a stale policy of guarding coastal enclaves instead of cutting inland.

Even when Union forces did cooperate, the results were often less than expected. Naval planners, wrongly convinced of their ironclads' omnipotence, failed to realize that they often needed a great deal of army help to subdue any entrenched enemy. The rate of fire from the ironclads was still too slow to annihilate a solidly built fortress, and the Confederates knew well how to fortify themselves against shelling. Sometimes, as at Battery Wagner, the Union navy would bombard a fortress heavily. Then, when the smoke had cleared, it would find that it needed more troops than it had asked for in order to take its target. Success against the enemy's coastal bastions meant cooperation between the navy and army—and more realistic planning by naval strategists.

River Operations

Since most of the regular officers who led the navy had been trained under sail on the open ocean, it comes as little surprise that they rarely enjoyed serving on the western rivers. Farragut's yearning to avoid brown water operations was characteristic. In the early days of the war, when river operations were actually conducted under army command, there was even less reason for a naval officer to wish to be posted west. Slapping at mosquitoes inside a noisy, hot metal shell, while sniper rounds ricocheted off the hull, was no one's idea of a desirable assignment. Aside from the regular officers, most of those on board were either midwestern farm boys or drafts taken up from the army. Given the choice, few seamen went west.

Despite its unattractiveness, naval service on the western rivers was, in fact, vital to Union victory. Scott, in his prophetic Anaconda Plan, had seen from the earliest moments of the war that the rivers were the key to Union strategy.

The most critical river operations took place in the western theater. Gunboats fought to control the waterways and provide secure arteries for moving men and matériel. Had the Confederates been allowed to maintain blocking points at places like Henry, Donelson, Island Number Ten, and Vicksburg, it is difficult to imagine how Grant and his lieutenants could have waged successful campaigns. Considering the great distances involved and the often swampy terrain, moving armies cross-country through the Mississippi River borderlands would have been nearly impossible. What Rodgers, Davis, Foote, Porter, and the others did was to change the war in the West to one of movement along the rivers rather than a slogging march across fetid lowlands.

Ease of movement was not the only asset the navy brought to the western theater. Its gunboats offered potent firepower. To be sure, the navy was wont to exaggerate the ability of big guns to reduce an enemy. Nevertheless, without big-bore Dahlgrens, Parrotts, and mortars, it is hard to conceive how the army alone could have reduced Confederate river fortifications.

One final note ought to be mentioned in regard to the service of the Federal navy on western waters. Although the Confederates were never able to marshal the resources to offer a significant challenge to Union power on the rivers, they were quite capable, when opportunities arose, of causing havoc with the limited forces at hand. The *Arkansas*'s rampage is probably the best example. Without Federal gunboats to pursue and restrain river scamps, Confederate steamers would have posed a real threat to Union operations.

Raiders

Of all the naval activities during the war, none generated more interest than those of the high-seas raiders *Alabama* and her sisters. Stephen Mallory, hypnotized by the rhapsody of raiding, mistook folklore for history. The American romance with privateers and brave naval captains was a vital part of the nation's culture and was rehearsed every time naval accounts of the Revolution and War of 1812 appeared. The difficulty that Mallory and most Americans had was in separating ends and means. The outcome of both those wars, while favorable to the nation, had little or nothing to do with American prowess at sea.

Mallory's investment of scarce Confederate resources in building vessels abroad was a mistake. While the raiders did manage to take hundreds of Union merchantmen and whalers, their efforts had no demonstrable effect on the Union's ability to wage war. In fact, the North's foreign trade actually increased between 1861 and 1865.

Neither did the raiders provide much in the way of positive news for the South. They aggravated its delicate relations with Britain and France and did little to cement alliances elsewhere. The scene of *Alabama* passing out of Cherbourg to cheers from the French navy is a romantic one; however, that exchange was a French salute to a gallant lost cause, not a demonstration of confidence. In fact, although citizens in Melbourne, Bahia, and Cape Town crowded the quays to catch a glimpse of *Florida* or *Alabama,* local officials were always glad to see the raider's top-mast slipping over the horizon.

Nor did the raiders make any positive financial contribution to the war effort. Unable to bring prizes to port, they were always a costly venture. During the Revolution and War of 1812, warships and privateers were able to bring a good number of captures to port, but the Confederates could never do so. For most, as for *Shenandoah,* it was a one-way voyage.

On the other side of the Potomac Gideon Welles played a close hand when it came to the raiders. Mallory had hoped that the raiders would divert large numbers of Federal vessels from the blockade. Northern merchants who feared for their profits called for such action, but Welles and Fox were too wise for that. Welles did dispatch vessels to pursue the Confederates but never so many as to weaken the main thrust of his strategy. By misreading history and his opponent, Stephen Mallory wasted resources on a glamorous but not very useful enterprise.

Indeed, perhaps the raiders stand as enduring symbols of

the Confederate navy. With few economic resources at hand the South sought the beau geste. Although ill planned and frequently futile, Rebel ventures never lacked flamboyance and romance, qualities so characteristic of their "Lost Cause."

The overwhelming advantages of manpower, industrial might, organization, and logistics helped the Union win victory at last. All the North's advantages may be seen in its navy: the number of men in the service; hundreds of vessels built and bought; fleets and squadrons effectively managed; and food, fuel, and munitions provided in seemingly endless quantities. The Union navy was a powerful partner to the northern army, and its share in the Battle for the Republic should not be forgotten.

Endnotes

———◆———

ABBREVIATIONS USED IN NOTES

B and L *Battles and Leaders of the Civil War: Being for the Most Part Contribu-
tions by Union and Confederate Officers.* Based upon "The Century
War Series," ed. Robert Underwood Johnson and Clarence Clough
Buel of the editorial staff of "The Century Magazine." 4 vols.
Secaucus, N.J.: Castle, 1983 reprint.

DANFS *Dictionary of American Naval Fighting Ships.* 8 vols. Washington, D.C.:
Naval History Division, 1959–81.

ORA *The War of the Rebellion: A Compilation of the Official Records of the
Union and Confederate Armies.* 128 vols. Washington, D.C.: Government Printing Office, 1880–1901.

ORN *Official Records of the Union and Confederate Navies in the War of the
Rebellion.* 303 vols. Washington, D.C.: Government Printing Office,
1894–1922.

SFD John D. Hayes, ed. *Samuel Francis du Pont: A Selection from His Letters.* 3 vols. Ithaca, N.Y.: Cornell University Press, 1969.

CHAPTER 1

1. Bruce Catton, *The Coming Fury* (New York: Doubleday and Company, 1961), p. 311.

2. Frank Luther Mott, *A History of American Magazines* (Cambridge: Harvard University Press, 1938), vol. 1, p. 422.

3. For a discussion of the navy's support of commerce, see John H. Schroeder, *Shaping a Maritime Empire: The Commercial and Diplomatic Role of the American Navy, 1829–1860* (Westport, Conn.: Greenwood Press, 1985); for diplomatic activities, see David Long, *Gold Braid and Foreign Relations* (Annapolis, Md.: U.S. Naval Institute Press, 1988).

4. There is a considerable bibliography on both voyages. Both commanders made their own contributions. Charles Wilkes, *Narrative of the United States Exploring Expedition During the Year 1838, 1839, 1840, 1842, 1849*, 5 vols. (Philadelphia: C. Sherman, 1844); Matthew C. Perry, *Narrative of the Expedition of an American Squadron to the China Seas and Japan, Reformed in the Years 1852, 1853, and 1854, Under the Command of Commodore M. C. Perry, United States Navy by Order of the Government of the United States*, 3 vols. (Washington, D.C.: A. O. P. Nicholson, 1856). See also Herman J. Viola and Corolyn Margolis, eds., *Magnificent Voyagers: The U.S. Exploring Expedition, 1838–1842* (Washington, D.C.: Smithsonian Institution Press, 1985), and William J. Morgan, ed., *Autobiography of Rear Admiral Charles Wilkes, USN, 1798–1877* (Washington, D.C.: Washington Historical Center, 1979).

5. Hans Busk, *The Navies of the World: Their Present State and Future Capabilities, a Comparison Study on Steam and Screw Propelled Ships* (London: Routledge, 1859), p. 106; Frank M. Bennett, *The Steam Navy of the United States* (Westport, Conn.: Greenwood Press, 1974), pp. 48–176.

6. Spencer Tucker, *Arming the Fleet: U.S. Navy Ordnance in the Mussle-Loading Era* (Annapolis, Md.: U.S. Naval Institute Press, 1989), p. 206.

7. Hugo Hammar, "The *Monitor* and the *Merrimac*," *Mariners Mirror*, vol. 26 (April 1940), p. 163.

8. *Congressional Globe*, 2 March 1861.

9. There are several biographies of Welles. Among the ones I consulted are John Niven, *Gideon Welles: Lincoln's Secretary of the Navy* (New York: Oxford University Press, 1973), and Richard West, Jr., *Gideon Welles: Lincoln's Navy Department* (Indianapolis: Bobbs-Merrill, 1943). Welles also kept a diary: *Diary of Gideon Welles*, with an introduction by John T. Morse, Jr., 3 vols. (Boston: Houghton Mifflin Co., 1911). Paolo Coletta, one of Welles's biographers, wisely urges scholars to be careful when using these diaries. According to him, "they must always be considered as reflecting the biases, and the distortions of a strong-minded, opinionated man who was ever conscious of his own particular role. Only recently have historians placed him in proper perspective." Paolo Coletta, "Gideon Welles," *American Secretaries of the Navy* (Annapolis: U.S. Naval Institute Press, 1980), vol. 1, p. 357. The better edition to use, and

the one used here, is Howard K. Beale, ed., *The Diary of Gideon Welles* . . . 3 vols. (New York: W. W. Norton, 1960).

10. Quoted in Niven, *Gideon Welles*, p. 284.

CHAPTER 2

1. The best biography of Mallory is Joseph T. Durkin, *Stephen B. Mallory: Confederate Navy Chief* (Chapel Hill, N.C.: University of North Carolina Press, 1954).

2. Jefferson B. Browne, *Key West, the Old and the New* (St. Augustine, Fla.: 1912).

3. Durkin, *Mallory*, p. 136.

4. Thomas Scharf, *History of the Confederate States Navy* (Barre, Vt.: Fairfax Press, 1977 reprint), pp. 28–30.

5. William N. Still, Jr., *Iron Afloat: The Story of the Confederate Armorclads* (Nashville, Tenn.: Vanderbilt University Press, 1971), pp. 7–9.

6. Mallory to C. M. Conrad, chairman, Committee on Naval Affairs, 10 May 1861, ORN, Series 2, vol. 2, p. 57; William S. Dudley, *Going South: U.S. Navy Officers Resignations and Dismissals on the Eve of the Civil War* (Washington, D.C.: Naval Historical Foundation, 1981), pp. 18–19.

7. ORN, Series 2, vol. 2, p. 69.

8. G. T. Sinclair to Mallory, 22 April 1861, ORN, Series 1, vol. 4, p. 306.

9. Horace Greeley, *The American Conflict* (Hartford, Conn.: O. D. Case, 1864–66), vol. 1, p. 473.

10. Theodore Ropp, "Anacondas Anyone?," *Military Affairs* vol. 27 (Summer 1963), p. 71.

11. *Diary of Gideon Welles* (New York: W. W. Norton, 1911), vol. 1, p. 68.

12. Fox needs a biographer. For his wartime activities, see Robert Means Thompson and Richard Wainwright, eds. *The Confidential Correspondence of Gustavus V. Fox*, 2 vols. (New York: Naval Historical Society, 1919).

13. John Niven, *Gideon Welles: Lincoln's Secretary of the Navy* (New York: Oxford University Press, 1973), p. 362.

14. S. F. Hughes, ed., *Letters and Recollections of John Murray Forbes* (Boston: Houghton Mifflin, 1899), vol. 1, pp. 227–32.

15. Edward W. Sloan, *Benjamin Franklin Isherwood* (Annapolis, Md. U.S. Naval Institute Press, 1965), is the best biography of Isherwood.

16. Ibid., pp. 30–33.

17. The report of 13 July may be found in ORA, Series 1, vol. 53, pp. 67–73. The remainder are in ORN as follows: 5 July, Series 1, vol. 12, pp. 195–98; 16 July, Series 1, vol. 12, pp. 198–201; 26 July, Series 1, vol. 12, pp. 201–06 and 9 August, Series 1, vol. 16, pp. 618–30. Since Samuel F. du Pont was president of the board, his letters are informative. SFD, vol. 1, passim. The board seems to have had no official title, although it is occasionally referred to as Conference.

CHAPTER 3

1. DANFS, vol. 2, p. 539, ORN, Series 1, vol. 6, p. 71; Series 1, vol. 6, p. 110. Early in 1862 a combined expedition was launched into the North Carolina sounds. Rowena Reed, *Combined Operations in the Civil War* (Annapolis, Md.: U.S. Naval Institute Press, 1978), pp. 39–42.

2. Benjamin Butler is among the most controversial figures in the Civil War. Businessman, lawyer, politician, and general, he managed at one time or another to alienate nearly everyone. Much of Butler's correspondence is published in Jesse Ames Marshall, ed., *Private and Official Correspondence of Gen. Benjamin F. Butler,* 5 vols (Norwood, Mass.: Plimpton, 1917). Among the best biographies is Richard S. West, Jr., *Lincoln's Scapegoat General: A Life of Benjamin F. Butler, 1818–1893* (Boston: Houghton Mifflin Co., 1965).

3. Welles to Stringham, 9 August 1861, ORN, Series 1, vol. 6, pp. 69–70; Reed, op. cit., pp. 9–14. Stringham to Welles, 26 July 1861, ORN, Series 1, vol. 6, p. 39. Welles to Stringham, 14 August 1861, ORN, Series 1, vol. 6, p. 82; Major General John Wool to C. C. Churchill, 25 August 1861, ORN, Series 1, vol 6, p. 112.

4. Stringham to Welles, 26 July 1861, ORN, Series 1, vol. 6, p. 39.

5. Churchill to Butler, 25 August 1861, ORN, Series 1, vol. 6, p. 112.

6. In addition to the detailed accounts left by officers on the scene, Stringham's report is in ORN, Series 1, vol. 6, pp. 120–23. News reporters present also filed stories. See, for example, *New York Daily Tribune,* 3 September 1861, and *New York Times,* 3 September 1861.

7. William T. Adams, "The Ship-Shore Duel," *Ordnance,* vol. 45 (January–February 1961), p. 798; Bern Anderson, "The Naval Strategy of the Civil War," *Military Affairs,* vol. 26 (Spring 1962), p. 14; Richard V. Hamilton, "Facts Connected with the Naval Operations During the Civil War in the United States," *Journal of the Royal United Service Institute,* vol. 22 (1878), p. 617; and James M. Merrill, "Hatteras Expedition," *North Carolina Historical Review,* vol. 29 (April 1952), pp. 217–19.

8. Harold Peterson, *Notes on Ordnance of the American Civil War* (Washington, D.C.: American Ordnance Association, 1959), pp. 1–20.

9. A good deal has been written about Dahlgren. Shortly after the war his wife, Sophie Madeleine, published *Memoirs of John A. Dahlgren* (Boston: J. R. Osgood, 1882).

10. Reed, *Combined Operations,* passim.

11. Fox to Stringham, 14 September, 1861, ORN, Series 1, vol. 6, pp. 210–11; Stringham to Welles, 16 September 1861, ORN, Series 1, vol. 6, pp. 216–17.

12. Du Pont to Mme. Victor du Pont, 9 January 1816, SFD, vol. 1, p. xlv.

13. Du Pont to Mrs. du Pont, 17 September 1861, SFD, vol. 1, p. 149.

14. Du Pont to George Smith Blake, 27 September 1861, SFD, vol. 1, pp. 153–56; du Pont to Henry Winter Davis, 8 October 1861, SFD, vol. 1, p. 162.

15. Mrs. du Pont to du Pont, 16 October 1861, SFD, vol. 1, p. 169 n.

16. Report of Flag Officer Goldsborough, 29 October 1861, ORN, Series 1, vol. 6, p. 375. Various reports concerning the Port Royal expedition may be found in ORN, Series 1, vol. 12, and in *Report of the Secretary of the Navy for 1861* (Washington, D.C.: 1862), p. 7.

17. J. Cutler Andrews, *The North Reports the Civil War* (Pittsburgh: University of Pittsburgh Press, 1955), p. 142.

18. Ibid., p. 142.

19. *New York Herald*, 14 November 1861, quoted in Andrews, *The North Reports*, pp. 143–44.

20. Du Pont to Mrs. du Pont, 29 October 1861, SFD, vol. 1, p. 205.

21. Daniel Ammen, "Du Pont and the Port Royal Expedition," in B and L, vol. 1, pp. 671–91. Daniel Ammen also wrote about the expedition in Daniel Ammen, *The Atlantic Coast* (New York: Charles Scribner's Sons, 1883), pp. 13–45.

22. Report of Flag Officer du Pont, 11 November 1861, ORN, Series 1, vol. 12, p. 262.

23. Report of B. G. Drayton, 24 November 1861, ORN, Series 1, vol. 12, p. 302.

24. Ibid., p. 303.

25. Du Pont to Fox, 6 December 1861, quoted in James M. Merrill, "Strategy Makers in the Union Navy Department, 1861–1865," *Mid America*, vol. 44 (January 1962), p. 23.

26. ORA, Series 1, vol. 6, p. 367. Lee followed his own advice and was careful not to expose his own Army of Northern Virginia to the power of the Union navy. See John D. Hayes, "Lee Against the Sea," *Shipmate*, vol. 22 (November 1959), pp. 5–22.

CHAPTER 4

1. Mallory to C. M. Conrad, chairman, Committee on Naval Affairs, 10 May 1861, ORN, Series 2, vol. 2, p. 69.

2. John Niven, *Gideon Welles: Lincoln's Secretary of the Navy* (New York: Oxford University Press, 1973), p. 364.

3. Mallory to Ingraham, 20 May 1861, ORN, Series 2, vol. 2, p. 72.

4. Investigation of Navy Department, 26 February 1863, ORN, Series 2: vol. 1, p. 783. Precisely who was responsible for *Virginia*'s design was a matter of some controversy. J. Thomas Scharf, *History of the Confederate States Navy* (New York: Crown, 1977, reprint), pp. 145–51; George M. Brooke, Jr., *John M. Brooke: Naval Scientist and Educator* (Charlottesville, Va.: University of Virginia, 1980), pp. 234–54.

5. Niven, *Gideon Welles*, p. 365.

6. *Congressional Globe*, 19 July 1861.

7. Statistical data of U.S. ships, ORN, Series 2, vol. 1, p. 159; George Belknap, "Reminiscences of the Siege of Charleston," *Publications of the Military History Society of Massachusetts*, vol. 12, p. 159; DANFS, vol. 5, pp. 58–59.

8. Statistical data of U.S. ships, ORN, Series 2, vol. 1, p. 90; DANFS, vol. 3, pp. 6–7.

9. "Negotiations for the Building of the *Monitor*," in B and L, vol. 1, p. 748.

10. Ibid.

11. Quoted in William C. Davis, *Duel Between the First Ironclads* (Garden City, N.Y.: Doubleday, 1975), pp. 46–47. The history of *Monitor*'s design and building can also be found in Frank M. Bennett, *The Steam Navy of the United States* (Westport, Conn.: Greenwood Press, 1974 reprint), passim; and William N. Still, "*Monitor* Companies: A Study of the Major Firms That Built the USS *Monitor*," *American Neptune*, vol. 48 (Spring 1988), pp. 106–30.

12. R. E. Colston, "Watching the *Merrimac*," in B and L, vol. 1, p. 714.

13. Welles, *Diary*, vol. 1, p. 63.

14. Ibid., p. 67.

15. John Taylor Wood, "The First Fight of Ironclads," in B and L, vol. 1, p. 702.

16. Extracts from court-martial of Josiah Tattnall, 5 July 1862, ORN, Series 1, vol. 7, p. 792.

17. Report of Flag Officer Tattnall, 14 May 1862, ORN, Series 1, vol. 7, pp. 335–338; finding of the Court of Enquiry, 11 June 1862, ORN, Series 1, vol. 7, pp. 787–99.

18. Bankhead to Lee, 1 January 1863, ORN, Series 1, vol. 8, p. 347.

19. In 1973 a team of marine scientists aboard the research vessel *Eastward* located the *Monitor*'s wreck off Cape Hatteras.

CHAPTER 5

1. Craven to Welles, 29 March 1861, ORN, Series 1, vol. 4, p. 103.

2. Since the Federals held Fort Pickens, Pensacola, while in Confederate hands, was not useful as a port.

3. Mark Twain, *Life on the Mississippi* (New York: Harper and Brothers, 1911), p. 15.

4. First Report of Conference . . . 9 August 1861, ORN, Series 1, vol. 16, p. 623.

5. The original intention was for Mervine to command *Colorado*. Since that vessel could not be readied in time, his orders were changed. Welles to Mervine, 7 May 1861, ORN, Series 1, vol. 16, p. 519.

6. Mervine to Welles, 23 May 1861, ORN, Series 1, vol. 16, p. 525.

7. Alden to foreign consuls, 6 August 1861, ORN, Series 1, vol. 16, p. 607.

8. Foreign consuls to Alden, 5 August 1861, ORN, Series 1, vol. 16, p. 605.

9. Frank L. Owsley, *King Cotton Diplomacy* (Chicago: University of Chicago Press, 1959), p. 237. See also Stephen R. Wise, *Lifeline of the Confederacy: Blockade Running During the Civil War* (Columbia, S.C.: University of South

Carolina Press, 1989). This work became available too late to be used in this study.

10. Semmes wrote several accounts of his wartime services. See Raphael Semmes, *Memoirs of Service Afloat During the War Between the States* (Baltimore: Kelly, Piet, 1869); DANFS, vol. 2, pp. 569–70; J. Thomas Scharf, *History of the Confederate States Navy* (New York: Crown, 1977, reprint), p. 36; and Warren F. Spence, "Raphael Semmes: Confederate Raider," in *Captains of the Old Steam Navy* ed. James Bradford (Annapolis, Md.: U.S. Naval Institute Press, 1986), pp. 194–226.

11. Virgil Carrington Jones, *The Civil War at Sea* (New York: Holt, Rinehart & Winston, 1960), vol. 1, p. 151.

12. *The New York Times,* 3 August 1861.

13. Welles to Mervine, 16 July 1861, ORN, Series 1, vol. 16, p. 587.

14. Mervine to Pope, 11 September 1861, ORN, Series 1, vol. 16, pp. 664–65; Pope to Mervine, 15 September 1861, ORN, Series 1, vol. 16, pp. 675–76.

15. James M. Merrill, "Confederate Shipbuilding at New Orleans," *Journal of Southern History*, vol. 38 (February 1962), pp. 87–89.

16. In nearly all the literature *Manassas* is referred to as a privateer— that is, a privately owned and armed vessel commissioned by the government to capture or destroy enemy shipping. Technically, however, *Manassas* was granted a letter of marque and reprisal. Historically this meant she was a vessel intended for commerce but armed so that should opportunity arise, she might seize an enemy vessel. Furthermore, the inclusion of the term "reprisal" in its strictest legal sense meant that the authority to seize other vessels was being granted to individuals so that they might take revenge for wrongs done to them even though an actual state of war might not exist. Whether the Confederate authorities appreciated these nuances is unclear. It is quite likely they simply intended to get "privateers" to sea to harass Federal shipping. If all this was an issue, it could be only one in the American Civil War since by international agreement (Declaration of Paris, 1856), such activities were outlawed. The United States did not sign the declaration. ORN, Series 2, vol. 1, pp. 382–84; vol. 2, pp. 61–63; DANFS, vol. 2, pp. 584–85; Charles Wye Kendall, *Private Men-of-War* (London: Philip Allan and Co., 1931), passim.

17. Report of Commander French . . . 22 October 1861, ORN, Series 1, vol. 16, p. 713.

18. Various reports on this fiasco may be found in ORN, Series 1, vol. 16, pp. 703–30a.

19. First Report of Conference . . . 9 August 1861, ORN, Series 1, vol. 16, p. 627.

20. For a firsthand account of the events leading to the attack on New Orleans see Gideon Welles, "Admiral Farragut and New Orleans. With an Account of the Origin and Command of the First Three Naval Expeditions of the War. First Paper," *The Galaxy*, vol. 12 (November–December 1871), pp. 669–83; also "The Second Paper," vol. 12 (November–December), pp. 817–

32; Fletcher Pratt, *Civil War on Western Waters* (New York: Holt, 1958); John Niven, *Gideon Welles: Lincoln's Secretary of the Navy* (New York: Oxford University Press, 1973), pp. 379–82.

21. David D. Porter, "The Opening of the Lower Mississippi," in B and L, vol. 2, pp. 23–24.

22. Ibid., p. 24.

23. Ibid., p. 26.

24. David Glasgow Farragut, "ZB File," operational archives, Naval Historical Center. There are several published biographies of Farragut, including one by Alfred Thayer Mahan, *Admiral Farragut: First Admiral of the United States Navy* (New York: D. Appleton, 1879). Farragut was born James Glasgow Farragut but changed his name to David to honor his stepfather. For a good summary of Farragut's career, see William N. Still, Jr., "David Glasgow Farragut: The Union's Nelson," in *Captains of the Old Steam Navy*, pp. 166–93.

25. Admiral Sir William Milbourne James, *The Durable Monument: Horatio Nelson* (London: Longmans, Green and Co., 1948), p. 299.

26. H. Paulding to G. V. Fox, 23 October 1861, Robert Means Thompson and Richard Wainwright, eds., *Confidential Correspondence of Gustavus Vasa Fox* (New York: Naval History Society, 1918), vol. 1, p. 387.

27. David D. Porter, "Opening," vol. 2, p. 28

28. Welles to McKean, 20 January 1862, ORN, Series 1, vol. 17, pp. 56–57.

29. Farragut to Fox, 30 January 1862, *Confidential Correspondence of Gustavus Fox*, vol. 1, p. 299–300.

30. Niven, *Gideon Welles*, p. 385.

CHAPTER 6

1. At first Fox and Welles thought these requests for additional vessels were related to the New Orleans expedition. That was particularly galling since both men believed that when Farragut left Washington, he was fully satisfied with all the arrangements. This was merely an unfortunate misunderstanding. Farragut wanted the additional support, not for his New Orleans campaign but for the blockade. Relations eased when this was explained to Welles and Fox. See, for example, letters in Robert Means Thompson and Richard Wainwright, eds., *Confidential Correspondence of Gustavus Vasa Fox* (New York: Naval History Society, 1918), vol. 1, pp. 299–302; John Niven, *Gideon Welles: Lincoln's Secretary of the Navy* (New York: Oxford University Press, 1973), pp. 384–85.

2. J. G. Barnard (enclosure), 28 January 1862, ORN, Series 1, vol. 18, p. 19.

3. The role of the Coast Survey has often been overlooked. R. Meade Bache, "What the Coast Survey Has Done for the War," *United States Service Magazine,* vol. 3 (June 1865), pp. 499–511.

4. John E. Stanchak, "Mansfield Lovell," in *Historical Times Illustrated*

Encyclopedia of the Civil War, ed. Patricia L. Faust (New York: Harper & Row, 1986), pp. 450–51.

5. Virgil Carrington Jones, *The Civil War at Sea* (New York: Holt Rinehart Winston, 1961), vol. 2, p. 71; Investigation of Navy Department, 23 January 1863, ORN, Series 2, vol. 1, p. 622.

6. Quoted in James Russell Soley, "The Union and Confederate Navies," in B and L, vol. 1, p. 628.

7. The confusion at New Orleans was revealed clearly by the investigations conducted by the Confederate Congress in the aftermath of the city's surrender. Investigation of Navy Department, ORN, Series 2, vol. 1, pp. 431–809 passim.

8. James M. Merrill, "Confederate Shipbuilding at New Orleans," *Journal of Southern History*, vol. 28 (February 1962),p. 87.

9. William N. Still, Jr., *Iron Afloat* (Nashville, Tenn.: Vanderbilt University Press, 1971), p. 54; Mallory to Mitchell, 15 March 1862, ORN, Series 2, vol. 1, pp. 466–67.

10. Chief Engineer Wilson Youngblood to Mitchell, 1 August 1862, ORN, Series 1, vol. 18, p. 318.

11. Still, *Iron Afloat*, p. 61.

12. ORN, Series 1, vol. 18, contains the official correspondence relating to the attack on New Orleans.

13. John Russell Bartlett, "The *Brooklyn* at the Passage of Forts," in B and L, vol. 2, p. 58.

14. Finding of Court of Enquiry, 5 December 1863, ORN, 1:18, p. 319. Between the force at the city and the vessels at the forts the Confederates had a total fleet of fourteen vessels available. Neither individually nor collectively was it an impressive force.

15. George Bacon, "One Night's Work, April 20, 1862," *Magazine of American History*, vol. 15 (March 1886), pp. 305–07. Bacon was an officer aboard *Itasca*.

16. David D. Porter, "The Opening of the Lower Mississippi," in B and L, vol. 2, p. 39.

17. Technically there were only two divisions. The first, or red, division was commanded by Captain Theodorus Bailey. The second, or blue, division was commanded by Captain Henry H. Bell. However, in the center a third de facto division was created under Farragut's personal command. The divisions were arrayed as follows:

FIRST DIVISION

Cayuga, Lieutenant Commander Napoleon Harrison, flag gunboat
Pensacola, Captain Henry W. Morris
Mississippi, Captain Melancton Smith
Oneida, Commander Samuel Phillips Lee
Varuna, Commander Charles S. Boggs

Katahdin,	Lieutenant Commander George H. Preble
Kineo,	Lieutenant Commander George M. Ransom
Wissahickon,	Lieutenant Commander Albert N. Smith

SECOND DIVISION

Hartford,	Commander Richard Wainwright, flagship
Brooklyn,	Captain Thomas T. Craven
Richmond,	Commander James Alden

THIRD DIVISION

Sciota,	Lieutenant Commander Edward Donaldson, flag gunboat
Iroquois,	Commander John DeCamp
Kennebec,	Lieutenant Commander John H. Russell
Pinola,	Lieutenant Commander Commanding Peirce Crosby
Itasca,	Lieutenant Commander Charles H. B. Caldwell
Winona,	Lieutenant Commander Edward T. Nichols

ORN, Series 1, vol. 18, p. 166. The Union fleet had 302 guns versus the 166 available to the Confederates. Even this understates the Union advantage since its guns were considerably heavier than anything the Confederates could muster.

18. Abstract log of USS *Cayuga,* ORN, Series 1, vol. 18, p. 754.

19. George Dewey, *Autobiography of George Dewey, Admiral of the Navy* (New York: Charles Scribner's Sons, 1913), pp. 63–65; Ronald Spector, *Admiral of the New Empire: The Life and Career of George Dewey* (Baton Rouge, La.: Louisiana State University Press, 1974), pp. 10–19.

20. Warley to Mallory, 13 August 1862, ORN, Series 1, vol. 18, p. 336.

21. Ibid., p. 337.

22. ORA, Series 3, vol. 1, p. 862.

23. Richard S. West, *Lincoln's Scapegoat General* (Boston: Houghton Mifflin Co., 1965), p. 126.

24. Porter, "Opening," vol. 2, p. 51.

25. Farragut to Welles, 6 May 1862, ORN, Series 1, vol. 18, p. 158.

26. Quoted in Robert H. Fowler, "Capture of New Orleans," *Civil War Times,* vol. 2 (May 1960), pp. 6–7.

27. West, *Scapegoat General,* pp. 150–51.

28. Quoted in Joseph T. Durkin, *Stephen R. Mallory: Confederate Navy Chief* (Chapel Hill, N.C.: University of North Carolina Press, 1954), p. 208.

29. Craven to Mrs. Craven, 16 May 1862, ORN, Series 1, vol. 18, pp. 195–96.

CHAPTER 7

1. Welles to Farragut, 20 January 1862, ORN, Series 1, vol. 18, p. 8.

2. Farragut to Welles, 29 April 1862, ORN, Series 1, vol. 18, pp. 148, 155; Rowena Reed, *Combined Operations in the Civil War* (Annapolis, Md.: U.S. Naval Institute Press, 1978), pp. 195–96.

3. Jesse Ames Marshall, ed., *Private and Official Correspondence of Gen. Benjamin F. Butler* (Norwood, Mass.: Privately printed, 1917), vol. 1, p. 428.

4. Fox to Porter, 17 May 1862, Robert M. Thompson and Richard Wainwright, eds., *Confidential Correspondence of Gustavus Vasa Fox* (New York: Naval History Society, 1919), vol. 2, pp. 101–02.

5. Farragut to Craven, 3 May 1862, ORN, Series 1, vol. 18, p. 465.

6. Farragut to Bailey, 11 June 1862, ORN, Series 1, vol. 18, p. 551.

7. Private diary of Commander H. H. Bell, 6 June 1862, ORN, Series 1, vol. 18, p. 708.

8. Scott to McClellan, 3 May 1861, quoted in William E. Geoghegan, "Study for a Scale Model of U.S.S. *Carondelet*," *Nautical Research Journal*, vol. 17 (Fall–Winter 1970, 1971), p. 147.

9. For a summary of Eads's career, see James B. Eads, *Addresses and Papers of James B. Eads. Together with a Biographical Sketch*, ed. Estill McHenry (St. Louis: Slaivson, 1884).

10. James B. Eads, "Recollections of Foote and the Gunboats," in B and L, vol. 1, p. 338.

11. Eads to Welles, 29 April 1861, ORN, Series 1, vol. 22, p. 278.

12. Ibid.

13. Ibid., p. 279.

14. Welles to Eads, 14 May 1861, ORN, Series 1, vol. 22, p. 279–80.

15. Welles to Pook, 20 May 1861, ORN, Series 1, vol. 22, p. 280–81; Robert E. Johnson, *Rear Admiral John Rodgers, 1812–1882* (Annapolis, Md.: U.S. Naval Institute Press, 1967), p. 156.

16. For a complete biography of Meigs, see Russell F. Weigley, *Quartermaster General of the Union Army* (New York: Columbia University Press 1959). *Allegheny*'s career can be followed in Frank M. Bennett, *The Steam Navy of the United States* (Pittsburgh: N. T. Nicholson, 1896), pp. 53–57.

17. Report of Commander Rodgers, 8 June 1861, ORN, 1:22, p. 283. Rodgers tried to change the name *Tyler* to *Taylor* since her namesake, former President John Tyler, had become a secessionist. The name was not changed.

18. ORA, Series 3, vol. 11, pp. 814–15.

19. Johnson, *John Rodgers*, pp. 160–63; James M. Merrill, *Battle Flags South: The Story of the Civil War Navies on the Western Waters* (Rutherford, N.J.: Fairleigh Dickinson University Press, 1970), pp. 24–38; and John D. Milligan, *Gunboats down the Mississippi* (Annapolis, Md.: U.S. Naval Institute Press, 1965), pp. 11–17.

20. Among the best examinations of Frémont's turbulent career is Allan

Nevins, *Frémont: Pathmaker of the West* (New York: D. Appleton Century Co., 1939).

21. Foote to Meigs, 26 October 1861, ORN, Series 1, vol. 22, p. 378.

22. Frémont to Blair, 9 August 1861, ORN, Series 1, vol. 22, p. 297.

23. Johnson, *John Rodgers*, p. 166.

24. Welles to Rodgers, 30 August 1861, ORN, Series 1, vol. 22, pp. 307–08.

25. John Niven, *Gideon Welles: Lincoln's Secretary of the Navy* (New York: Oxford University Press, 1973), p. 11; John D. Milligan, "Andrew Foote: Zealous Reformer, Administrator, Warrior," in *Captains of the Old Steam Navy*, ed. James C. Bradford, (Annapolis, Md.: U.S. Naval Institute Press, 1986), pp. 115–41.

26. Report of Rear Admiral Foote, 13 November 1862, ORN, Series 1, vol. 22, p. 314.

27. On 8 September her name was changed to *Baron de Kalb*.

28. Charles D. Roland, "Albert Sidney Johnston and the Loss of Forts Henry and Donelson," *Journal of Southern History*, vol. 23 (February 1957), pp. 46–49. The most recent examination of this campaign is Benjamin Franklin Cooling, *Forts Henry and Donelson: The Key to the Confederate Heartland* (Knoxville, Tenn.: University of Tennessee Press, 1988).

29. Foote to Halleck, 28 January 1862, ORN, Series 1, vol. 22, p. 524.

30. Milligan, "Andrew Foote," p. 128.

31. Reports on the battle are to be found in ORN, Series 1, vol. 22.

32. Henry Walke, "The Gunboats at Belmont and Fort Henry," in B and L, vol. 1, p. 364.

33. Roland, "Albert Sidney Johnston," pp. 58–63.

34. Reports on the battle can be found in ORA, Series 1, vol. 7, and ORN, Series 1, vol. 22.

35. Foote to Welles, 15 February 1862, ORN, Series 1, vol. 22, p. 584.

36. U.S. Grant, *Personal Memoirs of U.S. Grant* (New York: Charles L. Webster, 1885–86), vol. 1, p. 303.

37. Roland, "Albert Sidney Johnston," p. 63.

38. John Y. Simon, ed., *The Papers of Ulysses S. Grant.* (Carbondale, Ill.: Southern Illinois University 1972), vol. 4, p. 218.

39. Quoted in Joseph T. Durkin, *Stephen R. Mallory: Confederate Navy Chief* (Chapel Hill, N.C.: University of North Carolina Press, 1954), p. 257.

CHAPTER 8

1. ORA, Series 1, vol. 3, pp. 681, 683; Jay Carlton Mullen, "The Turning of Columbus," *Registrar* of the Kentucky Historical Society, vol. 64 (July 1966), p. 215.

2. This movement helped set the stage for the Shiloh campaign. See Bruce Catton, *Grant Moves South* (Boston: Little, Brown and Co., 1960), pp. 198–264.

3. Jay C. Mullen, "Pope's New Madrid and Island Number 10 Campaigns," *Missouri Historical Review*, vol. 49 (April 1965), p. 325.

4. Pope to Brigadier General G. W. Cullum, 14 March 1862, ORN, Series 1:22, pp. 689–90; Mullen, "Pope's New Madrid . . . ," p. 333.

5. Pope to Foote, 26 March 1862, ORN, Series 1, vol. 22, p. 701; Henry Walke, "The Western Flotilla at Fort Donelson, Island Number Ten, Fort Pillow and Memphis," in B and L, vol. 1, pp. 440–41.

6. Foote had with him at Island Number Ten the following:

Benton, flagship, Lieutenant Commanding S. L. Phelps
St. Louis, Lieutenant Commanding Leonard Paulding
Cincinnati, Commander Roger N. Stembel
Pittsburgh, Lieutenant Commanding Egbert Thompson
Mound City, Commander A. H. Kitty
Carondelet, Commander Henry Walke
Eleven mortar boats, Captain Henry E. Maynadier, USA

Walke, "Western Flotilla," p. 463.
John D. Milligan, *Gunboats down the Mississippi* (Annapolis, Md.: U.S. Naval Institute Press, 1965), p. 53, asserts there were seven ironclads and ten mortar boats. According to Foote's report, *Louisville* was sent back to Columbus to repair a leaking broiler.

7. Foote to Welles, 17 March 1862, ORN, Series 1, vol. 22, pp. 639–94. *St. Louis* was renamed *Baron de Kalb* on 8 September 1862.

8. Ibid., p. 694.

9. Halleck to Foote, 21 March 1862, ORN, Series 1, vol. 22, p. 700.

10. Walke, "Western Flotilla," p. 442.

11. Foote to Welles, 26 March 1862, ORN, Series 1, vol. 22, p. 699; Mullen, "Pope's New Madrid and Island Number 10 Campaigns," p. 337.

12. Foote to Walke, 30 March 1862, ORN, Series 1, vol. 22, p. 704.

13. Pope to Halleck, 2 April 1862, ORN, Series 1, vol. 22, p. 708.

14. Walke, "Western Flotilla," pp. 434–44.

15. Foote to Welles, 9 April 1862, ORN, Series 1, vol. 22, p. 722–23; Walke, "Western Flotilla," p. 463.

16. During the crucial battle of 6 April Grant's left flank held in great measure because of the fire support provided by *Tyler* and *Lexington*.

17. ORN, Series 1, vol. 23, pp. 3–4; Robert Partin, ed., "A Confederate Sergeant's Report to His Wife During the Bombardment of Fort Pillow." *Tennessee Historical Quarterly*, vol. 15 (September 1956), pp. 243–44.

18. Pope to Foote, 16 April 1862, ORN, Series 1, vol. 23, p. 6.

19. Foote to Welles, 14 April 1862, ORN, Series 1, vol. 23, p. 5.

20. Foote to Welles, 9 May 1862, ORN, Series 1, vol. 23, p. 85.

21. John D. Milligan, "Andrew Foote: Zealous Reformer, Administrator, Warrior," in *Captains of the Old Steam Navy*, ed. James Bradford (Annapolis, Md.: U.S. Naval Institute, 1986), pp. 115–35.

22. Welles to Davis, 17 June 1862, ORN, Series 1, vol. 23, p. 213.

23. Several reports from the Confederate side of the engagement appear in ORN, 1:23, pp. 54–57. See also Walke, "Western Flotilla," pp. 447–49.

24. Davis to Welles, 6 June 1862, ORN, Series 1, vol. 23, p. 119.

25. There is a considerable literature on Ellet. See Gene Dale Lewis, "Charles Ellet, Jr., Early American Engineer, 1810–1862." (Ph.D. thesis, University of Illinois, 1957); Charles Ellet, Jr., *Coast and Harbour Defenses: The Substitution of Steam Battering Rams for Ships of War* (Philadelphia: John C. Clarke and Co., 1855); Stanton to Ellet, 27 March 1862, ORN, Series 1, vol. 22, p. 680.

26. Ellet to Stanton, 19 April 1862, ORN, Series 1, vol. 23, p. 65.

27. Ellet to Stanton, 25 April 1862, ORN, Series 1, vol. 23, pp. 73–74.

28. Milligan, *Gunboats down the Mississippi*, pp. 70–71.

29. Walke, "Western Flotilla," p. 456. In addition to Ellet's recollections, see the various reports in ORN, 1:23, pp. 118–39.

30. Walke, "Western Flotilla," pp. 451–52.

CHAPTER 9

1. Davis to Welles, 10 June 1862, ORN, Series 1, vol. 23, p. 162.

2. Welles to Davis, 10 June 1862, ORN, Series 1, vol. 23, p. 161.

3. Davis to Ellet, 11 June 1862, ORN, Series 1, vol. 23, p. 163. For the complete story of the expedition see Edwin C. Bearss, "The White River Expedition June 10–July 15, 1862," *Arkansas Historical Quarterly*, vol. 21 (Winter 1962), pp. 305–62.

4. Report of Lieutenant Wilson McGunnegle to Davis, 18 June 1862, ORN, Series 1, vol. 23, p. 166.

5. Dudley Taylor Cornish and Virginia Jeans Laas, *Lincoln's Lee: The Life of Samuel Phillips Lee, United States Navy, 1812–1897* (Lawrence, Kans.: University Press of Kansas, 1986). pp. 103–04.

6. Farragut to Butler, 22 May 1862, ORN, Series 1, vol. 18, p. 507.

7. Farragut to Welles, 30 May 1862, ORN, Series 1, vol. 18, p. 519–21.

8. Welles to Farragut, 19 May 1862, ORN, Series 1, vol. 18, p. 502.

9. Farragut's reports and those of his officers can be found in ORN, Series 1, vol. 18, pp. 575–652.

10. Ellet to Davis, 18 June 1862, ORN, Series 1, vol. 23, p. 214.

11. Farragut to Davis, 28 June 1862, ORN, Series 1, vol. 23, pp. 231–32.

12. Farragut to Welles, 28 June 1862, ORN, Series 1, vol. 18, p. 588.

13. Halleck to Farragut, 3 July 1862, ORN, Series 1, vol. 18, p. 593. See also Rowena Reed, *Combined Operations in the Civil War* (Annapolis, Md.: U.S. Naval Institute Press, 1978), pp. 190–223.

14. F. P. Rose, "The Confederate Ram, *Arkansas*," *Arkansas Historical Quarterly*, vol. 12 (Winter 1953), pp. 333–36; DANFS, vol. 2, pp. 499–500.

15. J. Thomas Scharf, *History of the Confederate States Navy* (Barre, Vt.: Fairfax Press, 1977 reprint), p. 309; William N. Still, Jr., *Iron Afloat: The Story of the Confederate Armorclads* (Nashville, Tenn.: Vanderbilt University Press, 1971), pp. 62–78.

16. Dabney Minor Scales to his father, 31 July 1862. A typescript of this letter was provided to the author through the kindness of James Ewin and his aunt Lucy Herndon Ewin, niece of Dabney Minor Scales.

17. Farragut to Welles, 17 July 1862, ORN, Series 1, vol. 19, p. 4.

18. Davis to Farragut, 20 July 1862, ORN, Series 1, vol. 19, p. 15.

19. For a discussion of this, see Reed, *Combined Operations*, pp. 219–22. J. F. C. Fuller, *The Generalship of Ulysses S. Grant* (Derby: Arden Library, 1929), pp. 124–25, also discusses the issue.

20. W. S. Rosecrans to Halleck, 16 August 1862, ORN, Series 1, vol. 23, p. 293.

21. Quoted in Joseph T. Durkin, *Stephen R. Mallory: Confederate Navy Chief* (Chapel Hill, N.C.: University of North Carolina Press, 1954), p. 224.

22. Ibid., p. 225.

23. Farragut to the people of Donaldsonville, Louisiana, ORN, Series 1, vol. 19, p. 143.

24. Phelps to Davis, 23 August 1862, ORN, Series 1, vol. 23, pp. 296–97.

25. Welles to Porter, 1 October 1862, ORN, Series 1, vol. 23, pp. 388–89.

26. Porter to Fox, 2 November 1862, Robert Means Thompson and Richard Wainwright, eds., *Confidential Correspondence of Gustavus Vasa Fox* (New York: Naval History Society, 1919), vol. 2, p. 146.

27. John Y. Simon, *The Papers of Ulysses S. Grant* (Carbondale, Ill.: Southern Illinois University Press, 1977), vol. 6, pp. 340, 341 n. Perhaps the two best biographies of Grant for this period are Bruce Catton, *Grant Moves South* (Boston: Little, Brown and Company, 1960), and the more recent William S. McFeely, *Grant: A Biography* (New York: W. W. Norton, 1981).

28. Porter to Walke, 21 November 1862, ORN, Series 1, vol. 23, pp. 495–96.

29. Reports of this expedition can be found in ORN, Series 1, vol. 23, pp. 544–56.

30. Milton F. Perry, *Infernal Machine: The Story of Confederate Submarine and Mine Warfare* (Baton Rouge, La.: Louisiana University Press, 1965), p. 33. One of the Confederacy's leading exponents of mine warfare was the recently departed General Pierre G. T. Beauregard. See Pierre G. T. Beauregard, "Torpedo Service in the Harbor and Water Defenses of Charleston," *Southern Historical Society*, vol. 5 (1878), pp. 145–61.

31. *Cairo* lives! After a long search she was discovered in 1956. Raised and partially restored, she and her artifacts are on exhibit at the Vicksburg National Military Park.

CHAPTER 10

1. Bruce Catton, *Grant Moves South* (Boston: Little, Brown and Company, 1960), pp. 340–42.

2. Porter to Sherman, 27 December 1862, ORN, 1:23, p. 577.

3. Stephen D. Lee, "The Campaign of Generals Grant and Sherman Against Vicksburg in December 1862, and January 1st and 2nd, 1863, Known as the 'Chickasaw Bayou Campaign,'" *Publications* of the Mississippi Historical Society, vol. 4 (1901), pp. 28–36.

4. Two interesting personal accounts for the Confederate side are L. V. Caraway, "The Battle of Arkansas Post," *Confederate Veteran*, vol. 14 (January–December 1906), pp. 171–73, and S. W. Bishop, "The Battle of Arkansas Post," *Confederate Veteran*, vol. 5 (January–December 1897), pp 151–52. Naval reports on the expedition may be found in ORN, Series 1:24, pp. 98–127.

5. Thomas W. Snead, "The Conquest of Arkansas," in B and L, vol. 3, p. 453.

6. John Y. Simon, ed., *The Papers of Ulysses S. Grant* (Carbondale, Ill.: Southern Illinois University Press, 1979), vol. 7, p. 209.

7. Ibid., p. 233; David D. Porter, *The Naval History of the Civil War* (Secaucus, N.J.: Castle, 1984 reprint), p. 293.

8. Porter to Fox, 10 September 1862, Robert Means Thompson and Richard Wainwright, eds., *Confidential Correspondence of Gustavus Vasa Fox* (New York: Naval History Society, 1920), vol. 2, p. 135.

9. Reports may be found in ORN, Series 1, vol. 24, pp. 243–93. Various aspects of the naval operations are covered by James Russell Soley, "Naval Operations in the Vicksburg Campaign," in B and L, vol. 3, pp. 551–81, as well as Porter, *Naval History*, pp. 295–302. As usual, these sources should be scrutinized for bias.

10. Smith to Porter, 17 March 1863, ORN, Series 1, vol. 24, pp. 280–81.

11. Porter, *Naval History*, p. 301.

12. Porter to Welles, 26 March 1863, ORN, Series 1, vol. 24, p. 479.

13. One of the vessels attempting to get past Vicksburg, *Lancaster*, was sunk by enemy fire.

14. Porter, *Naval History*, p. 311.

15. One of great handicaps the Confederates had in defending Vicksburg was confusion and disagreement among their leaders. Archer Jones, "Tennessee and Mississippi, Joe Johnston's Strategic Problem," *Tennessee Historical Quarterly*, vol. 18 (June 1959), pp. 134–47.

16. Edwin C. Bearss, "The Campaign Culminating in the Fall of Vicksburg: March 29–July 4, 1863," *Iowa Journal of History*, vol. 59 (April 1961), pp. 173–80. Grierson's raid is well told in D. Alexander Brown, *Grierson's Raid* (Urbana, Ill.: University of Illinois Press, 1954).

17. Although under heavy bombardment, several of the besieged found time and presence of mind to keep diaries detailing the ordeal. George W. Cable, ed., "A Woman's Diary of the Siege of Vicksburg," *Century Illustrated Magazine*, vol. 8 (September 1885), pp. 767–75; George C. Osborn, ed., "A Tennessean at the Siege of Vicksburg: The Diary of Samuel Alexander Ramsey Swan, May–July 1863," *Tennessee Historical Quarterly*, vol. 14 (December 1955), pp. 353–72.

18. L. Moody Simms, Jr., ed., "A Louisiana Engineer at the Siege of Vicksburg: Letters of Henry Ginder," *Louisiana History*, vol. 8 (Fall 1967), p. 377.

19. The most thorough treatment of the Red River foray can be found in Ludwell H. Johnson, *Red River Campaign: Politics and Cotton in the Civil War* (Baltimore: Johns Hopkins Press, 1958).

20. George Billias, "Maine Lumbermen Rescue the Red River Fleet," *New England Social Studies Bulletin*, vol. 16 (January 1958), pp. 5–8.

CHAPTER 11

1. Quoted in Alfred T. Mahan, *Admiral Farragut* (New York: Greenwood Press, 1968 reprint), p. 235.

2. Report of Commander Renshaw, 8 October 1862, ORN, Series 1, vol. 19, pp. 255–60.

3. Major William L. Burt to Major General N. Banks, 7 January 1863, ORN, Series 1, vol. 19, p. 455.

4. Captains Palmer and Smith and Lieutenant Commander Kimberly to Farragut, 12 January 1863, ORN, Series 1, vol. 19, pp. 447–50; Philip C. Tucker, "The United States Gunboat *Harriet Lane*," *Southwest Historical Quarterly*, vol. 21 (April 1918) pp. 364–69; Howard C. Westwood, "The Battle of Galveston," *Proceedings* of the U.S. Naval Institute, vol. 109 (January 1983), pp. 49–56.

5. Semmes wrote almost as well as he fought. For his career and that of *Alabama*, see, for example, Raphael Semmes, *Memoirs of Service Afloat During the War Between the States* (Baltimore: Kelly, Piet, 1869).

6. Farragut to Alden, 5 January 1863, ORN, Series 1, vol. 19, p. 489.

7. *Hatteras* went down in nine and a half fathoms. The next day, when a Union vessel arrived looking for *Hatteras*, the Federals sighted her topmasts poking above the waves with a night pennant still flying. Charles Grayson Summersell, *CSS Alabama, Builder, Captain, and Plans* (University, Ala.: University of Alabama Press, 1985), p. 46.

8. Report of Major Watkins, 23 January 1863, ORN, Series 1, vol. 19, pp. 564–566; "First Federal Defeat at Sabine Pass," *Confederate Veteran*, vol. 20 (1912), pp. 108–09.

9. Indeed, for the last two years of the war the Trans-Mississippi Department of the Confederacy functioned as a virtually separate command. Robert L. Kerby, *Kirby Smith's Confederacy: The Trans-Mississippi South, 1863–1865* (New York: Columbia University Press, 1972); Florence E. Holladay, "The Powers of the Commander of the Confederate Trans-Mississippi Department, 1863–1865," *Southwest Historical Quarterly*, vol. 21 (January–April 1918), pp. 279–98, 333–59. For traffic in the region, see Frank L. Owsley, *King Cotton Diplomacy* (Chicago: University of Chicago Press, 1959), and William Diamond, "Imports of the Confederate Government from Europe and Mexico," *Journal of Southern History*, vol. 6 (1940) pp. 470–503.

10. Ella Lonn, "The Extent and Importance of Federal Naval Raids on Salt-Making in Florida, 1862–1865," *Florida Historical Society Quarterly*, vol. 10 (July 1932), p. 167–84.

11. For a description of antebellum Mobile, see Peter J. Hamilton, *Mobile of the Five Flags* (Mobile, Ala.: Gill Printing Co., 1913), pp. 193–344.

12. Peter J. Guthorn, *United States Coastal Charts, 1783–1861* (Exton, Pa.: Schiffer, 1984), pp. 166–67.

13. Abstract log USS *Powhatan*, 26 May 1861, ORN, Series 1, vol. 4, p. 208.

14. Bruce Catton, *Never Call Retreat* (New York: Doubleday and Company, 1965), p. 233.

15. Buchanan's career may be followed in Charles Lee Lewis, *Admiral Franklin Buchanan* (Baltimore: Norman Remington Company, 1929), and Charles M. Todorich, "Franklin Buchanan: Symbol for Two Navies," in *Captains of the Old Steam Navy* ed. James Bradford (Annapolis, Md.: U.S. Naval Institute Press, 1986), pp. 87–112.

16. William N. Still, Jr., "The Confederate States Navy at Mobile, 1861 to August, 1864," *Alabama Historical Quarterly*, vol. 30 (Fall–Winter 1968), pp. 127–30.

17. Quoted ibid., p. 130.

18. Ibid., pp. 130–34; Lewis, *Admiral Franklin Buchanan*, pp. 209–15.

19. Report of Captain Jenkins, 13 January 1864, ORN, Series 1, vol. 21, pp. 30–31.

20. Charles Lewis, *David Glasgow Farragut*, 2 vols. (Annapolis, Md.: U.S. Naval Institute Press, 1941–43); William N. Still, "David Glasgow Farragut: The Union's Nelson," in *Captains of the Old Steam Navy*, pp. 166–93.

21. Reports of Captain Jenkins, 13 January 1864 and 15 January 1864, ORN, Series 1, vol. 21, pp. 30–31, 35–36.

22. Farragut to Porter, 17 January 1864, ORN, Series 1, vol. 21, p. 39; Farragut to Welles, 20 January 1864, ORN, Series 1, vol. 21, p. 45.

23. Drayton to Jenkins, 24 February 1864, ORN, Series 1, vol. 21, pp. 95.

24. Welles to Commander Nicholson, 7 June 1864, ORN, Series 1, vol. 21, p. 323; Porter to Canby, 1 July 1864, ORN, Series 1, vol. 21, p. 368.

25. Mahan, *Admiral Farragut*, p. 268.

26. General Orders 10, 12 July 1864, ORN, Series 1, vol. 21, pp. 397–98. Other documents regarding the Mobile expedition may be found in this same volume.

27. Loyall Farragut, *The Life of David Glasgow Farragut* (New York: D. Appleton and Co., 1879), pp. 414–15.

28. Ibid., pp. 416–17.

29. Report of Rear Admiral Farragut, 12 August 1864, ORN, Series 1, vol. 21, p. 417.

30. Farragut, *Life of David Glasgow Farragut*, p. 417.

31. Report of . . . Farragut, 12 August 1864, ORN, Series 1, vol. 21, p. 417.

32. Lewis, *Admiral Franklin Buchanan*, p. 234.

33. Page to Major General D. H. Maury, 30 August 1864, ORN, Series 1, vol. 21, p. 574.

34. Farragut to Welles, 27 August 1864, ORN, Series 1, vol. 21, p. 617.

35. Farragut to Welles, 22 September 1864, ORN, Series 1, vol. 21, p. 655.

CHAPTER 12

1. Between September 1862 and August 1863 only three major campaigns took place in the East: Fredericksburg, Chancellorsville, and Gettysburg. Two of these campaigns went in favor of the South, and the third, Gettysburg, was a northern victory that failed of full exploitation.

2. Reports may be found in ORN, Series 1, vol. 7, pp. 136–39.

3. Fox to Goldsborough, 27 March 1862, ORN, Series 1, vol. 7, p. 139.

4. These statistics are taken from Frank E. Vandiver, *Confederate Blockade Running Through Bermuda* (Austin, Texas: University of Texas Press, 1947), p. xix.

5. According to Rowena Reed, *Combined Operations in the Civil War* (Annapolis, Md.: U.S. Naval Institute Press, 1978), pp. 33–40, McClellan had a clear strategy in mind.

6. John G. Barrett, *The Civil War in North Carolina* (Chapel Hill, N.C.: University of North Carolina Press, 1963), p. 67; Robert Daly, "Burnside's Amphibious Division," *Marine Corps Gazette*, vol. 35 (December 1951), p. 34.

7. Goldsborough to Welles, 23 January 1862, ORN, Series 1, vol. 6, pp. 526–27; Barrett, *Civil War in North Carolina*, p. 71.

8. Report of Flag Officer Goldsborough, 18 February 1862, ORN, 1:6, pp. 550–56. The reports of individual commanders indicate the high consumption of ammunition.

9. *New York Commercial Advertiser* quoted in J. Cutler Andrews, *The North Reports the Civil War* (Pittsburgh: University of Pittsburgh Press, 1955), p. 223.

10. ORA, Series 9, vol. 1, p. 76.

11. Reed, *Combined Operations*, p. 189.

12. Beauregard demonstrated his pique to the public. In November 1861 he wrote a particularly inflammatory letter to the *Richmond Examiner*. For an explanation of this incident as well as an analysis of Beauregard and his relationship with Davis, see Douglas Southall Freeman, *Lee's Lieutenants* (New York: Charles Scribner's Sons, 1942–44), vol. 1, pp. 99–110.

13. Reports may be found in ORN, Series 1, vol. 13, pp. 589–623.

14. SFD, vol. 2, p. 97; Welles to du Pont, 6 January 1863, ORN, Series 1, vol. 13, p. 503.

15. *Montauk* was accompanied by three conventional warships—*Seneca, Wissahickon* and *Dawn*—as well as the mortar schooner *C. P. Williams*.

16. James M. Merrill *Du Pont: The Making of an Admiral* (New York: Dodd, Mead and Company, 1986), pp. 285–87.

17. Order of Battle and Plan of Attack, 4 April 1863, ORN, Series 1, vol. 14, pp. 8–9.

18. Beauregard took particular and justifiable pride in his role as designer

and promoter of devices used at Charleston. Pierre G. T. Beauregard, "Torpedo Service in the Harbor and Water Defenses of Charleston," *Southern Historical Society Papers*, vol. 5 (1878), pp. 145–61; Milton F. Perry, *Infernal Machines* (Baton Rouge: Louisiana State University Press, 1965), passim.

19. Quoted in Merrill, *Du Pont*, p. 291.

20. Battle reports may be found in ORN, Series 1, vol. 14, pp. 3–112.

21. *Keokuk* had an unusual configuration. She had stationary twin turrets housing nine-inch Dahlgrens. With great labor, and to the disbelief of the Federals, the Confederates managed to savage these guns. Ursula and James F. Harding, "The Guns of the *Keokuk*," *Historical Times*, vol. 1 (November 1962), pp. 22–25.

22. Joint Report of Officers, 25 May 1863, ORN, Series 1, vol. 14, pp. 214–16.

23. Report of Chief Engineer Stimers, 14 April 1863, ORN, Series 1, vol. 14, pp. 41–43; John D. Hayes, "Fox Versus du Pont," *Shipmate*, vol. 26 (April 1963), pp. 10–11.

24. Welles to du Pont, 3 June 1863, ORN, Series 1, vol. 14, p. 230.

25. Quoted in William N. Still, Jr., *Iron Afloat: The Story of the Confederate Armorclads* (Nashville, Tenn.: Vanderbilt University Press, 1971), p. 98.

26. Joseph T. Durkin, *Stephen R. Mallory: Confederate Navy Chief* (Chapel Hill, N.C.: University of North Carolina Press, 1954), p. 260 n.

27. Union and Confederate reports describing these fifty-eight days may be found in ORN, Series 1, vol. 14, pp. 317–640.

28. See, for example, Warren Ripley, ed. *Siege Train: The Journal of a Confederate Artilleryman in the Defense of Charleston* (Columbia, S.C.: Published for the Charleston Library Society by the University of South Carolina Press, 1986).

29. Finding of the Court of Enquiry, ORN, Series 1, vol. 15, p. 167.

30. Perry, *Infernal Machine*, pp. 105–08.

31. Report of Rear Admiral Dahlgren, 16 January 1865, ORN, Series 1, vol. 16, pp. 171–75; Perry, *Infernal Machines*, pp. 168–69.

32. According to *Nahant*'s captain, Commander John Downes, he and his crew did not get proper recognition for their role in *Atlanta*'s capture. Downes to Welles, 8 July 1863, ORN, Series 1, vol. 14, pp. 285.

33. James M. Merrill, ed., "The Fort Fisher and Wilmington Campaign: Letters from Rear Admiral David D. Porter," *North Carolina Historical Review*, vol. 35 (October 1958), p. 466. For the blockade before Porter's arrival, see Dudley Taylor Cornish and Virginia Jeans Laas, *Lincoln's Lee: The Life of Samuel Phillips Lee, United States Navy, 1812–1897* (Lawrence, Kan.: University of Kansas Press, 1986), pp. 108–39.

34. Edgar Holden, "The *Albemarle* and the *Sassacus*," in B and L, vol. 4, pp. 628–33.

35. Daniel Ammen, "The Career of Commander William B. Cushing," *The United Service*, vol. 2 (June 1880), pp. 692–94.

36. David D. Porter, *The Naval History of the Civil War* (Secaucus, N.J.:

Castle, 1984 reprint), p. 688. Cushing's own report makes the best reading: ORN, Series 1, vol. 10, pp. 611–12.

37. Report of Richard Delafield, general and chief engineer, 18 November 1864, ORN, Series 1, vol. 11, pp. 207–14.

38. William Lamb, "The Defense of Fort Fischer," in B and L, vol. 4, pp. 642–45.

39. Butler to Porter, 25 December 1864, ORN, Series 1, vol. 11, p. 251.

40. Some historians have laid the blame at the feet of both Butler and Porter, who they claim never got along and therefore did not cooperate. Others have suggested that there is no evidence to suggest the two did not get along before this battle. What is certain is that they despised each other after the battle.

In view of Porter's personality and distrust of the army, coupled with Butler's reputation as the penultimate political general, it seems likely Porter had a well-developed distaste for this officer long before the Fort Fisher fiasco.

41. Fox to Grant, 4 January 1865, ORN, Series 1, vol. 11, p. 409.

42. Merrill, "Fort Fisher and Wilmington Campaign," p. 467.

43. Porter to Grant, 3 January 1865, ORN, Series 1, vol. 11, p. 405.

44. Special Order 8, 3 January 1865, ORN, Series 1, vol. 11, p. 427.

45. General Orders 81, 4 January 1865, ORN, Series 1, vol. 11, p. 427.

46. Report of Rear Admiral Porter, 15 January 1865, ORN, Series 1, vol. 11, p. 434.

47. Semmes, *Memoirs*, pp. 805–6.

CHAPTER 13

1. There are numerous historians of privateering and the American navy for the early period. See, for example, my own *Rebels Under Sail: The American Navy in the Revolution* (New York: Charles Scribner's Sons, 1976) and *Jack Tars and Commodores: The American Navy 1783–1815* (Boston: Houghton Mifflin Co., 1984). Privateering may be examined in Edgar S. Maclay, *A History of American Privateers* (New York: Appleton, 1899).

2. Carlton Savage, *Policy of the United States Toward Maritime Commerce on War* (Washington, D.C.: Government Printing Office, 1934), vol. 1, p. 76.

3. Ibid., p. 389.

4. Ibid., pp. 418–19.

5. Ibid., p. 90.

6. R. D. Oliver, "The Destruction of Sea-Borne Commerce: Some Lessons of the American Civil War," *Journal of the Royal United Service Institution*, vol. 83 (February 1938), p. 105; J. P. Baxter III, "The British Government and Neutral Rights, 1861–1865," *American Historical Review*, vol. 34 (October 1928), pp. 9–29.

7. Proclamation by the president of the Confederate States, 17 April 1861, ORN, 2:3, p. 97. It is not clear why Davis used the term "letters of marque

and reprisal" rather than "privateer." Although there are legal and historical differences between the two terms, in practice there was very little distinction. Charles Wye Kendall, *Private Men of War* (London: Philip Allan and Co., 1931), pp. 4–6; Karen Kauffman-Mucci, "American Letters of Marque: Their Role in the Quasi-War with France." Seminar Paper, Munson Institute, Mystic Seaport, Summer 1985.

8. J. P. Benjamin to John T. Gordon, 13 August 1862, ORN, 2:1, p. 403. An account of privateering devolving into piracy may be found in Casper F. Goodrich, "Our Navy and the West Indian Pirates: A Documentary History," *Proceedings*, of the U.S. Naval Institute vol. 42 (1916), pp. 1171–92, 1461–82, 1923–29; vol. 43 (1917), pp. 83–98, 313–24, 483–96, 683–98, 973–84, 1197–1206, 1449–61, 1727–38, and 2023–35.

9. Aside from destroying the captured vessel, the victor had another option: sending her into port under a bond. This was a curious measure by which the prize was sent into port with the understanding that when the South won, she would be seen as a legitimate prize and proper adjudication would follow. The process was an act of faith. An Act Recognizing the Existence of War Between the United States and the Confederate States, 6 May 1861, ORN, Series 2, vol. 1, pp. 335–40.

10. Report of the secretary of the navy, 26 April 1861, ORN, Series 2, vol. 2, p. 51. For a general treatment of these cruisers, see James R. Soley, *The Blockade and the Cruisers* (New York: Charles Scribner's Sons, 1883).

11. See pages 99–100.

12. List of vessels captured by CSS *Sumter*, ORN, Series 1, vol. 1, p. 744.

13. David D. Porter, *The Naval History of the Civil War* (Secaucus, N.J.: Castle, 1985 reprint), p. 602.

14. Report of Commander Palmer to Welles, 28 November 1861, ORN, Series 1, vol. 1, pp. 215–16.

15. Extracts from journal of CSS *Sumter*, 3 January 1862, ORN, Series 1, vol. 1, p. 733.

16. Ibid., 24 February 1862, ORN, Series 1, vol. 1, p. 742.

17. Report of Lieutenant Pelgram to Mallory, 10 March 1862, ORN, Series 1, vol. 1, p. 746.

18. Gordon H. Warren, *Fountain of Discontent: The Trent Affair and Freedom of the Seas* (Boston: Northeastern University Press 1981), pp. 1–69, 130. William James Morgan, ed., *Autobiography of Charles Wilkes* (Washington, D.C.: Naval Historical Center, 1978), pp. 755–82.

19. Report of Lieutenant Pelgram, 10 March 1862, ORN, Series 1, vol. 1, pp. 747.

20. Craven to Welles, 3 February 1862, ORN, Series 1, vol. 1, p. 299.

21. Report of Lieutenant Pelgram, 10 March 1862, ORN, Series 1, vol. 1, p. 748.

22. DANFS, vol. 2, p. 552.

23. Bulloch's career can be followed in his *The Secret Service of the Confederate States in Europe*, 2 vol. (New York: Thomas Yoseloff, 1959, new ed.).

24. Bulloch to Mallory, 21 July 1862, ORN, Series 2, vol. 2, pp. 222–26;

Mallory to Bullock, 8 August 1862, ORN, Series 2, vol. 2, pp. 234–39; Bulloch to Mallory, 18 December 1862, ORN, Series 2, vol. 2, pp. 309–11; Bulloch, *Secret Service,* vol. 1: passim; Charles G. Summersell, *CSS Alabama, Builder, Captain and Plans* (University, Ala.: University of Alabama Press, 1985), pp. 16–19.

25. Extracts from journal of CSS *Florida,* 15 January 1862, ORN, Series 1, vol. 2, p. 667.

26. Report of Lieutenant Maffitt to Mallory, 26 February 1863, ORN, Series 1, vol. 2, p. 642.

27. Welles to Collins, 27 January 1864, ORN, Series 1, vol. 2, p. 593.

28. Letter from U.S. consul at Bahia and reply from the president of province of Bahia, 5 October 1864, ORN, Series 1, vol. 3, pp. 252–54, 634.

29. Summersell's *CSS Alabama* is the authoritative work.

30. Bulloch, *Service Service,* vol. 1, pp. 61–62.

31. Hull 290 was at various times known as *Barcelona Enrica,* and *Alabama.* Summersell, *CSS Alabama,* p. 12.

32. Ibid., p. 14.

33. Bulloch, *Secret Service,* p. 245; Bulloch to Mallory, 11 August 1862, ORN, Series 2, vol. 2, p. 236.

34. Bulloch to Mallory, 10 September 1862, ORN, Series 2, vol. 2, p. 264.

35. *Alabama*'s cruise is detailed by Semmes in his *Memoirs.*

36. *Rappahannock* was a British-built steamer purchased by the Confederates. She escaped from England but had to put in at Calais because of engine failure. She never left the port. DANFS, vol. 2, p. 560.

37. ORN, Series 1, vol. 3, contains details of the battle and the ships.

38. Semmes to Admiral Bonfils, 14 June 1864, ORN, Series 1, vol. 3, p. 648.

39. Semmes, *Memoirs,* p. 756.

40. Mallory to Bulloch, 21 March 1864, ORN, Series 2, vol. 2, p. 613.

41. Collins to Welles, 11 April 1864, ORN, Series 1, vol. 3, p. 11.

42. Thomas H. Dudley to Craven, 13 November 1864, ORN, Series 1, vol. 3, p. 372; Charles Lining, "The Cruise of the Confederate Steamship 'Shenandoah,' " *Tennessee Historical Quarterly,* vol. 8 (July 1924), p. 103.

43. James D. Horan, ed. *CSS Shenandoah: The Memoirs of Lieutenant Commanding James I. Waddell* (New York: Crown, 1960, reprint), pp. 22–51.

44. Bulloch to Waddell, 5 October 1864, ORN, Series 1, vol. 3, p. 754.

45. Communications between Waddell and officials at Melbourne may be found in ORN, Series 1, vol. 3, p. 761, 812; Waddell, *Memoirs,* p. 138. *Shenandoah*'s stay in Melbourne is described in Benjamin Franklin Gilbert, "The *Shenandoah* Down Under: Her Sojourn at Melbourne." *Journal of the West,* vol. 5 (July 1966), pp. 321–35.

46. Waddell, *Memoirs,* p. 145.

47. Extracts from notes on CSS *Shenandoah,* ORN, Series 1, vol. 3, p. 832.

48. *Historical Statistics of the United States,* part 2 (Washington, D.C.: Government Printing Office, 1975), p. 750.

49. For a full discussion of the issue, see George W. Dalzell, *The Flight from the Flag: The Continuing Effect of the Civil War upon the American Carrying Trade* (Chapel Hill, N.C.: University of North Carolina Press, 1940), and H. David Bess and Martin T. Farris, *U.S. Maritime Policy History and Prospects* (New York: Praeger, 1981), pp. 23–25.

CHAPTER 14

1. Joseph T. Durkin, *Stephen R. Mallory: Confederate Navy Chief* (Chapel Hill, N.C.: University of North Carolina Press, 1954), p. 357.

2. For an interesting analysis of technology and the navy in this period, see Elting E. Morison, *Men, Machines and Modern Times* (Cambridge, Mass.: MIT Press, 1966), pp. 98–122, and Robert Bruce, *The Launching of Modern American Science, 1846–1876* (New York: Knopf, 1987).
The decline of the navy is lamented in the standard naval histories.

3. Paul Buck, *Road to Reunion* (Boston: Little Brown, 1938).

4. William N. Still, Jr., surveys the literature on blockade and comes to a well-founded contrary opinion in "A Naval Sieve: The Union Blockade in the Civil War," *Naval War College Review,* vol. 36 (May–June 1983), pp. 38–45. See also Richard E. Beringer, Herman Hattaway, Archer Jones, and William N. Still, Jr., *Why the South Lost the Civil War* (Athens, Ga.: University of Georgia Press, 1986), pp. 53–63.

5. Raimondo Luraghi, *The Rise and Fall of the Plantation South* (New York: New Viewpoints, 1978) p. 128.

Bibliographic Note

———————◆———————

Americans have always had strong feelings about their Civil War. In the decades following Appomattox participants and observers, blue and gray, anxiously rushed into print to offer their notions of what had happened. The public, too, wanted to know, so through dozens of magazines and hundreds of books the story of the war emerged, not always clear, not always accurate, but always in abundance.

Bibliographies provide a good starting place for those interested in the naval side of the war. Among the best are Myron J. Smith, *American Civil War Navies: A Bibliography of American Naval History* (Metuchen, N.J.: Scarecrow Press, 1972); Paolo E. Coletta, *A Bibliography of American Naval History* (Annapolis, Md.: U.S. Naval Institute Press, 1981); and Robert G. Albion, *Naval and Maritime History: An Annotated Bibliography* (Mystic, Conn.: Marine Historical Association, 1972). The Albion bibliography should be used with Benjamin W. Labaree, *A Supplement to Robert G. Albion's Naval and Maritime History: An Annotated Bibliography* (Mystic, Conn.: Mystic Seaport Museum, 1988).

For the historian the first recourse ought always to be the primary documents. Fortunately for those interested in the naval history of the Civil War the most important documents have been published in two monumental series. The 31-volume, *Official Records of the Union and Confederate Navies in the War of the Rebellion* (Washington, D.C.: Government Printing Office, 1894–1922), are indispensable, as is the 128-volume *The War of the Rebellion: A Compilation of the Official Records of the Union and Confederate Armies* (Washington, D.C.: Government Printing Office, 1880–1901). Three other useful government publications are *Atlas to Accompany the Official Records of the Union and Confederate Armies* (Washington, D.C.: Government Printing Office, 1891–95); *Civil War Naval Chronology 1861–1865* (Washington, D.C.: Naval History Division, 1971); and *Dictionary of American Naval Fighting Ships*, 8 vols. (Washington, D.C.: Naval History Division, 1959–81).

The private papers of naval participants have not been as quick to appear in print as those of their army colleagues. Nevertheless, good sources are available. These include Howard K. Beale, ed. *The Diary of Gideon Welles*, 3 vols. (New York: W. W. Norton, 1960); Robert M. Thompson and Richard Wainwright, eds., *Confidential Correspondence of Gustavus Vasa Fox*, 2 vols. (New York: Naval History Society, 1918); and John D. Hayes, ed., *Samuel Francis du Pont: A Selection from His Civil War Letters*, 3 vols. (Ithaca, N.Y.: Cornell University Press, 1969).

Not unexpectedly David Dixon Porter contributed to the flood of postwar literature. His two principal works, both of which need to be approached with caution, are *Incidents and Anecdotes of the Civil War* (New York: D. Appleton, 1885) and *The Naval History of the Civil War* (New York: Sherman, 1886). Porter was also a contributor to *Battles and Leaders of the Civil War*, a four-volume collection of essays published by *Century* magazine in 1887. These volumes, too need, to be used with care, as does Frank Moore, ed., *The Rebellion Record*, 11 vols. (New York: D. Van Nostrand, 1864–68).

Journals have not been afraid to publish Civil War essays. Historical societies of the states involved in the war have often published, in their own journals or via special publications, important works on naval aspects of the War. In addition, such journals as *The American Neptune, Proceedings of* the U.S. Naval Institute, *Military Affairs*, and *Civil War History* ought to be sought.

The Confederate side of the naval war may be glimpsed in J. Thomas Scharf, *History of the Confederate States Navy* (New York: Rogers and Sherwood, 1887); James D. Bulloch, *The Secret Service of the Confederate States*, 2 vols. (New York: Putnam, 1884); Raphael Semmes, *Memoirs of Service Afloat During the War Between the States* (Baltimore: Kelly, Piet, 1869); and more recently the various works by William N. Still, Jr.

Among the secondary studies I have found useful are Bern Anderson, *By Sea and by River: A Naval History of the Civil War* (New York: Alfred Knopf, 1962); C. B. Boynton, *The History of the Navy During the Rebellion*, 2 vols. (New York: D. Appleton and Company, 1867–68); Robert Carse, *Blockade: The Civil War at Sea* (New York: Rinehart and Company, 1958): Virgil Carrington Jones, *The Civil War at Sea*, 3 vols. (New York: Holt, Rinehart & Winston, 1960); and Howard P. Nash, *A Naval History of the Civil War* (New York: A. S. Barnes, 1972).

Index

Page numbers in *italics* refer to illustrations.

INDEX

"River Defense Fleet," Confederate, 175–76

River War, 100–106, 111–223, *162*
  Confederate guerrilla tactics in, 196, 200–201, 210, 212–13
  critical assessment of, 306–7
  rationale and strategy in, 57, 58, 102–6, 128–30, 187
  seasonal conditions as factor in, 143, 154–55, 190–91, 193, 208–10, 214, 222
  sickness in, 190–91, 193
  Union harassment and retaliation in, 196–97
  see also specific battles and campaigns

Roanoke Island, 77–78, 249–50
Roanoke River, 264, 266
Rodgers, C. R. P., 70, 73, 76
Rodgers, John (father), 27, 61, 139
Rodgers, John (son), 132–36, 139, 262, 307, 321n
  Foote preferred to, 137–38
Roosevelt, Theodore, 282
Ross, Leonard, 210, 211
Rousseau, Lawrence, 114
Rowland, Thomas, 83
Russia:
  in Crimean War, 32
  privateering law and, 275
  U.S. gunboats contracted by, 52

Sabine City, Tex., 225, 228
Sachem, 84, 118
St. Andrew Bay, Fla., 109, 230
St. Augustine, Fla., 55, 56, 69, 230
St. Charles, Ark., Confederates defeated at, 184–85
St. Helena Sound, S.C., 55, 70
St. Louis, 139, 143, 145, 146, 152–53, 184
St. Mary's River, Fla., 54, 56
salt production, in Florida, 229–30
San Jacinto, 280, 281
Savannah, Ga., 55, 235, 251, 253, 263, 282
  Union naval attack on, 261–62
Scales, Dabney Minor, 191, 295, 297, 325n
Scharf, J. Thomas, 298
Scott, Winfield, 47–48, 64, 135, 251
  Anaconda Plan of, 48, 68, 78, 104, 130, 221, 306
Sea King, 294–95
Selfridge, Thomas, 201–2
Selma, 242, 243
Seminole, 75, 240

Seminole wars, 40, 70
Semmes, Raphael, 31, 44, 99–100, *170,* 272, 279–81, 317n, 327n, 333n
  as *Alabama* commander, 226–27, 288–92
  as *Sumter* commander, 280–81
  leadership qualities of, 99
  naval reputation of, 279–80
Seneca, 75, 329n
Seven Days Battles, 195–96
Seward, William Henry, 36–38, 48, 64
  Lincoln's admiration for, 36–37
  privateering law and, 275, 276
  Welles opposed by, 37–38
Shaw, Robert Gould, 260
Shenandoah, 294–98
  raiding activities of, 295–98
  Sea King renamed as, 295
  surrender of, 297
Sherman, Thomas W., in Port Royal capture, 70–72, 74, 76, 77
Sherman, William Tecumseh, 199, 237, 261, 262, 289
  Atlanta surrendered to, 245
  Chickasaw Bayou defeat of, 204–5, 207, 216
  Fort Hindman captured by, 205–6
  at Vicksburg, 212, 213, 217
  on Yazoo River, 202–4, 220
Shiloh, Battle of, 173, 252
Shimoda, Japan, 31
shipbuilding:
  Confederate navy and, 41–43, 46, 114–16, 140, 147
  Confederate raiders and, 282–84, 286, 287
  neutrality and, 277
  sloops of war and, 53
  Union blockade and, 52–53
Ship Island, Miss., 57, 58, 110, 111, 116
Shreveport and Vicksburg Railroad, 186
side-wheel steamers, 30
  disadvantages of, 31
  double-ended, 53
Signal, 200, 201
Sinclair, Arthur, 124
Sinclair, G. T., 46
Slidell, John, 281
sloops of war, 53
Smith, Joseph, 9, 81
Smith, Watson, 210–12
smoothbore guns, 67, 81
"soda-water bottle" guns, 66
Soley, James R., 304
Somers mutiny, 28–29
Southard, Samuel, 28

349